Biscuits

by
THE EDITORS OF TIME-LIFE BOOKS

TIME-LIFE BOOKS·AMSTERDAM

TIME-LIFE BOOKS
EUROPEAN EDITOR: Kit van Tulleken
Design Director: Louis Klein
Photography Director: Pamela Marke
Planning Director: Alan Lothian
Chief of Research: Vanessa Kramer
Chief Sub-Editor: Ilse Gray

THE GOOD COOK
Series Editor: Ellen Galford
Series Co-ordinator: Liz Timothy

Editorial Staff for *Biscuits*
Text Editor: Margot Levy
Anthology Editors: Markie Benet, Anne Jackson
Staff Writers: Tim Fraser, Thom Henvey, Alexandra Carlier, Sally Crawford
Researcher: Margaret Hall
Designer: Michael Morey
Sub-Editors: Sally Rowland, Charles Boyle, Kate Cann, Frances Dixon
Anthology Researcher: Deborah Litton
Anthology Assistants: Debra Dick, Stephanie Lee
Design Assistant: David Mackersey
Proofreader: Judith Heaton
Editorial Assistant: Molly Sutherland
EDITORIAL PRODUCTION FOR THE SERIES
Chief: Ellen Brush
Quality Control: Douglas Whitworth
Traffic Co-ordinators: Linda Mallett, Helen Whitehorn
Picture Co-ordinators: Steven Ayckbourn, Sarah Dawson
Art Department: Julia West
Editorial Department: Theresa John, Lesley Kinahan, Debra Lelliott, Sylvia Wilson

TIME
LIFE
BOOKS

PEOPLES OF THE WILD
THE EPIC OF FLIGHT
THE SEAFARERS
WORLD WAR II
THE GOOD COOK
THE TIME-LIFE ENCYCLOPAEDIA OF GARDENING
HUMAN BEHAVIOUR
THE GREAT CITIES
THE ART OF SEWING
THE OLD WEST
THE WORLD'S WILD PLACES
THE EMERGENCE OF MAN
LIFE LIBRARY OF PHOTOGRAPHY
THIS FABULOUS CENTURY
TIME-LIFE LIBRARY OF ART
FOODS OF THE WORLD
GREAT AGES OF MAN
LIFE SCIENCE LIBRARY
LIFE NATURE LIBRARY
YOUNG READERS LIBRARY
LIFE WORLD LIBRARY
THE TIME-LIFE BOOK OF BOATING
TECHNIQUES OF PHOTOGRAPHY
LIFE AT WAR
LIFE GOES TO THE MOVIES
BEST OF LIFE

Cover: A final golden macaroon is added to the array just before presentation. No flour was used in the making of these biscuits, which derive their light, chewy texture from a paste of almonds pounded in a mortar and blended with egg whites and sugar. This mixture was spooned on to a baking sheet, cooked for 10 minutes in a hot oven, then decorated with icing sugar and pine-nuts (*page 56*).

THE CHIEF CONSULTANT:
Richard Olney, an American, has lived and worked since 1951 in France, where he is a highly regarded authority on food and wine. He is the author of *The French Menu Cookbook* and the award-winning *Simple French Food,* and has contributed to numerous gastronomic magazines in France and the United States, including the influential journals *Cuisine et Vins de France* and *La Revue du Vin de France.* He has directed cooking courses in France and the United States and is a member of several distinguished gastronomic and oenological societies, including *L'Académie Internationale du Vin, La Confrérie des Chevaliers du Tastevin* and *La Commanderie du Bontemps de Médoc et des Graves.*

THE STUDIO CONSULTANT:
Pat Alburey is a Member of the Association of Home Economists of Great Britain. Her wide experience includes preparing foods for photography, teaching cookery and creating recipes. She was responsible for the majority of the step-by-step demonstrations in this volume.

THE PHOTOGRAPHERS:
Bob Komar is a Londoner who trained at both the Hornsey and Manchester Schools of Art. He specializes in food photography and in portraiture.
John Elliott, based in London, trained at the Regent Street Polytechnic. He has extensive experience in advertising and magazine photography, as well as in his special interest, food photography.
Tom Belshaw was born near London and started his working career in films. He now has his own studio in London. He specializes in food and still-life photography, undertaking both editorial and advertising assignments.

THE INTERNATIONAL CONSULTANTS:
Great Britain: *Jane Grigson* was born in Gloucester and brought up in the north of England. She is a graduate of Cambridge University. Her first book on food, *Charcuterie and French Pork Cookery,* was published in 1967; since then, she has published a number of cookery books, including *Good Things, English Food* and *Jane Grigson's Vegetable Book.* She became cookery correspondent for the colour magazine of the London *Observer* in 1968. *Alan Davidson* is the author of *Fish and Fish Dishes of Laos, Mediterranean Seafood* and *North Atlantic Seafood.* He is the founder of Prospect Books, which specializes in scholarly publications on food and cookery. **France:** *Michel Lemonnier* was born in Normandy. He began contributing to the magazine *Cuisine et Vins de France* in 1960, and also writes for several other important French food and wine periodicals. The co-founder and vice-president of the society *Les Amitiés Gastronomiques Internationales,* he is a frequent lecturer on wine and a member of most of the vinicultural confraternities and academies in France. **Germany:** *Jochen Kuchenbecker* trained as a chef, but worked for 10 years as a food photographer in many European countries before opening his own restaurant in Hamburg. *Anne Brakemeier,* who also lives in Hamburg, has published articles on food and cooking in many German periodicals. She is the co-author of three cookery books. **Italy:** *Massimo Alberini* divides his time between Milan and Venice. He is a well-known food writer and journalist, with a particular interest in culinary history. Among his 14 books are *Storia del Pranzo all'Italiana, 4000 Anni a Tavola* and *100 Ricette Storiche.* **The Netherlands:** *Hugh Jans,* a resident of Amsterdam, has been translating cookery books and articles for more than 25 years. He has also published several books of his own, including *Bistro Koken* and *Sla, Slaatjes, Snacks,* and his recipes are published in many Dutch magazines. **The United States:** *Carol Cutler,* who lives in Washington, DC, is the author of three cookery books, including the award-winning *The Six-Minute Soufflé and Other Culinary Delights. Judith Olney* received her culinary training in England and France and has written two cookery books.

Valuable help was given in the preparation of this volume by the following members of Time-Life Books: *Maria Vincenza Aloisi, Joséphine du Brusle* (Paris); *Janny Hovinga,* (Amsterdam); *Elisabeth Kraemer* (Bonn); *Ann Natanson, Mimi Murphy* (Rome); *Bona Schmid* (Milan).

CONTENTS

A Sampler of Simple Pleasures

Biscuit-making is the art of turning simple ingredients into wonderful things. It takes only a peaceful hour or two in the kitchen to transform such staples as flour, sugar, honey, butter and eggs into crisp discs of golden pastry, light sponge fingers, fragile cat's-tongue wafers, savoury twists of cheese-flavoured puff paste; tender madeleines with a buttery crumb, sugar and egg whites whipped into frothy meringue, or figures fashioned from warm brown honey doughs, redolent of spices.

The earliest biscuits were a good deal less inviting—simple pastes of flour and water baked without leavening in a crude oven or on a hot stone. Often, a piece of dough was baked twice to dry it out completely, thus prolonging its storage life. These rudimentary biscuits had little culinary charm, but what they lacked in subtlety they made up for in utility; for centuries, no ship left port without its supply of bone-hard biscuit in the hold to last for the months or even years of a long voyage.

While sailors and other travellers chewed their way through unyielding hardtack, another culinary tradition was developing. Medieval cooks compounded breadcrumbs, honey, wine and spices into an unbaked gingerbread, and introduced eggs, cream and butter into flour and water doughs to create all sorts of light sweetmeats. In wealthy households these little cakes were baked—twice, like their plainer precursors—on metal plates or in buttered moulds and served at the end of banquets. Meanwhile street pedlars did a lively trade in filled and flavoured wafers; the 14th-century cooking manual *Le Ménagier de Paris* explains these were made by pressing a batter between two hot, greased irons. Like so many medieval foods, the wafers combined sweet and savoury elements: in an early recipe, wafers made from flour, egg white, ginger and sugar are filled with cheese and fish.

By the 17th century, sweet biscuits were commonplace. Any reasonably prosperous household was capable of producing little slabs of sugared puff paste, iced biscuits shaped like lovers' knots, or wafers made with cream and rose-water, such as those recommended in the 1605 cookery book *Delights for Ladies*. The original sweetening was honey and, although it was gradually supplanted by sugar, honey remained a prevalent ingredient in the Middle East and parts of Europe.

Over the years, other flavourings were introduced reflecting regional preferences and produce. Then as now, almonds and pine-nuts, for example, marked many Mediterranean recipes; rye and oats betokened the colder lands of northern Europe; sour cream and poppy seeds hinted at a Russian origin. Many biscuits from Scandinavia and Central Europe are flavoured with ginger, cardamom, nutmeg, allspice and aniseeds—all prized in these regions since the days of the medieval spice trade. Greek and Arab biscuits are often perfumed with waters distilled from flowers. And new foods from the New World—molasses, pecan nuts, peanuts and sweet potatoes—have found an appropriate place in many American favourites.

But variety in the world's biscuits is not just a matter of flavouring. Much biscuit-making is an exercise in sculpting and moulding. Although some shapes are chosen only because of their decorative appeal, others have traditional associations with holiday celebrations: no German Christmas is complete without *springerle,* pale sugary plaques embossed with fruits, animals and human figures (*page 66*). In Marseilles, the feast of Candlemas is the occasion for baking biscuits shaped like ships or shuttles (*recipe, page 98*). On Palm Sunday in Albi, in southern France, small biscuit rings are carried on laurel and rosemary branches (*page 90*). Some shapes have roots older than Christianity: for example, some folklorists believe that the notched round of Scottish shortbread, served on New Year's Eve, once symbolized the rays of the Celtic Sun God.

For most cooks, however, the mechanics of shaping depend more upon the consistency of a biscuit's dough than on its historic origins. Some mixtures are firm enough to stamp out with metal cutters (*opposite and page 38*), or force through a mechanical biscuit press (*page 45*); others, such as the shell-shaped madeleines on page 70, are so soft they can only be baked in moulds. Some very thin mixtures, such as creamed egg white batters, bake into wafers that, when hot, are flexible enough to wrap round a rolling pin or the handle of a wooden spoon.

This book explains how to mix and shape virtually every biscuit dough. The first section provides a guide to flavourings and garnishes: chopped nuts, morsels of chocolate, dried fruits (*page 6*); thick icings and transparent glazes (*page 8*); creamy mousses, sweet nut pastes and other fillings (*pages 10-13*). This is followed by five chapters that demonstrate the uses of five basic mixtures; pastry doughs, creamed doughs, meringue and other egg-white mixtures, doughs made with beaten eggs, and doughs incorporating honey or syrup. The final chapter explores unusual cooking methods—the use of a griddle to cook oatcakes and flatbreads, the technique of scalding yeast dough before it is baked, and how to bake a soft dough in two stages to make rusks.

The second half of the book is an anthology chosen from among the world's best biscuit recipes. These come from many different ancient and modern sources; they include 18th-century recipes preserved as treasured heirlooms, as well as a generous supply of new ideas from the leading cookery writers of the present day.

Small Additions that Enhance and Embellish

A sprinkling of small, solid ingredients provides a pleasant contrast to the texture of a basic biscuit dough. Chocolate, nuts and crystallized or dried fruits are often used to complement sweet biscuits, while their savoury counterparts benefit from the addition of cheese, herbs, coarse salt, caraway seeds or poppy seeds. These elements are sometimes mixed into the dough. In other instances they are pressed into the surface of uncooked biscuits, or on to cooked ones, as a decorative finish.

Garnishes are usually simple; in most cases, a single ingredient is used to add to a biscuit's appeal without masking its flavour. Exceptions to this principle are found in elaborate assemblies such as the traditional gingerbread house shown on page 78, which calls for a variety of ornaments, lavishly applied.

Some garnishes need to be prepared before they can be incorporated into a dough or placed on the biscuits. Nuts must be shelled, and the smooth-surfaced ones must be freed of their thin, bitter skins (*right, above*). The nuts are first parboiled or roasted to loosen these membranes, then rolled in a towel to detach them. Nuts with relatively loose skins, such as pistachios or the almonds shown here, are skinned by parboiling—a process called blanching; nuts with tighter skins, such as Brazils or hazelnuts, should be roasted for 10 minutes in a moderate oven.

Once they are peeled, any nuts can be lightly toasted to intensify their flavour. Depending on the texture you want, the nuts can be left whole, chopped with a knife (*centre, right*), or finely ground in a processor or mortar.

Cheese needs to be grated and fresh herbs should be chopped. Chocolate can either be grated or chopped into small pieces with a sharp knife (*right*).

Dried fruits, such as raisins and sultanas, need no preparation. Crystallized citrus peels and angelica will be easier to handle if they are briefly softened in boiling water to reduce their stickiness (*far right*). You can chop these ingredients and mix them into a dough, or you can cut them into crescents, diamonds or other decorative patterns to press on to shaped biscuits before or after baking.

Blanching and Toasting Almonds

1 **Parboiling almonds.** Bring a large pan of water to the boil; tip in the nuts (*above*). Maintain a steady boil for 1 to 2 minutes in order to loosen the skins of the nuts. Remove the pan from the heat.

2 **Draining the almonds.** Set a strainer over a deep heatproof bowl or place a colander in a sink. Carefully pour the almonds and their cooking water into the strainer or colander (*above*).

Cutting Chocolate Chips

Chopping chocolate. With a sharp knife, slice a bar of plain chocolate into slivers about 5 mm ($\frac{1}{4}$ inch) thick (*above, left*). The chocolate will fragment as you cut it. Heap the pieces of chocolate together. Holding the knife blade over the pile, steady the knife tip with your free hand. Using the tip as a pivot, move the blade backwards and forwards in the form of an arc across the chocolate, at the same time rocking the blade up and down (*above, right*). Continue chopping until the pieces are the size that you require.

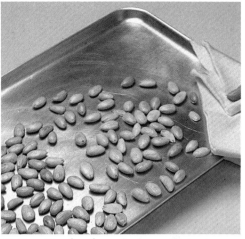

3 **Peeling the almonds with a towel.** Lay a towel on a work surface; tip the hot drained nuts over the middle of the towel. Bring the edges of the towel over the almonds. With the palms of your hands, rub the nuts between the folds of the towel for about 2 minutes, to remove most of the skins (*above*).

4 **Finishing the peeling.** Place the skinned nuts on a baking sheet. If any nuts still remain unpeeled, they should be rubbed between your fingers and thumb in order to remove the stubborn skin (*above*).

5 **Toasting the almonds.** Spread the nuts on the baking sheet in a single layer. Bake them in a preheated 180°C (350°F or Mark 4) oven for 10 to 15 minutes stirring the nuts occasionally—until they are evenly browned (*above*).

An Efficient Way with Nuts

Chopping nuts. Heap peeled nuts— here, pistachio nuts—on a chopping board. Position the blade of a heavy, sharp knife above the nuts. Holding the knife tip with one hand, use your other hand to rock the blade backwards and forwards across the pile of nuts (*above*).

Handling Crystallized Peel

1 **Softening in boiling water.** Bring a pan of water to the boil. Drop pieces of crystallized peel and angelica into the pan and boil them for 1 to 2 minutes until they are soft. Remove the peel and angelica with a slotted spoon (*above*).

2 **Cutting decorative shapes.** Place the angelica and peel on a chopping board. Slice the angelica into matchstick strips (*background*). Using a small, sharp knife or, as here, an aspic cutter, cut out little geometric shapes from the peel (*above*).

Icings and Glazes for a Finishing Touch

A smooth glaze or icing can be used to embellish the surface of any biscuit. A glaze gives a biscuit a sheen without obscuring its appearance (*right*). An icing—a thick, opaque mixture—is usually spread over a biscuit to mask its surface and provide a contrast in texture (*below*).

The glazes most commonly used for biscuits are those based on eggs. Brushed over an uncooked dough, egg glazes will set while the biscuits bake. Depending on the effect you want, you can make the glaze from whites, yolks or whole eggs. Egg whites, applied on their own, will give a colourless sheen, while whole eggs or yolks, beaten with a little water to thin them, will set to a shiny, transparent gold. Egg yolks can also be blended with caramel—an amber sugar syrup—to produce a reddish-brown glaze (*right*), or with very strong coffee, to flavour the coating.

Sweetened milk will provide another simple glaze. Milk and sugar, stirred over a low heat until the sugar dissolves, can be brushed over biscuits just out of the oven in order to give them a light, subtle gloss.

To give the baked biscuits a light matt finish, you can paint them with an icing sugar glaze. This is made by blending the icing sugar with warm water until it reaches a thin, coating consistency (*opposite page, below, right*). You can flavour the mixture by replacing a small amount of the water with liqueur or spirits, such as the rum used here, or you can squeeze in a dash of lemon juice to offset the sweetness of the sugar. A fruit purée will colour the glaze: a few raspberries, for example, can be passed through a sieve and mixed in to tinge the mixture a delicate pink.

Another way to colour the surface of a cooked biscuit is to apply a layer of sieved jam (*opposite page, below, left*). The jam can also be applied as an undercoat, then covered with a glaze of icing sugar and water; the two layers of different glazes will give the biscuits a brilliant shine.

In contrast to glazes, icings need to be stiff enough to coat biscuits thickly and evenly. Icings are always applied after the biscuits are baked. Royal icing (*below; recipe, page 167*) is a hard coating made from icing sugar beaten with egg whites. Beating the mixture until it is smooth and thick will take about 15 minutes by hand, or about 5 minutes with an electric mixer. The firm icing is easily spread with a metal spatula or forced through a piping bag on to the biscuit.

Another thick topping can be made from plain chocolate. No beating is necessary; the chocolate will achieve a thick coating consistency if it is simply broken into pieces, placed in a bowl set over a pan of hot water, and allowed to melt.

Glazes and icings can also be used in combination with biscuit garnishes. For example, sugar and chopped nuts can be sprinkled over an uncooked dough that has been washed with an egg glaze; gently rolled into the dough, it will become part of the biscuit's surface. A garnish such as a halved almond can be pressed on to an uncooked dough, then glazed after baking. A decoration can also be placed on a moist topping; as the glaze or icing sets, the garnish will adhere to the biscuit.

A Sturdy Icing Made with Egg Whites

1 **Adding icing sugar.** Crack an egg on the side of a mixing bowl. Open the shell and drop the yolk from one half to the other, letting the white fall into the bowl. Separate the remaining eggs in the same way. Add a few spoonfuls of sifted icing sugar to the whites (*above, left*). Stir the sugar into the whites, then beat the mixture until smooth. Add the rest of the sugar, a little at a time (*above, right*), beating well after each addition.

2 **Finishing the icing.** When all the icing sugar has been incorporated, continue beating the mixture until it is stiff (*above*). The icing is ready for use immediately or it can be set aside, covered with a damp cloth, for 30 minutes; if it is kept longer, the icing will begin to set.

A Brilliant Sheen from Caramel and Egg Yolks

1 **Beating egg yolks.** Break up egg yolks with a fork (*above*). Put sugar and cold water in a heavy saucepan; place the pan over a medium heat. Gently stir until the sugar has dissolved. With a brush dipped in hot water, brush down any sugar crystals sticking to the side of the pan: these might cause the syrup to crystallize. Bring the mixture to the boil.

2 **Thinning caramel.** Maintaining a light, steady boil, cook the syrup just until it turns a rich, red brown. Turn off the heat immediately lest the caramel burns. Pour a little hot water into the caramel to thin it and prevent it from setting (*above*).

3 **Mixing eggs and caramel.** Pour a little of the caramel and water mixture into the beaten egg yolks, stirring as you pour (*above*). Gradually add more caramel until the glaze is a deep golden-brown.

Sieving Jam for Smoothness

Forcing jam through a sieve. Put jam—in this case, apricot—into a heavy pan and heat it gently until it becomes runny. Set a sieve over a bowl and pour the jam into the sieve. Push the jam through the mesh with a wooden spoon or a pestle. Scrape off the jam that sticks to the bottom of the sieve and add it to the bowl.

A Light Coating with a Taste of Rum

1 **Adding rum.** Sift icing sugar into a bowl and make a well in the centre of the sugar. Add a spoonful of warm water, and stir it in. Gradually mix in more water to make a fairly thick paste. Pour a spoonful of rum into the mixture (*above*).

2 **Checking the consistency.** Mix the rum into the glaze. Lift the spoon above the bowl; the consistency is right if the glaze coats the back of the spoon (*above*). If necessary, stir in more water to thin the glaze, or add more sugar to thicken it.

Foundations for Fillings

Fillings are indispensable elements in biscuit assemblies. Mixtures based on nuts, butter and sugar, chocolate, fruit and other ingredients can be used to sandwich two biscuits together, or they can fill hollow shapes such as cups, cornets and cigarettes. These additions give biscuits a very special appearance, offering a pleasant contrast of colour, flavour and texture to a relatively dry biscuit dough.

Some fillings must be combined with a dough before it is baked. Those based on nuts, for example, are often too dry to adhere to a cooked biscuit, so it is best to shape the uncooked dough round them. This applies to smooth, firm mixtures such as marzipan—a stiff paste made of finely ground almonds and sugar bound with egg (*below; recipe, page 167*)—as well as to much looser blends of coarsely chopped nuts. A combination of walnuts, sugar and rose-water is shown here (*opposite page, below; recipe, page 166*), but you could also use hazelnuts or pistachio nuts and a different liquid, such as orange-flower water, for a similar effect.

Fillings based on fruit can be combined with an uncooked dough or they can be added to a biscuit that is already baked. You can fill biscuits with a fruit jam that has been sieved for smoothness, adding a few chopped nuts to vary the texture. Dried fruits, such as apricots, prunes and figs, can be cooked and chopped (*right, centre*) or they can be ground, then bound with honey to form a paste.

Some fillings are best added to biscuits after they are cooked. Icing sugar, bound with water or any liquid flavouring and melted butter, will make a firm, smooth paste that is ideal for sandwiching two biscuits together. You can flavour the resulting cream with the juice and grated rind of oranges or lemons (*right, above; recipe, page 167*), with a few sieved redcurrants or blackberries, or with very strong coffee. A dash of brandy, rum or any sweet liqueur can also be added.

Cooked biscuits can also be filled with a chocolate paste such as ganache—a blend of melted chocolate and cream that is whipped into a light mousse (*page 12, above; recipe, page 167*). It is easy to pipe into elaborate shapes and swirls that make a decorative filling for a cornet or other hollow biscuit.

Softened butter, beaten until fluffy, will also make a rich filling base that can be flavoured with puréed fruit, sugar and brandy or with praline, a mixture of powdered nuts and sugar (*page 12, below; recipe, page 166*). To make the praline, nuts and sugar are cooked together. This toasts the nuts, intensifying their flavour, and also melts the sugar to a rich, dark caramel. As this caramel cools, it will encase the nuts in a hard, brittle sheet that is easily pounded into a fine powder.

A Subtle Lemon-Flavoured Cream

1 **Adding lemon juice.** Melt butter in a small pan. Sift icing sugar into a bowl. Grate lemon rind and add it to the bowl. Squeeze the juice from the lemons and pour it into the bowl (*above*).

Softening Dried Fruits

1 **Preparing dried figs.** Place dried figs and water in a pan; simmer for 10 minutes, or until the figs have softened. Drain the figs, reserving the cooking water. Remove their stalks (*above*).

Marzipan: a Sweet Paste of Ground Almonds

1 **Mixing almonds and sugar.** Beat eggs with a fork until blended. Blanch almonds (*page 6*) and grind them in a processor. Place nuts, sugar and grated lemon rind in a bowl; mix with your hands (*above*).

2 **Adding the eggs.** Pour a little of the beaten egg into the bowl. Stir the egg into the almond and sugar mixture (*above*). Add more egg, a little at a time, until the mixture begins to cohere.

3 **Gathering the paste together.** When the mixture is sufficiently moistened by the eggs to hold together, gather it with your hands. Press it into a ball (*above*). Knead briefly until the paste is smooth.

2 Stirring. Add the melted butter to the bowl. Place the bowl over a pan of boiling water and stir until the mixture is smooth (*above*). Turn off the heat and leave for 10 minutes; stir occasionally.

3 Beating the cream. Remove the bowl from the pan and beat the warm mixture with a wooden spoon (*above, left*). Continue beating the lemon cream as it cools, until it has a thick, spreading consistency (*above, right*).

2 Chopping. Heap the figs on a chopping board. Place a heavy knife across the pile. Steadying the knife tip with one hand, rock the blade up and down across the figs, to chop them coarsely.

3 Cooking the filling. Place the chopped figs, sugar and the reserved cooking water in a heavy pan. Stir the contents of the pan over a moderate heat (*above, left*). Bring the mixture to the boil, then reduce the heat and simmer for about 10 minutes, until the filling is thick (*above, right*).

An Exotic Blend of Nuts and Rose-Water

1 Mixing nuts and sugar. Coarsely chop walnuts (*page 7*). Place them in a bowl with an equal quantity of castor sugar. Mix the nuts and the sugar (*above*).

2 Moistening the filling. Pour in a spoonful of rose-water (*above, left*). Stir the rose-water into the nut and sugar mixture. If necessary, add more rose-water to give the filling the consistency of coarse breadcrumbs (*above, right*).

Ganache: a Whipped Mousse of Chocolate and Cream

1 **Adding double cream.** Break or cut plain chocolate into little pieces. Place the pieces of plain chocolate in a heavy bottomed pan. Then pour double cream into the pan (*above*).

2 **Blending the chocolate and cream.** Place the pan over a low heat and melt the chocolate. Stir continuously to prevent the chocolate from scorching (above, left). When the chocolate has melted, continue stirring until the mixture is smooth and dark, and thickly coats the back of the spoon (above, right).

Praline: a Powdered Amalgam of Sugared Nuts

1 **Mixing almonds and sugar.** Oil or butter a baking sheet. Place blanched almonds and sugar in a heavy saucepan. Stir the contents of the pan over a low heat with a wooden spoon (*above*). Continue to stir the mixture until the sugar has melted to an amber caramel.

2 **Cooling the nuts and caramel.** Tip the pan over the baking sheet. With the spoon, push the contents on to the sheet (*above*). Spread the mixture with the spoon and leave it to cool.

3 **Pounding the nuts and caramel.** Place the cooled, hard, nut and caramel mixture in a sturdy, clear plastic bag. Holding the end of the bag to prevent the contents from spilling out, pound the mixture with a mallet or rolling pin (*above*).

3 **Cooling the chocolate mixture.** Pour the hot melted chocolate and cream into a mixing bowl (*above*). Set the mixture aside until it is cool. At this stage it is ready to use as an icing, if you like.

4 **Whipping the filling.** To make the chocolate mixture into a mousse that is suitable for piping, whisk it with a circular motion, steadying the bowl with your free hand (*above, left*). Continue to whisk until the filling has incorporated enough air to make it increase in bulk and become light and fluffy (*above, right*).

4 **Sieving the mixture.** When some of the mixture has been reduced to a powder, tip the contents of the bag into a sieve set over a bowl. Stir the mixture with your hand to allow the powder to fall through the sieve (*above*). Return the lumps to the bag and repeat the process until all the mixture has been powdered.

5 **Mixing butter and praline.** Let butter soften at room temperature; place it in a bowl. Beat the butter until it is pale and fluffy. Add some of the praline powder to the bowl and stir it into the butter (*above*).

6 **Beating the praline butter.** Beat the praline powder and butter mixture until it becomes a smooth paste. Gradually incorporate more praline into the butter, beating well after each addition (*above*).

1
Biscuits made from Pastry Doughs
A Repertoire of Simple Techniques

Pastry dough is the foundation of a variety of biscuits that range from plain savoury crackers to flaky, sugared confections. Most of these biscuits are made from the classic pastry doughs, such as shortcrust and puff dough; these doughs, which are also used for larger pies and tarts, provide a medium for devising many different biscuits. Other doughs, unique to biscuits, employ the techniques of pastry-making for special effects.

The art of pastry-making is sometimes shrouded in mystery, but if you understand your ingredients and handle them lightly, you can easily achieve perfect results. The base of any pastry dough is a mixture of flour, which provides bulk, and fat—usually butter—which provides tenderness. These ingredients are combined, and then moistened with liquid to form a dough. Always keep ingredients cold and handle them as little as possible; this prevents the fat from becoming oily. It is also important not to overwork the dough; this would strengthen the gluten network in the flour and make the biscuits tough.

The texture of the finished biscuits depends on the amount of fat in the dough, the kind of fat used and the way in which the ingredients are blended. Rubbing in a small quantity of lard will produce a simple water cracker (*page 16*); a much higher proportion of butter can be cut into the flour for crisp shortcrust (*page 18*); you can produce even richer results by including sugar and binding the mixture with egg (*page 22*). By a sequence of rolling, folding and chilling, a rich shortcrust dough can be transformed into a rough-puff which yields both sweet and savoury biscuits of exquisite flakiness (*page 26*).

A sheet of pastry dough provides an opportunity for devising many different biscuits. Plain shortcrust can be enlivened with sweet or savoury fillings, then rolled into a cylinder and sliced into thin biscuits (*page 18*), but you can also use this dough to encircle a more substantial filling, such as a log of marzipan (*page 24*). In this case, the dough can be flavoured with spices to provide a crisp, spicy casing for the almond filling. Rough-puff dough, which rises in flaky layers when baked, can be given a couple of turns in sugar or grated cheese to flavour the dough. Because of the way it rises, rough-puff dough provides a special opportunity for imaginative shaping (*pages 28-32*)—some examples of this are shown opposite.

An alluring assortment of biscuits, in a variety of shapes, have been created from a single batch of rough-puff dough. The twisted sticks are embellished with almonds, the tiny cases are filled with jam, while extra sugar provides the heart-shaped palmiers and pastry butterflies with a gleaming caramelized surface.

Basic Steps for a Savoury Cracker

The simplest pastry dough—a mixture of fat and flour, bound with water—forms the base for a wide range of biscuits. If the proportion of fat to flour is low, the result is a dough that is easy to roll out thinly, to make crisp savoury crackers called water biscuits (*right; recipe, page 161*).

Here, the dough is made with one part of lard for every four parts of white flour; the relatively small quantity of lard, and its unassertive taste, determine the dry texture and mild flavour of the biscuits. If you use butter instead of lard, the biscuits will be more brittle, while other flours, such as whole wheat, will yield a coarser, more crumbly biscuit.

Whenever you make pastry, it is essential to keep the dough cold, and to handle it quickly and lightly. Use your fingertips to rub cold fat into the flour, so that the heat of your hands does not melt the fat and make the mixture oily. Here, a little baking powder is sifted with the flour, to leaven the dough slightly and to help produce the characteristic bubbled surface of the water biscuits.

Always use cold water to bind the dough; the amount of water needed may vary according to the type of fat and flour used. Start by adding less water than you think you may need—if the dough feels crumbly, you can always add a little more, but too much liquid will make the dough sticky. Light handling is important at this stage, too, since overworking would strengthen the gluten, making the dough too elastic to roll out, and the biscuits tough when baked.

The dough should be rolled out immediately on a lightly floured surface—marble is ideal as it helps to keep the dough cool. In this instance, the sheet of dough is pricked with a fork before it is cut into rounds; during baking, steam will rise through the tiny pricked holes and prevent the dough from buckling.

You can add a subtle, savoury flavour to the biscuits by sprinkling them with a little coarse salt, caraway seeds or poppy seeds before baking. Plain or flavoured, water biscuits are an ideal accompaniment to cheese and savoury spreads.

1 Sifting the dry ingredients. Measure the flour and transfer it to a fine-meshed sieve set over a large mixing bowl. Add a pinch of salt and baking powder. To sift, gently shake the sieve, tapping the side with the palm of your hand. Alternatively, you can use a flour sifter.

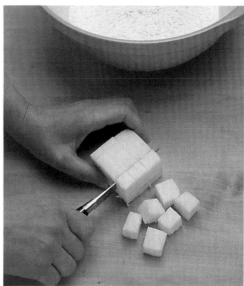

2 Cutting the fat into cubes. Use chilled fat—in this case, a block of lard—and cut it into rough cubes. To make cubes, first slice the fat in half horizontally, then lengthwise and crosswise (*above*).

5 Gathering the dough. Using one hand, gather together the mixture in the bowl. Press the dough lightly against the base and the side of the bowl and form it into a smooth ball. If the mixture is too crumbly to form a ball, add a little more water.

6 Rolling out the dough. Place the dough on a lightly floured work surface. To prevent the rolling pin from sticking, sprinkle a little flour over the surface of the dough. With firm, light strokes, roll the dough forwards. Then turn the dough clockwise, by 45 degrees—known as a quarter turn—and roll it again. Repeat until it is about 3 mm ($\frac{1}{8}$ inch) thick.

3 **Rubbing the fat into the flour.** Transfer the fat to the bowl of sifted flour. Pick up small amounts of fat and flour, and rub them lightly between the tips of your fingers and thumbs; let the mixture fall through your fingers back into the bowl in large flakes (*above, left*). Continue the process for about 3 minutes, scooping in the unrubbed ingredients, until all the fat is rubbed into the flour (*above, right*). The mixture will form coarse-textured crumbs.

4 **Adding water.** Make a small well in the centre of the mixture and pour in cold water very gradually, stirring it in with a knife, until the dough forms a cohesive mass. If the dough is too dry to cohere, add more cold water, a little at a time, until the dough clings together.

7 **Cutting out the biscuits.** Prick the sheet of dough all over with a fork. Then, using a biscuit cutter—here, 9 cm (3½ inches) in diameter—cut out circles from the dough (*above*); with a spatula, place them on a lightly greased baking sheet. Gather up the scraps of dough into a ball, roll it out and cut more shapes. If you like, sprinkle the biscuits with coarse salt.

8 **Baking and serving.** Bake the biscuits in a preheated 180°C (350°F or Mark 4) oven, for 10 to 15 minutes, or until they colour slightly. Transfer them to a rack to cool. Here, the biscuits are presented in a napkin-lined basket. □

Buttery Spirals with Cinnamon and Sugar

A dough rich in butter will produce crisp, golden biscuits with a flaky texture. The shortcrust dough shown here (*right; recipe, page 165*) is made with three parts of butter for every four parts of flour. The butter can be rubbed into the flour (*page 17*) but, if you cut the butter into the flour instead (*Step 2*), the butter will remain in larger pieces, and the dough, when baked, will produce a flakier biscuit.

The high proportion of butter makes it especially important to keep the dough cold and to handle it lightly, so that the butter does not become oily. To firm the butter, the dough is chilled before use. This resting period will also relax the gluten in the flour, making the dough less elastic and easier to roll out.

The rolled-out dough can be shaped with biscuit cutters, or you can sprinkle a sheet of dough with a light filling—such as sugar and spice, jam, chopped nuts or dried fruit—roll it into a log, then slice it. You can also make savoury biscuits by sprinkling the dough with grated cheese, or herbs such as chives and tarragon.

1 **Preparing the ingredients.** Sift flour and salt together into a large mixing bowl; set it aside. Cut a block of chilled butter horizontally through the middle; then slice the block lengthwise and crosswise into 1 cm (½ inch) cubes (*above*).

2 **Cutting in the butter.** Put the cubes of butter into the bowl of flour. With two table knives, cut the butter into the flour: repeatedly cross the blades of the knives and draw them apart, making sure that you cut right through the mixture so that the knife tips touch the bottom of the bowl (*above*). Continue cutting until the butter is reduced to small pieces.

6 **Adding flavourings.** Prepare a filling of your choice—a mixture of castor sugar and freshly ground cinnamon is used here for a sweet, spicy taste. Sprinkle the mixture evenly over the surface of the dough (*above*). With a rolling pin, lightly roll over the flavouring to ensure that it clings to the dough.

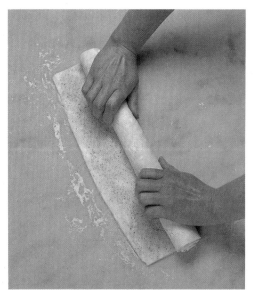

7 **Forming a roll.** Pick up a long edge of the rectangle and fold it over, to make a narrow hem that will form the centre of the finished biscuits. Then, applying light pressure and starting from the hem, roll up the dough into a log shape (*above*). To make the roll firm and easier to slice, chill it in the refrigerator, or in the freezer, for 10 to 15 minutes.

8 **Slicing the roll.** Place the chilled roll on a work surface. Using a sharp knife with a narrow blade, slice the roll at intervals of 5 mm (¼ inch) to make thin biscuits. Transfer the slices to a baking sheet.

3 **Stirring in the water.** Pour a little cold water over the mixture and stir it in lightly with a fork or, as here, a knife (*above*). Continue to add water, stirring quickly, until the mixture just clings together.

4 **Gathering the dough.** With your hand, gather up the dough. Firmly press the dough together and form it into a ball. Wrap the dough in plastic film to prevent it from drying out, and then chill it in the refrigerator for at least 15 minutes or in the freezer for half that time.

5 **Rolling out the dough.** Place the dough on a lightly floured work surface—here, a marble surface to help keep the dough cold. Roll out the dough into a rectangle about 3 mm (⅛ inch) thick. With a long, sharp knife, trim off the uneven edges. Roll the trimmings into a ball and reserve them; you can roll them out and cut individual biscuits.

9 **Baking and serving.** Place the baking sheet in a preheated 180°C (350°F or Mark 4) oven for about 10 minutes, or until the biscuits are firm to the touch and golden-brown. Remove the sheet from the oven and, with a spatula, transfer the biscuits to a wire rack to cool (*above*). Piled high on a napkin-lined plate (*right*), the honey-gold, buttery spirals make an attractive presentation.□

Forming a Round of Crumbly Shortbread

A simple rubbed dough containing flour, sugar and a generous amount of butter will produce rich, crumbly shortbread (*right; recipe, page 94*). No liquid will be needed to bind together the ingredients, since the moist crumbs formed by rubbing a large quantity of butter into flour and sugar can be pressed together by hand.

There are many ways to vary the flavour and texture of shortbread. A plain dough can be made with wheat flour alone, but many traditional recipes, such as that demonstrated here, combine two parts of wheat flour with one part of rice flour, yielding shortbread with a lighter texture. If you mix wheat flour with fine semolina, the shortbread will be very crunchy, while ground almonds blended with the flour will give the biscuits a delicate, nutty taste.

A few drops of concentrated flavouring, such as almond extract, are often added. Or, for a more pronounced effect, you can substitute one or two tablespoons of vanilla sugar—sugar stored for a week or more with a vanilla pod in a closed jar—for ordinary sugar in the dough.

The ingredients for shortbread are always rubbed together until they form a fine, consistent, crumbly mass that is gathered into a neat ball. The dough is too crumbly to roll out, but it is easily pressed into shape by hand. Here, the dough is formed into a flat round and a fork is used to neaten and decorate the edge.

You can decorate the shaped dough by pressing a round wooden mould over it; a traditional Scottish shortbread board is stamped with a thistle, but you can print the dough with other patterns as well. The dough is pricked with a fork to allow the steam to escape during baking; this will prevent the shortbread from buckling while it cooks.

Since the baked shortbread quickly cools to a crumbly biscuit that is tricky to cut, the surface of the dough is scored into portions with a knife before it is placed in the oven. After baking, but while still warm and tender, the shortbread is cut along the pre-scored lines; it can be re-assembled into a round when you serve it.

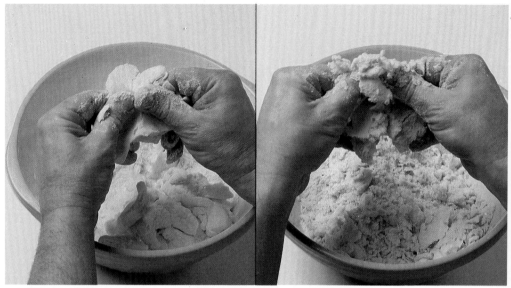

1 **Rubbing the butter into sugar and flour.** Sift sugar, a pinch of salt and flour—here, a mixture of plain wheat flour and rice flour—into a large mixing bowl. Cut butter into cubes and add them to the bowl. With the tips of your fingers and thumbs, pick up small amounts of the butter and the dry ingredients and rub them together, letting the mixture form large flakes that fall back into the bowl (*above, left*). Continue rubbing for 2 to 3 minutes, until the entire mixture is even and crumbly (*above, right*).

4 **Finishing the dough.** For a decorative edge, press the prongs of a fork round the circumference of the shaped round (*above, left*). Prick the dough all over with the fork. Using a long knife, score the surface of the dough into wedge-shaped portions (*above, right*).

2 **Gathering the dough.** Using fingertips and thumbs, press the mixture so that it gradually clings together (*above*). When the mixture has formed a cohesive mass, gather it into a ball.

3 **Shaping the dough.** Transfer the ball of dough to a lightly greased baking sheet. Steadying the dough with one hand, use the heel of your other hand to flatten the ball into a rough round (*above, left*). Then, with the outstretched fingers of one hand, pat the dough into a flat, evenly shaped disc, keeping the edge of the disc smooth with your free hand as you work (*above, right*).

5 **Baking and serving.** Place the baking sheet in a preheated 180°C (350°F or Mark 4) oven for about 20 minutes, or until the shortbread is pale golden. Slide a metal spatula under the shortbread to ease it from the baking sheet and cut it into wedges while it is still hot. Leave the cut shortbread on the baking sheet. After about 15 minutes, when the wedges are firm enough to handle, transfer them to a rack to cool. To serve, rearrange the pieces into the original round (*right*).□

Rich Shortcrust with an Amber Glaze

A rich shortcrust dough, containing sugar and eggs, yields tender, golden biscuits that owe their full flavour to these extra ingredients (*right; recipe, page 96*). Like plain shortcrust (*page 18*), the dough is rich in butter, but the flour is sweetened with sugar and the mixture is bound with eggs instead of water.

For a fine, crumbly texture, the butter is rubbed into the flour and sugar until the mixture forms sand-like particles. If you like, the dough can be flavoured with spices or grated lemon rind.

The addition of eggs makes the dough sticky, so it requires gentle kneading to make it smooth and pliable. Since it contains sugar, this dough is harder to roll out than plain shortcrust, but after it has been chilled—to firm the butter and to relax the gluten—it will be easier to handle.

Once rolled, the dough can be stamped out with biscuit cutters, then coated with any glaze or icing. An egg glaze coloured with caramel (*page 9*) gives a rich red-brown finish; when mixed with strong coffee, it will add flavour.

1 Assembling the ingredients. Sift flour into a large bowl with the sugar—here, icing sugar, for a fine texture. Add small cubes of cold butter and, if you like, grate the rind of a lemon into the bowl (*above*).

2 Rubbing in the butter. Using your fingers and thumbs, pick up small amounts of the mixture and rub them together, letting them fall back into the bowl in large flakes (*above*). With continued rubbing, the flakes will become smaller, and they will eventually form fine, even crumbs.

5 Kneading the dough. Transfer the dough to a lightly floured work surface and knead it gently: press the heel of your hand into the centre of the dough and gently push it forwards (*above, left*); fold the extended section of dough backwards on to the mass (*above, right*). Give the dough a quarter turn and knead it once again. Shape the dough into a ball and wrap it in plastic film. To make it easier to roll, chill the dough in the refrigerator for about 30 minutes.

6 Rolling out the dough. Place the chilled dough on a lightly floured work surface. Flatten the ball of dough slightly with a rolling pin. Using firm, light strokes, roll the dough forwards; then give the dough a quarter turn and roll it forwards again. Continue to roll the dough forwards and turn it, until it forms an even round about 3 mm ($\frac{1}{8}$ inch) thick (*above*).

3 **Adding eggs.** Make a well in the centre of the mixture and add one whole egg. Over a small bowl, crack another egg; separate the egg by passing the yolk from one half-shell to the other, while allowing the white to drip into the small bowl (*above*). Add the egg yolk to the ingredients in the mixing bowl; reserve the white for another use.

4 **Blending the dough.** With a fork or, as here, the blade of a knife, cut the eggs into the rubbed mixture. Start by drawing in the flour round the well in the centre (*above, left*) and gradually work outwards until all the flour is incorporated; the mixture will become moist and crumbly (*above, right*). Gather it into a ball with your hands.

7 **Shaping the dough.** With a biscuit cutter, cut out as many shapes as possible from the sheet of dough. Pull away the dough trimmings (*above*) and stack them up. Transfer the biscuits to a lightly greased baking sheet with a spatula. Press the trimmings together, chill them, and then roll them out to cut out more biscuits.

8 **Glazing the biscuits.** Prepare an egg glaze—here, it is coloured with caramel. Using a pastry brush, evenly coat the surface of the biscuits with the glaze (*above*); allow the first coat to dry, and then apply a second layer. Decorate the biscuits by drawing the prongs of a fork across the egg glaze before it dries.

9 **Baking and serving.** Bake the biscuits in a preheated 200°C (400°F or Mark 6) oven for about 12 minutes, or until the undersides of the biscuits are golden: the tops will in any event be brown from the egg glaze. Transfer the finished biscuits immediately to a wire rack and leave them to cool before serving.□

A Spicy Wrapping for a Marzipan Filling

By enclosing a filling in a long strip of pastry dough, you can assemble a roll that, when baked and sliced, will yield a quantity of filled biscuits. Shortcrust dough, whether it is plain (*page 18*) or enriched (*page 22*) makes an excellent wrapping, since it is strong enough to support a bulky filling. Here, enriched shortcrust—lightly leavened with baking powder and flavoured with spices—encircles a cylinder of marzipan (*page 10*). The rich, aromatic blend of spices—known in Holland as *speculaas* spice—complements the sweetness of the filling, and the finished assembly is decorated with almonds (*recipe, page 109*).

If you prefer, the dough can be left plain, or it can be flavoured with a single spice, such as cinnamon. Fillings containing figs, dates or mixed dried fruits (*page 10*) can be used instead. These soft fillings are spooned on to the rolled-out dough, then enclosed by pressing the long sides of the dough together. Whatever the filling, the rolls are then glazed, baked and sliced.

1 Starting the dough. In a small bowl, beat eggs lightly with a fork. Sift flour and baking powder into a large bowl, add cubes of cold butter and rub the mixture until it forms crumbs (*page 16, Steps 1 to 3*). Add sugar, grated lemon rind and ground spices—in this case, cinnamon, nutmeg, cloves, ginger, cardamom and white pepper. Mix well by hand (*above*).

2 Blending the dough. Make a well in the centre of the dry ingredients and pour in the eggs. With a fork or knife, blend in the eggs (*page 23, Step 4*). Gather the dough with your hand (*above*) and press it into a ball. Wrap the dough in plastic film and chill it for at least 1 hour, to make it easier to roll out.

6 Forming the assembly. To make the dough and the filling adhere, brush the surface of the dough with beaten egg—a whole egg and an extra yolk are used here. Lay a roll of marzipan in the centre of a strip of dough. Roll the dough round the marzipan in order to form a tight cylinder (*above*). Assemble the other rolls in the same way.

7 Glazing and garnishing the rolls. Place the rolls on a lightly greased baking sheet, so that their seams are facing downwards. Brush the surface of the rolls with beaten egg (*above*). Press a row of halved, blanched almonds along the top of each roll. Place them close together and at a diagonal slant.

8 Finishing and baking. For extra gloss, coat the rolls once again with the beaten egg (*above*). Bake them in a preheated 180°C (350°F or Mark 4) oven for about 25 minutes. Remove the baking sheet from the oven and slide a metal spatula underneath the rolls to loosen them from the sheet. Since the rolls are fragile, leave them on the baking sheet to cool.

3 **Shaping marzipan.** Prepare marzipan for the filling. Place the ball of dough on a lightly floured surface. Cut the marzipan into pieces—here, divided in four. Roll each piece of marzipan by hand into a cylinder about 2.5 cm (1 inch) in diameter and as long as your baking sheet; in this instance, 35 cm (14 inches) long.

4 **Rolling out the dough.** Set the marzipan aside. With quick, firm strokes, roll out the dough until it is about 3 mm ($\frac{1}{8}$ inch) thick, turning the dough to roll it into an even rectangle that is slightly longer than your baking sheet (*above*).

5 **Trimming the dough.** With a long, sharp knife, trim the edges of the dough to make an even rectangle—here, 40 by 35 cm (16 by 14 inches). Cut the rectangle into strips, each about 10 cm (4 inches) wide and as long as the rolls of marzipan. Gather up the trimmings and use them to make individual biscuits.

9 **Slicing and serving.** Transfer the cooled rolls to a wooden board and slice each roll diagonally between the almonds (*above*). Each slice forms an attractive chunky biscuit decorated with a nut; here, the biscuits are arranged to show their rich, pale filling (*right*). □

The Secrets of Rough-Puff

A puff dough that rises into crisp, flaky layers in the oven's heat yields a range of biscuits distinguished by their melting lightness. The rough-puff dough here begins as a simple cut shortcrust (*page 18*), but is transformed by repeated rolling, folding and chilling (*recipe, page 165*).

The structure of rough-puff depends upon the fact that the butter is not evenly incorporated into the flour. Instead, the butter remains in distinct pieces; these are reduced to a thin film when the dough is rolled. Each folding sequence creates more layers of dough, and air is trapped between them. During baking, the air expands, the butter melts, and moisture in the dough becomes steam, lifting the layers into tender flakes.

The basic ingredients of the dough are flour, butter and liquid; sugar is mixed with the flour for a sweet dough. Equal weights of butter and flour are used, and the dough must be kept cold so that the butter does not become oily. Cutting the butter into the dry ingredients leaves it in fairly large pieces—when rolled out, the dough displays streaks of butter (*Step 6*).

Rough-puff dough can be bound just with water, or with milk, cream or egg yolks thinned with a little water. Here, a binding of egg yolk, rum and cream gives an especially full flavour.

The dough must be chilled as soon as the liquid has been added, and chilled again between each of the rolling and folding sequences—known as "turns"—that follow. Chilling will firm butter, and during the resting periods the gluten in the flour will relax, making the dough easier to roll. You can chill the dough in the freezer, but remove it immediately if particles of ice form on its surface.

The completed dough can also be rolled in sugar before it is shaped. Sweetened rough-puff is used to make the heart-shaped biscuits known as palmiers (*page 28*). The rich, sugared dough may distort slightly during baking, so that some of the heart shapes may be imperfect. But the sugar caramelizes during baking, giving the biscuits an attractive, amber colour.

1 Starting the dough. Cut cold butter into cubes. Sift flour into a large mixing bowl; add sugar. Cut the butter rapidly into the dry ingredients with two knives (*page 18, Step 2*), until the cubes become fairly large pieces. Put an egg yolk into a small bowl, add water or, as here, rum; pour in cream (*above*). Stir the liquids together lightly with a fork.

2 Mixing the dough. Pour the liquid mixture all at once over the ingredients in the large bowl. With a fork, stir in the liquid lightly (*above*), distributing the liquid evenly throughout the mixture to ensure that it does not form clumps.

6 Rolling and folding. With light, forward strokes, roll the dough into a rough rectangle about 1 cm (½ inch) thick. If necessary, sprinkle on a little more flour to prevent sticking. At this stage, the edges of the dough will be uneven. Fold over the ends of the rectangle, so that they meet in the centre (*above*).

7 Forming a square package. Fold the dough in half so that it forms a roughly square package, resting one hand in the crease as you fold over the end (*above*). The original ends, folded into the centre in Step 6, should now be enclosed in the package, which comprises four layers.

3 **Gathering the dough.** When the liquid is incorporated, gather the dough together with your hands (*above*). Press it lightly into a ball, wrap it in plastic film and chill it in the refrigerator for 45 minutes, or in the freezer for half that time, to rest the dough and make the butter firm.

4 **Flattening the dough.** Lightly flour a cool work surface. Place the cold dough, which will be quite hard, on the surface. Sprinkle the dough lightly with flour. Press down on the ball of dough with the heel of your hand to flatten it (*above*).

5 **Beating the dough.** To make the dough more supple and to flatten it into a rough oval shape for rolling out, beat it with a rolling pin. Strike the surface of the dough with the pin until the dough is about 2 cm (¾ inch) thick. So that the pin will not stick to the dough, sprinkle the dough with a little flour, brushing off any excess.

8 **Turning and rolling.** Turn the package 90 degrees so that the folded ends are at the side and an open end is directly in front of you. Roll the dough forwards into a rectangle three times as long as it is wide (*above*). Repeat Steps 6 and 7, folding the dough into a square. Wrap the dough in plastic film and chill it in the refrigerator for at least 30 minutes.

9 **Completing the sequence.** Remove the dough from the refrigerator. With an open end in front of you and the folded edges at the side, roll out a rectangle (*Step 8*). Then fold the dough into a square (*Steps 6 and 7*) and chill it again. The dough is now ready for use, but if you want an even flakier dough, you can roll, fold and chill it again.

10 **Preparing to use the dough.** After its final turning and chilling, remove the dough from the refrigerator. With a long, sharp knife, cut off as much dough as you need for shaping into biscuits. Wrap the rest of the dough in plastic film and refrigerate until you are ready to use it; it can be stored in the refrigerator for up to two days. ▶

11 **Rolling the dough in sugar.** Sprinkle a work surface with castor sugar. Place the dough on the sugared surface and sprinkle a little more sugar over the dough (*above, left*). Roll the dough forwards into a rectangle—here, 30 cm (12 inches) long (*above, centre*). Fold the ends of the rectangle to the centre (*above, right*), then fold the dough in half to make a square package. For an even sweeter dough, give the dough a quarter turn, roll it in sugar again and fold as above. Wrap it in plastic film, and chill it in the refrigerator for at least 30 minutes before use.

14 **Slicing the strip.** Chill the dough until it is firm—about 20 minutes in the refrigerator, or half that time in the freezer—to make it easier to slice. Using a sharp, narrow-bladed knife, slice across the strips at 5 mm ($\frac{1}{4}$ inch) intervals (*above*).

15 **Baking the biscuits.** Place the slices on a baking sheet; since they will expand when baked, leave plenty of space between the biscuits. Place the baking sheet in the refrigerator for 20 minutes—or in the freezer for half that time—to firm the shapes, then bake in a preheated 200°C (400°F or Mark 6) oven for 6 to 7 minutes.

16 **Turning the biscuits over.** Remove the sheet from the oven. With a metal spatula, turn the biscuits over; work quickly, lest the caramelized surface hardens as it cools and the biscuits stick to the sheet. To colour both sides evenly return the biscuits to the oven for 2 to 3 minutes; the second side takes less time than the first.

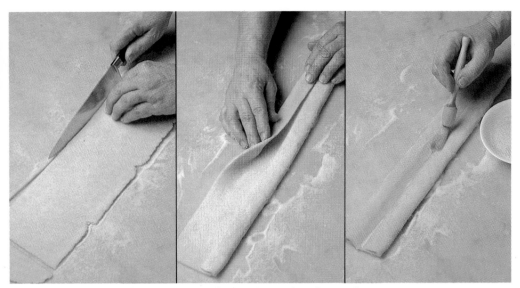

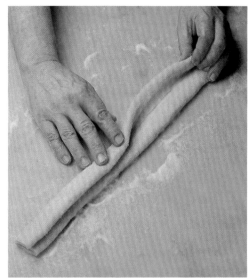

12 **Trimming and shaping the dough.** Dust the work surface with castor sugar. Roll the dough into a long, narrow rectangle no more than 5 mm (¼ inch) thick; with a sharp knife, trim the uneven edges (*above, left*). Here, the trimmed rectangle measures 45 by 10 cm (18 by 4 inches). Fold in the two long edges of the rectangle almost to the middle so that they do not quite meet (*above, centre*). Press a rolling pin lengthwise down the middle to seal the edges, creating an indented channel. Mix an egg yolk with water and brush this egg mixture along the channel (*above, right*).

13 **Folding the strip.** Fold the dough in half lengthwise, so that the folded edges meet (*above*). To ensure that the four layers stick together, gently roll the shaped strip with a rolling pin.

17 **Cooling and serving.** Remove the sheet from the oven. Use the spatula to transfer the biscuits to a wire rack (*above*); they are very fragile while warm. Cool, then serve them on a napkin-lined plate (*right*). □

Ingenious Shapes of Melting Tenderness

Because rough-puff dough rises in crisp, flaky layers when baked, it can be used to make unusual, individually shaped biscuits. If the layers lie flat, the dough will rise upwards, but if the layers stand upright, the dough will puff outwards. Thus a simple twist will swell lightly (*right*), a complex arrangement of twisted strips will fan out to form butterfly wings (*below*), while the sides of tiny shells will rise so that they can hold a little jam (*page 32*).

The dough can be varied by sprinkling it with a flavouring such as chopped nuts (*page 7*), grated citrus rind or spices—cinnamon or nutmeg. These flavourings are pressed firmly into the surface of the dough with a rolling pin.

You can shape the dough by cutting it with a very sharp knife, or with biscuit cutters. To help the biscuits hold their shape, they should be thoroughly chilled before baking. Certain shapes will create trimmings. These trimmings can be carefully reassembled into a level sheet, and rolled out again (*box, page 32*).

Twists of Nut-Encrusted Dough

1 Incorporating nuts and sugar. Roll out rough-puff dough (*page 26, Steps 1 to 10*) 5 mm (¼ inch) thick. With a sharp knife, cut out a rectangle—in this case, 20 cm (8 inches) wide. Brush with egg yolk beaten with water. Mix together equal amounts of chopped nuts—here, almonds—and granulated sugar, and sprinkle over the dough. Roll in lightly (*above*).

2 Turning the dough. With both hands, pick up one end of the sheet of dough and turn it over (*above*), so that the nut-coated side rests face-down on the work surface. Brush the uncoated side of dough with the egg yolk and water mixture; sprinkle on more of the mixed nuts and sugar, and roll in.

Strands that Spread to Butterfly Wings

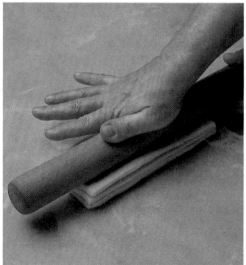

1 Cutting bands of dough. Roll out rough-puff dough (*page 26, Steps 1 to 11*) to a thickness of 5 mm (¼ inch). Cut a rectangle of dough—in this case, 30 cm (12 inches) wide—then cut it into four bands, each 7.5 cm (3 inches) wide. Beat egg yolk with water and brush a strip of egg mixture down the centre of three bands (*above*), leaving the fourth one uncoated.

2 Stacking the bands. Place the three brushed bands of dough on top of one another, with the strips of egg facing upwards (*above*). Carefully align the edges to form a neat stack, and then lay the unbrushed band on top.

3 Sealing the centre of the stack. To stick the bands together, and to seal the layers down the centre, press a rolling pin along the middle of the stack (*above*). Avoid pressing the edges of the stack, which must remain in well-separated layers. Cut the stack at 1 cm (½ inch) intervals into slices, each comprising four thin strips joined at the centre.

3 **Cutting and twisting.** Cut the rectangle in half, lengthwise, then cut each half crosswise into strips about 1 cm (½ inch) wide. Hold a strip at each end and twist the ends in opposite directions (*above*); lay the twist on a baking sheet. To prevent it from untwisting, press the ends of the strip flat against the sheet. Shape the remaining strips in the same way.

4 **Baking and serving.** Place the baking sheet in the refrigerator for 20 minutes or in the freezer for 10 minutes. Bake the twists in a preheated 200°C (400°F or Mark 6) oven until they are evenly golden—about 10 minutes. Cool on a wire rack before serving. □

4 **Shaping the butterflies.** Hold a slice loosely at one end; with your free hand, twist the other end towards you (*above*); lower the slice on to a baking sheet, allowing the thin strips to fan out, with their cut edges facing upwards. Shape the remaining slices in the same way. Place the sheet in the refrigerator for 20 minutes, or in the freezer for 10 minutes.

5 **Baking the biscuits.** Bake the biscuits in a preheated 200°C (400°F or Mark 6) oven for 6 to 7 minutes, until lightly browned. With a spatula, turn the biscuits over; bake them for 3 more minutes, then transfer them to a rack to cool. To serve these fragile butterfly biscuits, arrange them on a napkin-lined plate. □

Fragile Shells to Fill with Jam

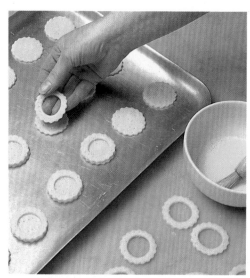

1 Cutting the dough. Roll out rough-puff dough (*page 26, Steps 1 to 10*) 3 mm (⅛ inch) thick; to prevent the dough from rising too much, prick it all over with a fork so that steam can escape during baking. With a fluted cutter, cut as many rounds as possible; place half on a baking sheet. With a smaller, plain cutter, cut out the centre of the remaining rounds (*above*).

2 Forming shells. Beat an egg yolk with a little water. Brush the rim of each round base with the egg mixture, then place a ring of dough on top (*above*). Brush the surface of the ring with egg, taking care that no egg touches the cut sides and prevents the dough from rising. Put the baking sheet in the refrigerator for 20 minutes or in the freezer for 10 minutes.

3 Baking and filling the shells. Transfer the sheet to a preheated 230°C (450°F or Mark 8) oven. After a few minutes, lower the heat to 180°C (350°F or Mark 4) and continue baking the biscuits; they require a total of 12 to 15 minutes. Cool on a wire rack. Warm some jam (*page 8*)—here, raspberry jam—and spoon a little into each of the shells (*above*).☐

A Patchwork of Trimmings

1 Assembling the pieces. Assemble scraps of chilled, rough-puff dough on a lightly floured work surface. Arrange the trimmings in a rough rectangle, overlapping the pieces slightly to form a solid sheet (*above*). The dough must not be gathered into a ball, since this would destroy its intricate layers.

2 Rolling the dough. Using short, light strokes, rolling forwards only, roll the rectangle into a smooth-surfaced sheet about 5 mm (¼ inch) thick and three times as long as it is wide (*above*). Fold, roll and chill the dough twice (*page 26, Steps 6 to 9*). The dough is then ready to be rolled out and cut into shapes.

A Cheese Enrichment for Savoury Straws

Made without sugar, rough-puff dough (*page 26*) can be used to make savoury biscuits such as the cheese straws demonstrated here. In this instance, the dough is bound with water; if you like, you can substitute a richer binding such as milk or cream, or egg yolk thinned with a little water.

Here, the flavouring is incorporated by rolling the dough on both sides in finely grated cheese, then folding the dough and chilling it. This entire sequence is repeated so that cheese is distributed between the thin layers of dough and butter, as well as coating the surface of the rolled-out dough. The cheese will melt into the dough during baking. You can use any hard cheese, such as Parmesan, Cheddar or Gruyère. A light sprinkling of cayenne pepper sharpens the flavour of the biscuits.

Once flavoured, the dough can be shaped into twists (*Step 3*), or it can be cut into rounds with a small biscuit cutter. These biscuits make an excellent accompaniment to aperitifs.

1 **Rolling the dough in grated cheese.** Make a rough-puff dough and chill it for 1 hour (*page 26, Steps 1 to 10*). Give the dough two more turns and chill it for at least 30 minutes. Evenly sprinkle grated cheese—here, Parmesan—over the work surface and the dough. Roll out the dough into a rectangle 5 mm (¼ inch) thick and three times as long as it is wide. Fold the ends to meet in the centre (*above, left*), then fold the dough in half (*above, centre*) to make four layers. Turn the dough so the folds are at the side; roll out (*above, right*) and fold into four as before. Chill for a further 30 minutes.

2 **Cutting into strips.** Sprinkle more grated cheese over the work surface and roll the dough into a rectangle. Sprinkle more cheese, then a little cayenne pepper, over the dough. Roll the flavouring lightly into the surface. Turn the sheet over and flavour the other side. With a sharp knife, cut the dough widthwise into strips about 1 cm (½ inch) wide (*above*).

3 **Forming twists.** Hold the ends of a strip of dough between your fingers, and twist the ends in opposite directions (*above*). Lay the strip on a baking sheet, pressing the ends down flat to prevent them from untwisting. Shape the remaining strips in the same way. Place the baking sheet in the refrigerator for 30 minutes or in the freezer for 15 minutes.

4 **Baking and serving the straws.** Bake the straws in a preheated 230°C (450°F or Mark 8) oven for about 7 minutes, or until they are evenly coloured. Transfer the biscuits carefully to a rack; they are very fragile when warm from the oven. Leave them to cool or serve them while they are still slightly warm. Here, the straws are presented on a napkin-lined plate.

2
Creamed Doughs
Opportunities for Improvisation

Of all the doughs in the cook's repertoire, creamed dough is the most versatile—it is the starting point for more biscuits than any other dough. The dough takes its name from creaming, the process of beating together butter and sugar so that air bubbles are forced into the butter. The aerated mixture is then moistened with eggs and blended with flour. Provided you follow the proportions given in your recipe, and avoid overworking the dough—this would strengthen the gluten in the flour and make the biscuits tough—a few minutes' baking will transform this simple creamed dough into crisp, crumbly biscuits.

A firm creamed dough is ideal for combining with other ingredients; its robust structure and unassertive flavour provide a vehicle for the addition of nuts or chocolate (*page 36*) or crystallized fruit (*page 38*). You can assemble the dough with a sweet filling before or after baking it (*pages 46 and 53*), and embellish the baked biscuits with any of the icings and glazes described on page 8.

Creamed doughs provide many opportunities for imaginative shaping. A firm dough can be simply dropped from a spoon to produce chunky, irregular shapes (*page 36*), but it can also be rolled out and cut into any design: circles—plain or fluted—hearts and diamonds, crescents and rosettes are among the many shaped biscuit cutters available. While firm enough to roll out, the dough is also sufficiently malleable to mould by hand; if a portion of the dough is coloured a deep brown with cocoa powder, you can roll and mould it to make patterned, particoloured biscuits (*page 40*). Fanciful forms such as looped pretzels can be created by hand moulding (*page 43*); you can also shape the dough with a tool such as a piping bag, a mechanical biscuit press or even a sieve (*page 44*).

Further variations arise through changing the proportion of the basic liquid added to the creamed butter and sugar. For example, a large quantity of eggs will produce a soft batter that bakes into a cake-like biscuit (*opposite and page 38*). Creamed batters can also be thinned with egg whites, and these loose batters will spread when baked, yielding light, dry wafers (*page 48*). The wafers are brittle when cold, but while still warm can be shaped into decorative containers for creamy fillings (*page 50*).

These golden biscuits, decorated with raisins, derive their brilliant sheen from being glazed twice—first with a coating of sieved apricot jam, then with a thin icing sugar glaze, flavoured with rum. The biscuits, made from a creamed dough rich in eggs, have a tender, sponge-like interior.

Rich Rewards from a Simple Beginning

Many moist, crumbly biscuits begin with a combination of butter and sugar, blended by the process known as creaming. To aerate it, the butter is first beaten alone until it is pale and creamy, and then beaten vigorously with sugar. The sharp edges of the sugar crystals help force air into the butter. As air bubbles are incorporated, the mixture increases in volume, becoming pale and fluffy. This creamed base is moistened with egg and strengthened with flour, and the result is a simple creamed dough (*right; recipe, page 166*).

The consistency of creamed doughs can be varied by using different amounts of egg or flour. The dough shown here contains only one egg and an extra yolk, and the resulting biscuits are close-textured. In some instances, more eggs are added, producing a softer dough and a lighter, more sponge-like biscuit (*page 38; recipe page 113*). The mixture may look curdled when you add the extra eggs, but the flour will bind it together again. In either case, the flour should be blended in gently, a little at a time. Avoid overworking the dough; this would strengthen the gluten, making the dough tough when baked.

A basic creamed dough can be varied in many ways. A light flavouring can be added by using one or two tablespoons of vanilla sugar, or by adding a few drops of flavouring essence, the grated rind of citrus fruit, or ground spices. You can also blend in more substantial additions such as currants, raisins or chopped crystallized fruit. The dough will have a fuller flavour and a deeper colour if it is made with brown sugar, and chopped nuts and chocolate can be incorporated for chunky, textured biscuits; the chocolate will blend into the dough without melting entirely (*box, right; recipe, page 124*).

There are also many ways to shape a firm creamed dough: it can be simply dropped from a spoon, as here, or rolled out and shaped with biscuit cutters (*page 38*). Soft creamed doughs are too thin for rolling, and are dropped from a spoon or piped through a piping bag.

Any of the icings, glazes and garnishes on pages 6-9 can be used to flavour and embellish the biscuits. They range from a dusting of castor sugar to a double coating of apricot glaze and water icing.

Crumbly Biscuits Dropped from a Spoon

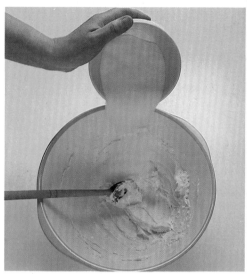

1 **Creaming the butter.** Allow the butter to stand at room temperature until it is soft enough to work easily. Place the butter in a large bowl set on a damp cloth to stop it slipping. With the back of a wooden spoon, mash the butter against the side of the bowl. Then beat the butter with the spoon or—for speed—an electric mixer, until it is pale and soft.

2 **Blending butter and sugar.** Pour the sugar into the creamed butter. With the spoon or an electric mixer, beat the butter and sugar until the mixture becomes fluffy and almost white. To ensure that all the sugar is blended in, scrape the sides of the bowl with the spoon or a rubber spatula from time to time.

Changing Texture with Nuts and Chocolate

1 **Adding nuts and chocolate.** Make a creamed dough with brown sugar. Finely chop chocolate and nuts (*page 6*); here, walnuts are used. Add the chopped nuts and chocolate to the dough (*above*), stirring the mixture in order to distribute the flavourings evenly.

2 **Baking the biscuits.** Drop portions of the dough on to a buttered baking sheet with a tablespoon. Bake the biscuits in a preheated 190°C (375°F or Mark 5) oven for 10 to 12 minutes, or until they are a deep golden-brown. Cool the biscuits on a rack before serving them.

3 **Adding eggs.** Break an egg into the creamed mixture. Separate a second egg over a small bowl (*above*); reserve the white to use as a glaze and add the yolk to the mixing bowl. Beat the egg and the yolk into the other ingredients.

4 **Adding flour.** Sift the flour into another bowl. Shake a little sifted flour into the mixing bowl (*above*). Fold it gently into the other ingredients with the wooden spoon, blending it evenly into the mixture.

5 **Gathering the dough.** Add the rest of the flour, a little at a time. When the dough becomes too stiff to stir, mix in the flour by hand (*above*). Gather the dough with your hands into a smooth, pliable mass.

6 **Shaping the dough.** Butter a baking sheet. Take teaspoonfuls of the dough and, with the back of another spoon, push them on to the sheet, leaving space for the dough to expand between each portion (*above*). With a fork, beat the reserved egg white lightly. Using a pastry brush, glaze the biscuits with egg white; if you like, sprinkle them with sugar.

7 **Baking the biscuits.** Bake the biscuits in a preheated 180°C (350°F or Mark 4) oven for 10 minutes, or until they are a pale, golden-brown. With a metal spatula, transfer the biscuits to a rack to cool. If you wish, dust them with icing sugar before serving. □

Scalloped Circles Flecked with Fruit

1 Mixing in fruit. Make a creamed dough (*page 36*) using one egg. Finely chop crystallized fruit—about 175 g (6 oz) of fruit is sufficient for the quantity of dough used here. Add the chopped fruit to the mixture (*above*) and stir it into the dough until it is evenly distributed.

2 Rolling out the dough. Lightly flour a work surface. Sprinkle a little flour over the surface of the dough to prevent the rolling pin from sticking. With quick, light strokes, roll out the dough to a thickness of about 5 mm (¼ inch).

3 Shaping the dough. Cut as many shapes as possible from the rolled dough, using a fluted biscuit cutter—here, 7.5 cm (3 inches) in diameter. Press the cutter firmly into the dough to ensure a clean cut. With a metal spatula, transfer the cut biscuits to a buttered baking sheet. Gather any remaining dough into a ball, roll it out and shape more biscuits.

Piping a Soft Creamed Batter

1 Filling a piping bag. Cream butter and sugar. Mix in the eggs one at a time; six eggs are used here (*recipe, page 113*). Blend in the flour. Insert a nozzle—in this case, 1 cm (½ inch) wide—into a piping bag. Fold back the top of the bag and spoon in the dough (*above*) until the bag is about two-thirds full. Twist the top of the bag, enclosing the dough.

2 Piping the batter. Lightly butter baking sheets. Pipe the batter on to the baking sheets in small mounds; use a small knife to stop the flow. Allow plenty of space between each mound (*above*), since the batter will spread during baking. If you wish, decorate the biscuits by pressing raisins on to their surface.

3 Glazing the biscuits. Cook the biscuits in a preheated 180°C (350°F or Mark 4) oven for about 10 minutes, or until lightly browned. Remove them from the oven. To colour the biscuits, brush on a little sieved apricot jam (*page 8*). The glaze will set in seconds. Prepare an icing sugar glaze—here, flavoured with rum (*page 8*)—and brush it over the apricot glaze.

4 **Baking the biscuits.** If you like, sprinkle the unbaked biscuits with granulated sugar (*above*). Place the baking sheet in a preheated 180°C (350°F or Mark 4) oven and bake for about 10 minutes until the biscuits are a pale golden colour.

5 **Serving the biscuits.** With a metal spatula, transfer the biscuits to a wire rack and leave them to cool before serving. Here, the biscuits are arranged on a plate in order to fully display their fluted edges and the multi-coloured flecks of crystallized fruit.☐

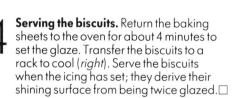

4 **Serving the biscuits.** Return the baking sheets to the oven for about 4 minutes to set the glaze. Transfer the biscuits to a rack to cool (*right*). Serve the biscuits when the icing has set; they derive their shining surface from being twice glazed.☐

Dramatic Effects from Contrasting Colours

Shaped into a cylinder and chilled, a moist creamed dough becomes firm enough to slice neatly into biscuits. For a striking effect, part of the dough can be coloured a deep brown with cocoa powder, and it can be shaped into a variety of patterned biscuits (*right and overleaf; recipe, page 114*). Because chilling is essential, these are often called refrigerator biscuits.

Refrigerator biscuits are tender and crumbly—the dough requires less flour than a basic creamed dough because chilling will make it firm. The dough should always be wrapped in an airtight covering, such as plastic film, so that it does not dry out in the refrigerator or freezer. It should be chilled until firm before you roll it out and shape it; this will take at least an hour in the refrigerator or half an hour in the freezer, and it can be chilled overnight if convenient.

The chilled dough is firm enough to roll out, but it is also sufficiently malleable to mould by hand; both of these shaping techniques are used for patterned biscuits. For example, trimmed sheets of plain and coloured dough can be rolled up together to produce a spiral design (*right*); four thin cylinders of alternating colours, wrapped in a layer of plain dough, will make chequered biscuits; while a log encircled by a contrasting wrapper becomes a simple rimmed disc (*page 42*). Whatever the finished result, a brushing of beaten egg white will help the surfaces of the plain and coloured doughs to cohere.

Refrigerator biscuits can also be made from plain or coloured dough used on its own. For a simple spiral design, you can roll out a sheet of dough, sprinkle it with chopped nuts or dried fruit, and roll it up (*page 18*). Or you can mould the dough into a log, and roll it in chopped nuts or chocolate so that the finished biscuits have rough-textured rims.

1 Colouring the dough. Make a creamed dough (*recipe, page 114*). When the flour has been incorporated, divide the dough into two equal parts and place half of it in a separate bowl. Add cocoa powder to one portion, stirring lightly to distribute the cocoa evenly.

2 Finishing the dough. Lightly flour a work surface. Gather up the plain dough, turn it out on to the work surface and shape the dough into a ball (*above*). Gather the coloured dough into a ball in the same way. Wrap the balls of dough in plastic film and then chill them in the refrigerator for at least 1 hour, or in the freezer for 30 minutes, until firm.

6 Forming a cylinder. Roll up the long edge of the stack, working away from you, to form a cylinder; the coating of egg white will make the layers stick together as you roll. Wrap the shaped dough in plastic film and chill it for 1 hour in the refrigerator, or for 30 minutes in the freezer, until it is firm.

7 Slicing the dough. Remove the chilled roll from the refrigerator or freezer. Place the seam of the roll against the work surface. With a sharp knife, slice the roll into thin rounds—here, about 5 mm ($\frac{1}{4}$ inch) thick (*above*). Use a light sawing action to achieve a smooth, clean cut.

3 **Rolling out the dough.** Roll the plain dough forwards and crosswise, without turning it, into a rectangle 3 mm (⅛ inch) thick and about twice as long as it is wide; here, the sheet of dough is 30 cm (15 inches) long and 20 cm (8 inches) wide. Then roll out the coloured dough into a rectangle of the same size.

4 **Stacking the dough.** In a small bowl, lightly beat an egg white with a fork until it begins to foam. Brush the surface of the plain dough with egg white. Carefully lay the coloured dough on top of the plain dough (*above*). To ensure that the two sheets are firmly fixed together, lightly roll the surface with the rolling pin.

5 **Trimming the dough.** With a long, sharp knife, trim away the ragged edges of the dough to form an even rectangle. Use the trimmings to make other biscuits. Brush the surface of the stacked dough with the lightly beaten egg white.

8 **Baking the slices.** Lightly butter a baking sheet; transfer the biscuits to the sheet and bake in a preheated 190°C (375°F or Mark 5) oven for 8 to 10 minutes until firm to the touch. With a metal spatula, lift the biscuits on to a wire rack to cool (*above*). Here, they are arranged on a plate to display their spiral pattern (*right*). □

Constructing a Chequerboard

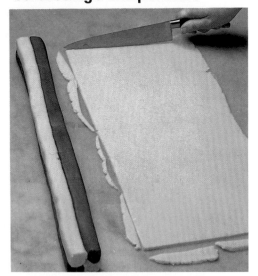

1 **Colouring the dough.** Make the dough and reserve one-fifth of it. Colour half of the remainder brown. Shape four long ropes of dough, two coloured and two plain, each 2.5 cm (1 inch) in diameter. Brush with egg white and arrange them as above. Roll out the reserved dough into a sheet as long as the stack and four times as wide; trim its edges (*above*).

2 **Wrapping the stack.** Brush the sheet of plain dough with egg white. Lift the stack and place it near to one edge of the sheet. Fold the sheet round the stack to form a wrapper. Refrigerate the dough for 1 hour or place it in the freezer for 30 minutes, until firm.

3 **Baking the biscuits.** Remove the roll from the refrigerator or freezer and slice it into thin biscuits. Lightly butter a baking sheet, and bake the biscuits in a preheated 190°C (375°F or Mark 5) oven for 8 to 10 minutes, until firm to the touch. Cool the biscuits on a rack before serving.□

Wrapping a Log for Concentric Circles

1 **Rolling out the dough.** Make the dough and reserve about one-fifth of it. Colour the remaining four-fifths of the dough with cocoa powder. Mould the coloured dough by hand into a log about 5 cm (2 inches) in diameter. With a rolling pin, roll out the reserved plain dough into a rectangle (*above*).

2 **Wrapping the cylinder.** Trim the sheet of plain dough so that it is as long as the log and wide enough to wrap round it. Brush the sheet of dough with beaten egg white. Place the log close to one edge of the rectangle. Roll the wrapper round the log (*above*). Refrigerate the log for 1 hour, or place it in the freezer for 30 minutes, to firm it for slicing.

3 **Baking the biscuits.** With a sharp knife, cut the log into slices about 5 mm (¼ inch) thick. Place the biscuits on a buttered baking sheet, and bake in a preheated 190°C (375°F or Mark 5) oven for 8 to 10 minutes. Transfer the biscuits to a rack and leave them to cool before serving.□

Chocolate Pretzels Fashioned by Hand

Intricate biscuits can be shaped by rolling a small portion of creamed dough into a thin rope, and then twisting it into any pattern you like. In the demonstration on the right, a firm creamed dough (*page 40*) is coloured brown with cocoa powder, and twisted into a loose knot.

Since the dough is so malleable, you can devise many different shapes, such as looped rings—for a figure-of-eight—bows, corkscrew twists, or numbers and alphabet letters. You can also twist one length each of plain and coloured dough together for a striking effect.

The moulded shapes require only a simple glaze of egg or egg white to give them a shiny surface; they can be garnished with chopped nuts before baking, or dusted with icing sugar when they are removed from the oven. Here, the knotted shapes are sprinkled with coarse sugar to resemble the salt crystals that garnish the hard savoury biscuits called pretzels.

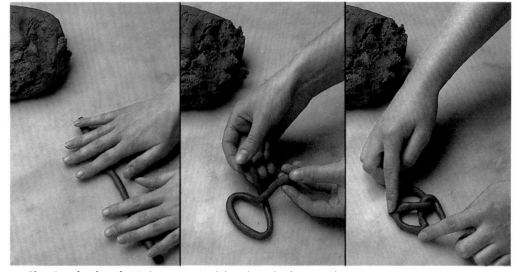

1 **Shaping the dough.** Make a creamed dough and colour it with cocoa powder. Refrigerate the dough for 1 hour or freeze it for 30 minutes. Sprinkle a work surface with flour. Pull a small portion off the dough and roll it into a thin, smooth rope (*above, left*), about 25 cm (10 inches) long. Lay it down in a curved shape with the ends towards you. Lift one end over the other and twist them (*above, centre*). Turn the ends back and press them down on to the centre of the curve (*above, right*). Shape the rest of the dough, then chill it.

2 **Baking the biscuits.** Place the dough shapes on a buttered baking sheet. Brush each one with lightly beaten egg white (*above*) and then sprinkle it with coarse sugar. Bake the biscuits in a preheated 190°C (375°F or Mark 5) oven for about 10 minutes. Cool the biscuits on a rack and then serve them.□

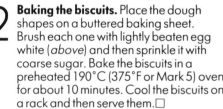

Shaping Techniques from a Trio of Tools

A creamed dough is ideal for shaping into decorative biscuits, since it can be made soft enough to force through a piping bag, a wire sieve or a mechanical biscuit press. Unlike a loose batter, which is also shaped with a piping bag, this dough will not spread, so that the biscuits will hold their shape when baked. In these demonstrations, a creamed dough (*recipe, page 166*) is pushed through three implements to create different effects. Light flavourings, such as vanilla, grated lemon rind or cocoa powder, can be added to the dough for additional variety.

Biscuits with a rough, mossy surface are made by pushing the dough through a wire sieve (*right*). As small portions of dough are pressed through the mesh, they form strands as thin as vermicelli. The strands cling together when scraped off the base of the sieve and blend together during baking, but they remain distinct on the surface of the biscuits. If you like, the moss biscuits can be garnished with chopped nuts; here, pistachio nuts provide a vivid contrast, but almonds or pine-nuts could be substituted.

A piping bag (*right, below*) can be used to make a great variety of designs—the rings, S-shapes and paired lines shown here, as well as other shapes such as latticed squares, figures-of-eight, coils and crescents. A starred nozzle will provide the shapes with a ridged surface. These biscuits are often dipped in melted chocolate, but they can also be served plain or dusted with icing sugar.

Very precise shapes can be formed using a biscuit press (*opposite page, below*). Essentially a mechanical piping bag, the biscuit press consists of a metal cylinder and a choice of decorative discs. When the handle is pressed, a limited amount of dough is forced through the holes in the disc. By changing the disc, you can make biscuits of different designs from the same batch of dough.

Using a Sieve for a Mossy Effect

1 Shaping the dough. Make a creamed dough. Pull off a small portion of the dough—about the size of a walnut—and shape it into a rough ball with your hands. Place the ball of dough in a metal sieve. Press it with the back of a spoon to force it through the mesh in thin strands. With a knife, scrape the ends of the strands from the underside of the sieve (*above*).

2 Lifting the dough. Lift the strands on the knife carefully and push them on to a buttered baking sheet with your fingers. Pull off more portions of dough from the mass and shape them in the same way.

Swirls from a Star-Shaped Nozzle

1 Piping the dough. Prepare a creamed dough. Butter a baking sheet. Fit a nozzle—here, a medium-sized star—in a piping bag. Spoon the dough into the bag until it is two-thirds full; twist the top of the bag to enclose the dough. Press the bag to pipe shapes—here, rings, S-shapes and paired lines; after piping each biscuit, stop the flow of dough with a knife.

2 Dusting with sugar. Place the baking sheet in a preheated 190°C (375°F or Mark 5) oven for about 15 minutes. Transfer the biscuits to a rack to cool. If you wish, dust them with icing sugar, tapping the sugar gently through a sieve over the warm biscuits (*above*). □

3 **Baking the biscuits.** If you like, sprinkle the biscuits with finely chopped nuts, such as pistachio nuts (*above*). Place the biscuits in a preheated 190°C (375°F or Mark 5) oven for about 15 minutes. Transfer the biscuits to a wire rack to cool before you serve them (*right*).□

Neat Rosettes from a Biscuit Press

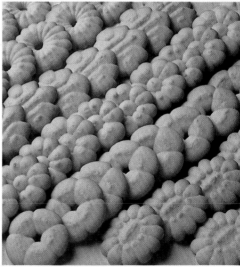

1 **Filling a biscuit press.** Make a creamed dough; spoon it into the body of a biscuit press (*above*). Select a decorative disc and place it in position over the dough. Screw on the end of the press tightly.

2 **Shaping the dough.** Butter a baking sheet. Place the end of the biscuit press flat against the baking sheet, press down the handle and then release it (*above*). Carefully lift up the press and place it alongside to shape another biscuit; here, the disc is changed after every row.

3 **Baking the biscuits.** Place the baking sheet in a preheated 190°C (375°F or Mark 5) oven and bake the biscuits for about 15 minutes, until they are a light golden-brown. Using a metal spatula, transfer the biscuits to a rack to cool. Here, the biscuits are displayed in rows, showing the variety of patterns made by the different discs.□

Frameworks for Fillings

By combining a plain dough with a rich filling, you can create a wide variety of filled biscuits. A firm creamed dough (*page 36*) makes an excellent base, since it is strong enough to contain a bulky filling, and its mild flavour will set off the flavour of any of the sweet ingredients described on page 10. The assembly may be prepared before baking, with the filling either concealed in the dough (*right*) or partly revealed in an open-face biscuit (*opposite page, below*). You can also sandwich a creamy filling between two baked biscuit shapes (*below*).

If you want to conceal the filling, choose a dry nut or fruit mixture that will neither spread during baking nor leak through the dough. Moist fillings, such as jam or lemon curd, should be reserved for sandwiched biscuits or for open-face assemblies—they will lend colour as well as a contrasting soft texture. Other decorative effects can be devised by colouring the dough with cocoa powder, and binding pairs of cooked biscuits with a filling flavoured with nuts or chocolate (*page 12*).

Fragrance Concealed in a Sugared Surround

1 **Filling the dough.** Prepare a nut filling—here, chopped walnuts flavoured with rose-water (*page 11*). Lightly butter a baking sheet. Roll a piece of dough, the size of a walnut, between your palms into a small ball (*above, left*). Press your finger into the ball to make a cavity and spoon a little filling into it (*above, centre*). Press the dough over the filling to seal it (*above, right*); place the biscuit on the baking sheet. Shape and fill the rest of the dough in the same way.

Heart Shapes Sandwiched with Lemon Cream

1 **Spreading the filling.** Roll out creamed dough until it is about 5 mm (¼ inch) thick. Shape the dough with a decorative cutter—here, a heart shape. Bake the biscuits in a preheated 180°C (350°F or Mark 4) oven for about 10 minutes. Transfer the biscuits to a wire rack to cool. Prepare a filling—in this case, a lemon filling (*page 10*). With a metal spatula, spread the underside of half of the biscuits with filling (*above, left*); place the other biscuits, underside down, on top of the filling to make sandwiches (*above, right*).

2 **Serving the biscuits.** When all the biscuits have been sandwiched together, leave them on the wire rack until the filling has set. Here, the biscuits are arranged on a plate for serving, in order to display the bands of lemon filling.□

2 **Baking the biscuits.** Bake the biscuits in a preheated 180°C (350°F or Mark 4) oven for 10 to 15 minutes, until they are lightly browned. Sift a thick layer of icing sugar on to a plate. While the biscuits are still warm, roll them in the icing sugar, which will cling to their surfaces (*above*). Cool on a wire rack. Here, one biscuit has been halved to reveal the filling (*right*). □

An Open Design to Reveal a Fruit Centre

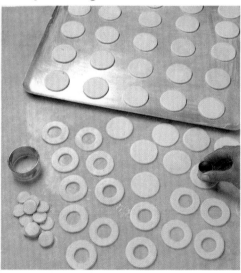

1 **Shaping the dough.** Roll out creamed dough to a thickness of about 5 mm (¼ inch) and cut out biscuits using a circular biscuit cutter. Place half of the rounds on a lightly buttered baking sheet. With a small cutter, cut out the centres from the remaining rounds (*above*).

2 **Filling the shapes.** Prepare a dried fruit filling (*page 10*)—here, figs are used. Spoon a little filling on to each of the biscuits on the sheet, leaving a margin as wide as the rings of dough round the edge (*above*). Lightly beat an egg; brush the egg round the filling, to serve as an adhesive. Firmly press the rings of dough on top of the rounds.

3 **Baking the biscuits.** Place the baking sheet in a preheated 180°C (350°F or Mark 4) oven and bake the biscuits for about 12 minutes—until the dough is a light golden-brown. Before serving them, transfer the biscuits to a rack to cool. □

Delicate Strips to Enjoy with Desserts

A creamed batter thinned with a large quantity of egg whites is the foundation of a range of light, fine-textured biscuits that are often served as an accompaniment to ice cream and creamy desserts. These thin wafers owe their exceptional lightness to the fact that they contain very little fat. To make the batter, a small amount of butter is creamed with sugar and the mixture is moistened with egg whites; the yolks are reserved for other uses. The soft batter spreads during baking, to yield a thin, crisp biscuit that melts in the mouth (*right; recipe, page 112*).

Any type of sugar can be used, but icing sugar will give the biscuits a finer texture than granulated sugar. The mixture can be flavoured by adding vanilla extract or by substituting a few spoonfuls of vanilla sugar for some of the plain sugar. Alternatively, you can use the grated rind of an orange or lemon, or a little orange-flavoured liqueur or rum.

When all the whites have been added to the creamed ingredients, the mixture will appear to be curdled; but there is no cause for alarm, since the batter binds together as soon as the flour is added. It is important to blend in the flour gently; vigorous beating would strengthen the gluten in the dough, making the texture of the finished biscuits tough.

Batters of this type are soft enough to be shaped by piping. In this demonstration, the batter is piped into strips to make the regular, elongated shapes known as "cat's tongues". Alternatively, you can spoon the batter into a shallow tin that is specially designed for finger wafers.

After baking and cooling, the biscuits may be served plain or, for variation, the ends of the biscuits may be dipped into melted chocolate. The wafers can also be sandwiched in pairs with a little jam or any creamy filling (*pages 10-12*).

1 **Incorporating egg whites.** In a large bowl, cream softened butter and sugar; here, sifted icing sugar is used. Flavour the mixture with vanilla. Separate eggs and reserve the yolks for another use. With a fork, break up the whites until they foam. Add the whites to the creamed ingredients, a little at a time (*above, left*). Gently stir in each addition with a wooden spoon (*above, centre*), until all the whites have been incorporated. As they are blended in, the mixture will begin to look curdled (*above, right*).

4 **Filling the piping bag.** Place a nozzle—here, 10 mm (⅜ inch)—in a piping bag. Fold back the top of the bag, and spoon in batter until the bag is two-thirds full. Twist the top, enclosing the batter.

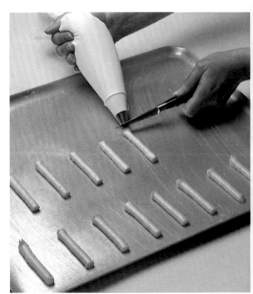

5 **Piping the batter.** Pipe the batter on to a lightly buttered baking sheet, in strips about 7 cm (2¾ inches) long. Use a knife to stop the flow of batter and give the piped strips a neat end; leave plenty of room between the strips (*above*) because the batter will spread during baking.

2 **Adding the flour.** Stir the mixture to incorporate the whites evenly. Sift the flour into another bowl; pour the sifted flour all at once into the ingredients in the mixing bowl (*above*).

3 **Folding in the flour.** With a spoon or spatula, blend the flour into the mixture, using a gentle cutting action and folding the batter over on itself. The flour will bind the mixture into a smooth, loose batter.

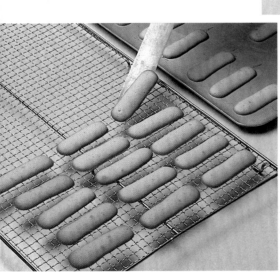

6 **Baking and cooling.** Bake the biscuits in a preheated 220°C (425°F or Mark 7) oven until their edges are brown—about 7 to 8 minutes. With a spatula, transfer the biscuits to a wire rack to cool (*above*); to serve, arrange them on a plate (*right*).□

Artfully Moulding Fragile Wafers

When they are still warm from the oven, thin wafers made from a creamed egg white batter are so flexible that they can be moulded into many different shapes (*right and overleaf; recipes, pages 111, 112 and 117*). The biscuits harden as they cool, and their brittle texture and simple flavour make an excellent contrast to rich fillings and garnishes.

For these decorative biscuits, you can use the basic creamed egg white batter demonstrated on pages 48-49, but after folding in the flour, a little cooled melted butter is added. The butter makes the batter very loose—it spreads to a thin sheet during baking—and it also enriches the biscuits. You can further enliven the batter by folding slivered almonds into it.

The key to successful shaping lies in moulding the biscuits while they are warm. It is best to bake only a few biscuits at a time, and shape them as soon as you remove them from the oven. Each wafer needs to be pressed against a mould for only a few seconds to take on its shape; it can then be placed on a rack to cool while you swiftly shape the next biscuit. If the wafers harden as you are shaping them, return them to the oven and warm them until they are pliable again.

A variety of implements can be used for shaping: a wooden spoon, for example, will produce "cigarettes" (*right, above*); and a rolling pin will form shapes that resemble Mediterranean roof tiles (*right*). A metal cream horn mould can be used to make cornets (*page 52*). The wafers can also be pressed into a tiny metal container, such as a chocolate mould or even a deep metal bottle top, to make small biscuit cases (*page 52*).

Cigarettes, cornets and cases all make attractive containers for fillings. For instance, you can use creamy fillings such as chocolate ganache or praline butter (*page 12*), whipped cream or sieved jam; and for a more elaborate presentation, you can garnish the filling with chopped nuts or grated chocolate.

Rolling Warm Biscuits Round a Wooden Spoon

1 **Piping the batter.** Make a creamed egg white batter. In a heavy pan, melt about 2 tablespoons of butter over a low heat. Allow it to cool slightly, then fold it into the batter. Butter a baking sheet. Fill a piping bag fitted with a 10 mm (⅜ inch) nozzle two-thirds full with the batter. Pipe small mounds of batter on to the sheet, leaving plenty of space between mounds.

2 **Baking the biscuits.** Place the sheet in a preheated 230°C (450°F or Mark 8) oven and bake the biscuits until they are lightly browned at the edges—about 5 minutes; during baking, the batter will spread, forming thin discs. Remove the sheet from the oven. Using a metal spatula, loosen the wafers from the baking sheet.

Sculpting Curves on a Rolling Pin

1 **Spooning out batter.** Make a creamed egg white batter, thinned with melted butter. Add slivered almonds, mixing them into the batter with a spoon. Place small mounds of the mixture well apart on a lightly greased baking sheet, pushing the batter off the spoon with your finger.

2 **Distributing the almonds.** With the back of a wet fork, smooth the mounds of batter to distribute the almonds evenly. Wet the fork again if the batter sticks to it. Bake the biscuits in a preheated 230°C (450°F or Mark 8) oven until their edges are brown—about 5 minutes.

3 **Shaping the wafers.** Working quickly, take a wafer from the baking sheet and wrap it round the handle of a wooden spoon. Press down on the join to close the cylinder. Ease the shaped wafer off the spoon handle, place it on a rack to cool, and immediately shape the next one. Continue until all the wafers are shaped.

4 **Serving the cigarettes.** Allow the shaped wafers to cool: they will become crisp and brittle. Serve them plain or, if you wish, you can pipe a little filling into both ends of each cigarette (*above*)—here, praline butter is used, but any soft creamy filling is suitable.□

3 **Shaping the wafers.** Remove the wafers from the oven and loosen them from the baking sheet with a spatula. Place as many as will fit over a rolling pin (*above*), holding them gently against the pin for a few seconds. Slide the moulded wafers off the pin and place them on a rack to cool completely before serving (*right*).

Cornets to Hold a Rich Filling

Shaping wafers into cornets. Bake thin wafers (*page 50, Steps 1 and 2*). Remove the baking sheet from the oven, loosen the biscuits with a metal spatula and wrap a warm wafer round a small cream horn mould (*above*). After a few seconds, slide the shaped cornet off the mould and place it on a rack to cool. When all the cornets are cooled, pipe in a filling—here, chocolate ganache (*page 12*)—and sprinkle it with chopped pistachio nuts (*right*), if you like.

Forming Miniature Cups

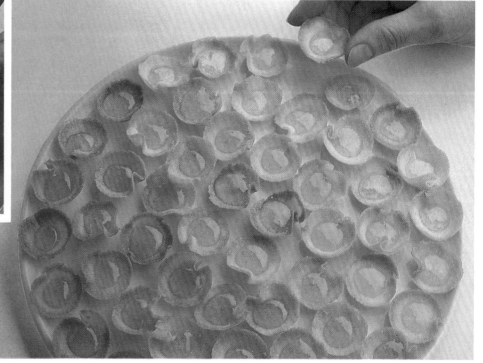

Moulding small cases. Make a thin creamed batter (*page 50*), piping it out in smaller mounds to bake the tiny wafers above. Press a warm wafer into a mould—here, a metal chocolate mould; the rim of the wafer will fold into pleats as you press it down. Gently lift out the shaped case and leave it to cool. Mould and cool the rest of the biscuits, and spoon in a little filling, such as sieved apricot jam (*right*).

An Easy Approach to Layered Assemblies

An easy and convenient method of assembling layered biscuits is to line a baking tin with a firm dough and cover it with a filling. The assembly is baked in a single slab, and sliced while warm into bars or squares. In the demonstration here, a creamed dough provides a crumbly base for a crunchy pecan nut topping; the chopped nuts are sweetened with brown sugar, thickened with a little flour and bound with egg (*right; recipe, page 108*).

Bar biscuits of this type can also be made with a plain or enriched shortcrust dough (*pages 18 and 22*). But whatever dough you use, the base must be partly baked before you spoon on the topping, which takes less time to cook.

Any sweet ingredients can be chosen for the topping; you can experiment with varying combinations of nuts, dried fruit—dates, figs or mixed fruit—and grated chocolate. If you like, the filling can be bound and sweetened with honey or jam, and the addition of eggs makes the topping moist and light.

1 **Spreading the dough base.** Make a firm creamed dough (*page 36*). Butter a baking tin. With the palm of your hand, press the dough to form an even layer covering the base of the tin (*above*).

2 **Preparing the topping.** Bake the dough base in a preheated 180°C (350°F or Mark 4) oven for 10 to 12 minutes. In the meantime, combine the dry ingredients for the topping—in this instance, brown sugar, chopped pecan nuts and sifted flour. Add eggs (*above*) and mix the ingredients together until they are all thoroughly blended.

3 **Cooking the assembly.** Remove the tin from the oven. Increase the oven heat to 190°C (375°F or Mark 5). Spread the topping over the dough, distributing the nuts evenly. Return the baking tin to the oven and bake the assembly until it is firm—about 20 minutes.

4 **Serving the biscuits.** Remove the tin from the oven. Holding the hot tin firmly with an oven cloth, slice the assembly into bars (*inset*) or squares. Leave them to cool in the tin, then lift them out with a spatula. Pile the biscuits on to a plate and serve them (*above*).□

3
Egg White Mixtures
Chewy Nut Pastes and Airy Meringues

Binding a blend of nuts and-sugar

Pounding almonds in a mortar

Decorative effects from baked marzipan

Tactics for whisking egg whites

Using sugar syrup for Italian meringue

Macaroons, marzipan crescents and delicate meringues are only three of the light biscuits that can be produced from egg white without the use of flour, fat or egg yolk. They owe their diversity to the different roles that egg whites can play in biscuit-making.

Unbeaten egg white is a viscous liquid. When lightly broken up with a fork, the whites become a loose foam which can be used to bind dry ingredients. Nuts are often used as the basis of such mixtures, replacing the flour that provides the body of most biscuit doughs. A blend of nuts and sugar, moistened with sufficient egg white to form a soft batter, will produce crisp, light macaroons. These biscuits will have a deliciously chewy texture if they are made with almonds pounded to a rough, moist paste in a mortar (*page 56*). Marzipan crescents contain the same ingredients—almonds, sugar and egg white—but in this case the nuts must be finely ground to achieve a smooth, even mixture. Hazelnuts, walnuts, coconut or a mixture of different nuts can also be used. Just enough egg white is added to make a stiff paste that can be moulded by hand into various shapes, then decorated, baked and glazed (*page 58*).

However, when egg whites are whisked, the proteins they contain form thin layers that trap air bubbles. Prolonged whisking breaks up these air cells into smaller and smaller bubbles until the whites increase dramatically in volume and mount into a dense, stable foam. Whenever you whisk egg whites, it is important to separate the eggs meticulously; no trace of yolk should be allowed to mar the whites, since the fat present in egg yolk will prevent the whites from mounting fully. For the same reason, use scrupulously clean utensils without a trace of grease. Glass, porcelain or stainless steel bowls are all suitable, but a copper bowl is a valuable asset, since a chemical reaction between egg whites and copper strengthens the walls of the air bubbles and assists the creation of a stable foam.

Plain meringue, a blend of beaten egg whites and sugar, is a confection in its own right (*opposite and page 60*); the addition of ground nuts will produce a firmer textured meringue. Another type of meringue—Italian meringue—is made with sugar syrup instead of sugar. The syrup can be used as a vehicle for incorporating a liquid flavouring, such as a fruit purée, into the meringue. A strawberry purée, for instance, will produce pastel-tinted biscuits tasting of the fresh fruit (*page 62*).

The frosty beauty of plain meringues is reflected in a sparkling glass serving dish. To make the meringues, egg whites were whisked to soft peaks; sugar was blended in until the mixture became stiff and glossy. Spoon-dropped on to baking sheets and dried out in the gentlest of ovens, the meringues slowly hardened and acquired a texture both crisp and meltingly light.

Macaroons: Pounding Nuts for Special Results

When almonds are pounded in a mortar, they become a rough, moist paste. Mixed with sugar, then bound and softened with egg white, this paste is the basis of the light biscuits known as macaroons (*right; recipe, page 129*). It takes time to pulverize almonds using a mortar and pestle, but macaroons made this way have a deliciously chewy, uneven texture.

A little egg white should be added to the nuts before you pound them, since the liquid will prevent the almonds from exuding too much oil. The white is added to the pounded nuts and sugar a little at a time, so that you can control the consistency of the mixture, which should be soft but not runny. Spooned out in small mounds, the batter will form irregularly shaped biscuits with an attractive, rough surface. For biscuits with a more uniform shape, the batter can be piped.

You can also make macaroons with almonds ground in a food processor or bought ready-ground. But such biscuits will have a drier and more uniform texture, and a less emphatic flavour.

1 **Pounding almonds.** Blanch almonds (*page 6*) and place them in a mortar with a little egg white. If you like, add a few bitter almonds to the sweet ones for extra flavour. Using a pestle, pound the almonds (*above, left*); after about 30 minutes they will have the consistency of coarse breadcrumbs and will form a moist paste (*above, right*).

3 **Completing the batter.** Add the rest of the sugar, stirring it into the mixture with the pestle. Gradually add more egg white, taking care not to pour in too much—the mixture should be just loose enough to drop from a spoon.

4 **Spooning out the mixture.** Lightly grease the corners of a baking sheet. Cut a piece of greaseproof paper to fit; lay it on the sheet, pressing it down at the corners to stay flat. Put spoonfuls of the macaroon mixture on the paper, leaving plenty of space between them (*above*) since the batter will spread during cooking.

5 **Cooking the biscuits.** Put the baking sheet in a preheated 220°C (425°F or Mark 7) oven for about 10 minutes, until the edges of the macaroons are golden. Remove the baking sheet from the oven. Press a blanched almond or—as shown here—a couple of pine-nuts on the top of each biscuit, and then sift a fine coating of icing sugar over them.

2 **Adding sugar and egg white.** In a small bowl, mix the egg whites with a fork until they begin to foam. Add half the sugar to the almond paste in the mortar (*above, left*). Mix the almonds and sugar together with the pestle (*above, centre*). Pour in half the egg white (*above, right*) and stir it into the almonds and sugar.

6 **Finishing the macaroons.** Put the biscuits back in the oven for a minute to set the icing sugar. Allow the macaroons to cool on the baking sheet; do not try to lift them from the paper while they are still warm—although they feel firm, they are soft inside and, if handled, would break. When the macaroons are cool, peel them off the paper and serve them.□

Marzipan Crescents with a Crunchy Coating

Nuts, sugar and egg whites, the same basic ingredients as macaroons (*page 56*), can be made into a stiff paste that is easily moulded into decorative shapes (*right; recipe, page 133*). For a smooth, even texture, the nuts should be finely ground in a food processor, or bought ready-ground. When made with almonds, the paste is called marzipan (*page 10*), but you could use walnuts or hazelnuts or mixed nuts.

The dry, powdery nuts are mixed with sugar; icing sugar will produce a finer paste than granulated sugar. A little jam or marmalade helps to bind the mixture, which is then moistened with just enough egg white to form a cohesive paste. The kneaded paste can be moulded by hand into individual shapes or a large cylinder for slicing into rounds. Or, it can be rolled out and shaped with biscuit cutters.

Before baking, the biscuits are coated with egg white and rolled in chopped nuts—almonds, as here, or pistachio or pine-nuts for a contrasting flavour. After baking, the biscuits are glazed with sweetened milk. They are crisp on the outside with a moist, chewy centre.

1 Binding the ingredients. Mix ground almonds and icing sugar in a bowl. Make a well in the centre of the mixture and add a spoonful of jam—here, apricot jam—and, if you wish, a few drops of flavouring essence. Beat egg whites with a fork until they foam. Pour about two-thirds of the egg white into the well in the middle of the nut mixture (*above, left*). Using a knife, stir the egg white and jam into the dry ingredients (*above, right*). Continue stirring in egg white, a little at a time, until the mixture is moist enough to hold together.

4 Coating the sticks. Chop nuts finely (*page 7*); almonds are used here. Place the chopped nuts on a plate. Using a pastry brush, coat a stick of the paste on all sides with lightly beaten egg white (*above, left*), then roll it in the chopped almonds (*above, right*) so that the stick is completely covered with nuts.

5 Shaping the crescents. Bend the nut-coated stick of paste into a crescent shape, and place it on a greased baking sheet. Coat and shape the other sticks in the same way. Put the crescents in a preheated 190°C (375°F or Mark 5) oven and bake them for 10 to 12 minutes, until they are a pale golden colour.

2 **Gathering the paste.** When the mixture becomes a cohesive paste, gather the ingredients in the bowl into a ball with your hand (*above*). The paste should be firm enough to shape by hand.

3 **Shaping the paste.** Transfer the ball of paste to a lightly floured work surface. Pull small pieces of paste—about the size of a walnut—off the ball, and roll them with the palm of your hand into sticks about 7 cm (3 inches) long.

6 **Glazing the crescents.** Stir a little icing sugar into cold milk in a small bowl. Remove the biscuits from the oven. While they are still warm, brush each one with a little of the sweetened milk to glaze its surface (*above*). When the biscuits feel firm, transfer them to a wire rack to finish cooling. Here, the crescents are served on a napkin-lined plate (*right*). □

A Two-Tiered Confection

When egg whites are whisked, they readily absorb air and mount to a stiff foam. Blended with sugar and flavoured with vanilla extract, spices or nuts, this mixture can be slowly and gently baked into delicate meringues. Here, plain and nut meringue mixtures (*recipe, page 166*) are juxtaposed for a two-tiered biscuit.

To make perfect meringue, the whites must be free of any trace of yolk—the fat present in yolk will prevent the whites from mounting—and all utensils should be absolutely clean. A copper bowl is ideal, since a chemical reaction between the metal and the whites helps to produce a stable foam. However, whites should not be left in a copper bowl for more than 5 minutes, lest they discolour. A wire whisk traps more air than an electric beater, and ensures more control; if the whites are overbeaten, the meringue will be too dry.

Piped or spooned out on a baking sheet, the meringues should be baked in a very cool oven for a minimum of 3 hours so that they dry out without taking colour.

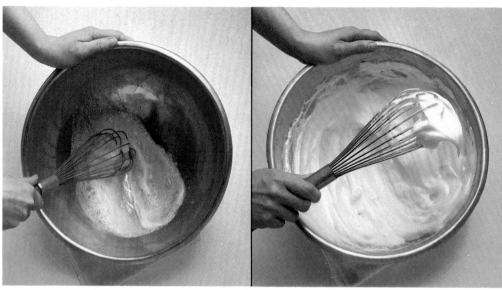

1 **Beating egg whites.** Separate an egg over a small bowl (*page 23*); let the white fall into the bowl and reserve the yolk for another use. Transfer the white to a large bowl set on a damp cloth to prevent it from slipping. Repeat this procedure with each egg in turn, so that any mishap will affect only one egg. With a wire whisk, beat the whites, using a regular figure-of-eight motion. When the whites start to foam (*above, left*), beat them with a rapid, lifting motion, until they form soft peaks (*above, right*).

3 **Flavouring the meringue.** Transfer two-thirds of the mixture to a separate bowl and add finely ground nuts—in this case, hazelnuts (*above, left*). With a spatula, fold the nuts into the larger quantity of meringue, lifting the mixture from the bottom of the bowl to the surface (*above, right*). Continue folding until the ground nuts are evenly distributed throughout the mixture.

4 **Layering the meringue.** Lightly grease a baking sheet and line it with greaseproof paper, smoothing the paper to create a wrinkle-free surface. Spoon small, even-sized mounds of nut-flavoured meringue on to the baking sheet, using your finger to slide the mixture from the spoon. Top each mound with a smaller amount of the plain meringue (*above*).

2 **Incorporating sugar.** Measure 45 g (1½ oz) of castor sugar for each white used. Sprinkle a small amount of the sugar over the whites and whisk it in (*above, left*). Repeat the process until about one-third of the sugar has been added and the mixture is fairly dense (*above, centre*). Incorporate the remaining sugar in larger batches than before, whisking vigorously, until the mixture forms stiff, glossy peaks (*above, right*).

5 **Baking and serving.** Bake the meringue on a low shelf in a 150°C (300°F or Mark 2) oven, or the lowest setting of your oven, until they are completely dry—at least 3 hours. If they start to brown during this time, leave the oven door slightly ajar; if necessary, wedge the door open with a wooden spoon. Warm meringues are fragile, so let them cool completely before removing them from the paper. If you like, serve the tiny meringues in individual paper cases, which will both enhance and protect them (*right*).□

Capturing the Flavour of Fresh Fruit

When meringue is made by blending whisked egg whites with a concentrated sugar syrup instead of sugar, the result is known as Italian meringue. This method enables you to incorporate a substantial quantity of liquid flavouring, such as a fruit purée. The amount of purée needed to flavour and colour the mixture would spoil the texture of an ordinary meringue. However, a purée may be blended into a thick syrup which is then whisked into beaten whites. Here, Italian meringue is made into delicate finger biscuits coloured and flavoured with fresh strawberries (*recipe, page 127*).

Sugar syrup is made by first dissolving sugar in water over heat, then boiling it until it thickens. A single, undissolved sugar crystal can make the whole mixture crystallize as it boils, so while the sugar dissolves, any crystals that collect on the sides of the pan should be brushed back into the mixture (*Step 2*). Alternatively, the pan can be covered, so the condensed steam washes the crystals down from the sides. Once the sugar has dissolved, the heat is increased and the mixture boiled until water evaporates and the syrup reaches the required degree of concentration; you can measure this accurately with a sugar thermometer.

To retain its fresh taste, the fruit is puréed in advance. The addition of the purée to the completed syrup will arrest cooking and thin the syrup a little. In this instance, the sugar is boiled to the stage known as hard crack (154°C or 310°F) because it will be diluted by fruit purée. If you are using a flavour such as coffee or liqueur, the syrup need only be boiled to the hard-ball stage (121°C or 250°F).

The flavoured syrup is poured into the beaten whites, cooking them slightly and thickening the mixture. Like ordinary meringue, Italian meringue is piped or spooned on to a baking sheet, and slowly dried out in a very cool oven. Fruit-flavoured meringue is best made with a red, acid fruit such as small strawberries or raspberries. Here, meringue fingers are served plain; they can also be sandwiched with jam or whipped cream.

1 **Puréeing fruit.** Remove the stalks from strawberries. Swirl the fruit briefly in water and immediately drain it in a colander. Place the fruit in a fine-meshed sieve over a bowl. Using a pestle or the back of a spoon, press the fruit through the sieve to make a smooth, liquid purée (*above*).

4 **Adding flavoured syrup to the beaten whites.** Pour the hot syrup at once into the beaten egg whites in a thin, steady stream, whisking continuously. Ask a helper to pour in the syrup while you use a hand whisk, as here (*above, left*), or whisk the whites with an electric beater while you add the syrup. Increase the flow slightly as you proceed (*above, centre*); the mixture may soften, but it will regain its stiffness when all the syrup has been added (*above, right*).

2 **Making the sugar syrup.** Put sugar and water in a heavy saucepan over a medium heat. Stir the mixture lightly with a wooden spoon to distribute the sugar evenly. When the liquid is clear, brush down the sides of the pan, using a pastry brush dipped in water (*above*).

3 **Finishing the syrup.** When the sugar has dissolved, place a sugar thermometer—warmed in hot water to prevent it cracking—in the pan. Bring the syrup to the boil (*above, left*). Beat egg whites in a large bowl until they form stiff peaks. When the syrup reaches 154°C (310°F), turn off the heat. Carefully pour fruit purée into the syrup (*above, right*); the syrup will bubble and the temperature will fall. Pour in purée until the temperature has dropped to 121°C (250°F). Holding the thermometer with a towel, stir the mixture once, then place the thermometer in a bowl of hot water to clean it.

5 **Piping the meringue.** Lightly grease a baking sheet and line it with greaseproof paper; smooth down the paper so that the lining does not wrinkle. Fit a piping bag with a nozzle—here, a fluted nozzle, 7 mm ($\frac{3}{8}$ inch) wide. Fill the bag two-thirds full with meringue and pipe strips about 7 cm (3 inches) long; use a knife to stop the flow and give the strips a neat finish.

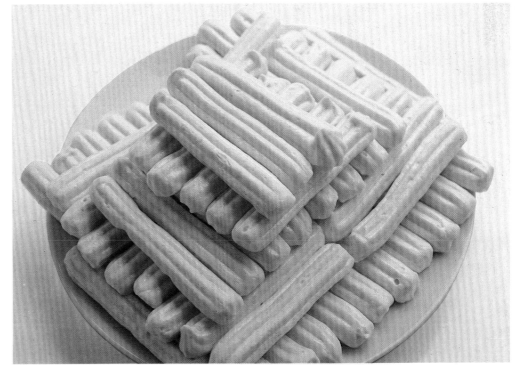

6 **Baking and serving.** Bake the meringues in a very slow oven— 130°C (250°F or Mark $\frac{1}{2}$) or the lowest setting—for at least 3 hours, until the biscuits are dry; do not let them colour. Here, the meringues are stacked on a plate to form a delicate pale-pink lattice.□

4

‛Beaten ‛Egg ‛Doughs
Capturing Lightness

The last biscuit is added to a plate of shell-shaped madeleines, that have been arranged in tiers for serving. The biscuits, made with a butter-enriched sponge batter, were baked in a moulded tin (*page 70*). After unmoulding, the biscuits were dusted with sugar in order to highlight their attractive ridged surface.

Among the pleasures of biscuit-making is discovering how the same basic ingredients can be used to produce very different results. This is particularly true when the foundation is a mixture of whole eggs whisked with sugar. Biscuits that begin with this base include pale domes with a risen surface, densely textured squares decorated with an embossed pattern and crumbly, shell-shaped madeleines.

When eggs and sugar are whisked together, air cells are trapped by the proteins in the eggs; the mixture increases in volume while the sugar dissolves and stabilizes the foam. The trapped air leavens the batter, because the air bubbles will expand in the oven's heat and raise the other ingredients. If aerated eggs and sugar are merely thickened with a little flour, they form a soft batter that can be piped or spooned in mounds on to the baking sheet. If left to stand before baking, the surface of the biscuits dries, helping to form a pale crust (*page 66*).

However, the aerated mixture can also be used to bind a more substantial quantity of flour, producing a dough firm enough for rolling out. Because kneading and rolling presses out much of the air, the biscuits will rise less than the others. This firm dough can be printed with a carved rolling pin or a stamped board to create an embossed design which springs up when the biscuits are baked (*page 66*).

For the lightest of egg batters, the whites are whisked separately, so that they form a stiff foam that is gently folded into the whisked yolks and sugar. The volume of air suspended in the snowy mass of beaten egg whites is responsible for the light, resilient texture of sponge fingers (*page 68*). Another variation is to enrich a whisked batter with melted butter. The addition of butter will make the mixture so soft that it must be baked in a moulded baking tin (*page 70*).

These biscuits derive their subtle flavour from a hint of anise, a few drops of orange-flower water or a sprinkling of grated lemon rind. Grains of crystallized sugar provide sponge fingers with an attractive beaded surface and a light dusting of sugar is all that is required to highlight the surface of biscuits baked in decorative moulds.

Traditional Shapes with a Sugary Crust

The simplest egg doughs are made from a base of whisked eggs and sugar, which is blended with flour. When eggs and sugar are whisked together, air bubbles are trapped by the proteins in the eggs; during baking, the air expands to raise and lighten the batter. By varying the amount of flour that is added to the aerated eggs and sugar, you can produce quite different types of biscuit—if a large quantity of flour is added, the biscuits will be hard and densely textured, as are the German *springerle* on the right (*recipe, page 142*); by lowering the proportion of flour, you can make light biscuits that rise during baking (*right, below; recipe, page 142*).

For all egg doughs, start by whisking the eggs and sugar together until the mixture trebles in volume and becomes firm enough to fall from the whisk in ribbons (*Step 1*). Flavourings can then be added: *springerle* traditionally have an anise flavour, imparted in this case by pastis— anise-flavoured liqueur—and aniseeds; you can also add lemon rind, as here, or spices such as cinnamon.

To make *springerle*, enough flour is added to the whisked eggs and sugar to make a firm dough, which is lightly kneaded and then rolled out. Here, a stamped rolling pin is pressed over the sheet of dough to emboss the biscuits with a variety of traditional designs. Stamped wooden boards or individual moulds can be used to achieve the same effect.

Before baking, the biscuits are left in a cool place to allow their surfaces to dry off and the designs to set. During baking, the embossed pattern appears to spring up, forming a decorative crust. The biscuits are very hard when baked; if you prefer a softer texture, they can be stored for about three weeks until moisture from the air softens them.

For biscuits with a lighter texture, a smaller proportion of flour is folded into the whisked eggs and sugar, a little at a time, to avoid driving out air. The resulting batter can be piped out or, as here, spooned on to baking sheets. The dough is left to settle for a shorter time, since the moist batter quickly forms a sugary crust. During baking, the air incorporated into the eggs will expand, creating the domed surface that is a feature of these biscuits.

1 **Combining eggs and sugar.** In a large mixing bowl, set on a damp cloth to prevent it from slipping, whisk whole eggs to blend the whites and yolks together. Sift sugar—here, icing sugar—into the bowl and whisk it together with the eggs (*above, left*). Continue whisking the mixture for about 20 minutes—or half that time with an electric mixer—until it increases in bulk and becomes pale and thick. It will fall smoothly from the whisk in wide ribbons that hold their shape and remain visible on the surface (*above, right*).

Snowy Domes Scattered with Aniseeds

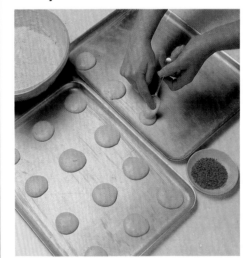

1 **Spooning the batter.** Whisk whole eggs and castor sugar in a bowl until the mixture reaches the ribbon stage (*Step 1, above*). Gradually fold in the sifted flour. Using a teaspoon, drop small portions of the batter on to greased baking sheets, pushing the batter off the spoon with your finger (*above*). Leave enough space for the batter to expand between portions.

2 **Serving the biscuits.** If you like, garnish the surface of the biscuits; here, they are sprinkled with aniseeds. Put the biscuits in a cool, dry place for 2 hours. Bake in a preheated 180°C (350°F or Mark 4) oven for about 10 minutes until they are slightly coloured. Cool the biscuits on a wire rack before serving them (*above*).

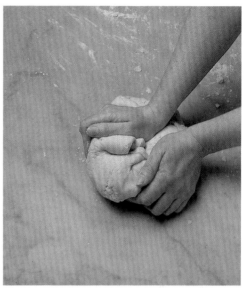

2 **Adding flour.** With the whisk, stir in flavourings—grated lemon rind and a little pastis are used here. Gradually add sifted flour (*above*), whisking it lightly into the egg and sugar mixture.

3 **Mixing the dough.** When the dough becomes too stiff to whisk, use your hands to mix in the rest of the flour. When the dough feels firm enough to knead, gather it into a ball in the bowl.

4 **Kneading the dough.** Transfer the ball of dough to a floured work surface. Knead the dough briefly, sprinkling it with more flour if it becomes sticky. Do not overwork the dough, or it will become too elastic and the biscuits will be tough.

5 **Rolling the dough.** With a lightly floured rolling pin, roll out the dough into a rectangle about 5 mm (¼ inch) thick. Using a knife, cut the dough into strips slightly wider than the carved rolling pin used here or a stamped board. Lightly flour the pin and roll it firmly over each strip of dough (*above*); if using a stamped board, press it into the dough.

6 **Transferring to baking sheets.** To add extra flavour to the biscuits, sprinkle aniseeds over greased baking sheets. Using a sharp knife, cut between the raised designs on the dough to make individual squares. With a metal spatula, transfer the biscuits to the baking sheets. Leave in a cool, dry place overnight, loosely covered with greaseproof paper.

7 **Baking and serving.** Bake the biscuits in a preheated 150°C (300°F or Mark 2) oven for 15 to 20 minutes—the biscuits are ready when their tops rise up to form a crisp, white crust and their bottom surfaces are lightly coloured. Put the biscuits on a wire rack to cool before serving them (*above*).□

Sponge Fingers with a Beaded Surface

The delicate biscuits known as sponge fingers are made from a separated egg batter, which owes its special lightness to the fact that egg whites whisked alone will trap much more air than when they are beaten with yolks. The aerated, snowy mass of beaten whites, folded into the yolks, sugar and flour, produces a particularly light batter (*right; recipe, page 139*). The heat of the oven will make the air bubbles in the batter expand, puffing up the biscuits and giving them their characteristic springy texture.

Although sponge fingers can be baked in moulded baking tins, here the batter is piped in strips and sprinkled with sugar. A few drops of water, scattered over the strips of batter and the baking sheet, will make the sugar coating crystallize during baking, and the tops of the biscuits will be frosted with little sugar pearls.

Also known as ladyfingers or *biscuits à la cuiller*—literally, spoon biscuits—these light biscuits are often served as an accompaniment to creamy desserts.

1 **Whisking yolks and sugar.** Separate egg yolks and whites. Put the yolks in a bowl; reserve the whites in another bowl. To stop it from slipping, set the bowl of egg yolks on a damp towel; add sugar and whisk until the mixture is pale and thick and falls smoothly from the whisk in wide ribbons (*page 66, Step 1*).

2 **Folding in flour.** Transfer the whites to a large bowl—here, a copper bowl to help stabilize the foam—and whisk until they form stiff peaks (*page 60, Step 1*). Stir a few drops of orange-flower water into the yolks; add sifted flour. Using a large spoon, fold in the flour: cut through the batter with the edge of the spoon, then fold the batter over on itself.

5 **Piping the batter.** Spoon batter into a piping bag fitted with a 9mm (⅜ inch) nozzle; twist the top of the bag to enclose the batter (*page 38*). Pipe strips of batter about 10cm (4 inches) in length on to a greased baking sheet. Use a knife to stop the flow of batter at the end of each strip (*above*). Leave plenty of space between each strip to allow for expansion.

6 **Sprinkling on sugar.** Through a sieve, sprinkle a generous amount of icing sugar over the biscuits. To remove excess sugar, tilt the sheet and then bang its underside so that the surplus sugar slides down the length of the batter strips and off the sheet. With your fingers, flick a few drops of water over the batter and sheet.

7 **Baking the biscuits.** To prevent the batter from deflating, place the baking sheet at once in a preheated 170°C (325°F or Mark 3) oven. Bake the biscuits for about 20 minutes, until they are very lightly coloured and feel firm. Using a spatula, transfer the biscuits to a wire rack to cool.

3 **Adding a little egg white.** To loosen the batter, in order to prevent lumps from forming when the bulk of the egg white is incorporated, add one or two large spoonfuls of the beaten egg whites to the whisked yolks and sugar mixture. With the spoon, cut and fold this first addition of egg white into the mixture (*above*).

4 **Completing the batter.** Transfer the rest of the beaten egg whites to the bowl of batter all at once, using a spatula to scrape the bowl (*above, left*). With the spoon, cut and fold the mixture over on itself, gradually incorporating the whites into the rest of the ingredients until the batter is smooth (*above, right*).

8 **Serving the biscuits.** When the biscuits have cooled, arrange them on a plate for serving. If you prefer a more elaborate presentation, you can coat the tips of the biscuits in melted chocolate, or sandwich pairs of biscuits together with jam or chocolate ganache (*page 12*). □

Madeleines Moulded in a Shell-Shaped Tin

By adding butter to a whisked egg batter, you can enrich and flavour the mixture, and give it a softer consistency. The butter is melted first, so that it will blend evenly into the other ingredients. The result is a batter so loose that it must be baked in a moulded baking tin. Here, the mixture is flavoured with lemon rind and then spooned into a moulded tin to make shell-shaped biscuits called madeleines (*right; recipe, page 140*). Similar biscuits can be made by adding alternative flavourings such as vanilla or grated orange rind to the batter, and using shallow moulds of other shapes.

Tins for moulding biscuits need very careful preparation. Before the batter is spooned in, the hollow indentations in the tin are brushed with melted butter (*Step 4*) and dusted with flour. This creates a fine, protective layer which prevents the biscuits from sticking to the tin. The moulds should be prepared in this way before each baking. After use, the tin should be wiped clean with paper towels; washing it would remove the protective film.

1 Sifting in flour. In a large bowl set on a damp cloth to prevent it from slipping, whisk whole eggs and castor sugar until the mixture is pale and thick (*page 66, Step 1*). Add flavourings—in this case, the finely grated rind of half a lemon. Sift flour into the mixture (*above*).

2 Folding in flour. Gently fold the flour into the eggs and sugar with a spoon or, as here, a spatula. Cut downwards through the batter with the spatula, then fold the batter over on itself until all the flour is incorporated and the batter is smooth.

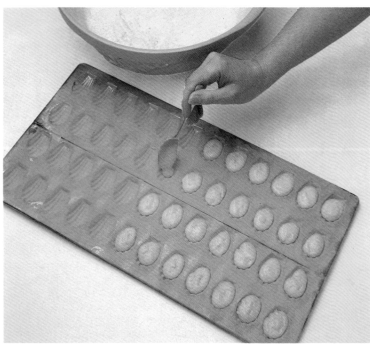

5 Filling the moulds. Using a teaspoon, spoon the batter into the prepared baking tin. To allow for the expansion of the batter during baking, spoon in just enough batter so that each of the hollow moulds is approximately two-thirds full.

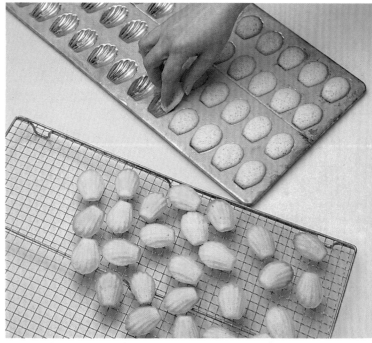

6 Baking the madeleines. Place the tin in a preheated 190°C (375°F or Mark 5) oven until the madeleines are firm and have shrunk away from the moulds—12 to 15 minutes, depending on the size of the moulds. Press down on the narrow ends of the madeleines to make them spring up out of the moulds (*above*) and put them on a rack with their patterned side upwards.

3 **Adding butter.** In a small, heavy pan, melt butter over a low heat; remove the pan from the heat and leave the butter to cool a little. Pour the melted butter into the batter, a little at a time, folding it in with the spatula (*above*).

4 **Preparing the baking tin.** With a pastry brush, lightly coat the individual moulds of a madeleine tin with melted butter (*above*). Sprinkle flour over the buttered surfaces. To remove any excess flour, invert the tin and then sharply tap its underside with your hand.

7 **Coating with sugar.** If you like, finish the madeleines by sprinkling them with a little sugar. Here, castor sugar is sifted over the surface of the biscuits while they are still warm; the sugar will cling to the warm biscuits, emphasizing their decorative ridges. Leave the madeleines on the rack to cool before serving them.☐

5
Syrup and Honey Doughs
Melting in Sweetness

Syrups such as honey, treacle and molasses provide biscuits with extra sweetness, a warm brown colour and a distinctive flavour. Honey has been used to sweeten biscuits since ancient times, but with the development of sugar refining, a wide variety of syrups has become available; these range from light golden cane syrup to heavy black treacle. Syrups are generally used in conjunction with sugar, and brown sugar—which varies from a pale soft brown to golden demerara and dark brown muscovado—intensifies the colour and flavour of lighter syrups. Many syrup doughs are enlivened with a lavish addition of spices—such as ginger, nutmeg, cinnamon, cardamom and fennel—to offset their sweetness.

Since syrups are thick and viscous, they are usually heated—often with sugar and butter—to make them more fluid. The resulting liquid, when blended with flour, will form a cohesive dough. Some recipes call for a lengthy resting period so that the dough will ferment and rise; while other recipes specify adding a chemical leavener, such as baking powder or bicarbonate of soda. These alkaline substances will react with the natural acids in the syrup and promote the release of carbon dioxide, which, in turn, will raise the dough during baking.

A firm syrup dough can provide many opportunities for imaginative shaping. It can be simply cut into bars (*page 74*), or shaped with cutters of various forms to make biscuits such as the traditional gingerbread men (*opposite and page 76*). The dough can also be pressed into a decorative wooden mould; in many parts of Europe, these traditional moulds were carved with elaborate designs, such as animals, human figures or ornate medallions. A modified version of these biscuits can be made with a carved wooden rolling pin (*page 67*) or a mould. A robust syrup dough can be used to construct a gingerbread house—a festive centrepiece which is easy to make if you follow the plan on page 78. Firm syrup doughs produce close-textured biscuits that can be glazed with a thin icing, which will gild their surfaces without obscuring their warm brown colour. A heavy royal icing cements and embellishes the gingerbread house.

For more delicate biscuits, the melted ingredients can be thinned with cream; the batter spreads during baking to form brittle wafers. Enriched with a lavish quantity of crystallized fruit and nuts, this batter forms the basis of chocolate-coated florentines (*page 80*).

Arranged in a napkin-lined basket, a cluster of gingerbread men stand ready to be presented. The biscuits are made from a syrup dough, which is spiced with ginger, cinnamon, cloves and aniseeds. Supple and malleable when it is rolled out, the dough bakes to a hard and densely textured biscuit.

Balancing Sweetness and Spice

Many biscuits gain in sweetness as well as in flavour when syrups such as honey, treacle or molasses are used in conjunction with sugar. Since syrup is thick and viscous, the best way to blend it into a dough is to melt it so that it can easily be combined with other ingredients. Here, a mixture of warmed honey, brown sugar and butter is blended with flour, to make a firm dough that will yield sturdy, close-textured biscuits (*right; recipe, page 165*).

The full flavour and the warm brown colour of these biscuits come not only from syrup and brown sugar, but from a liberal addition of spices, offsetting the dough's sweetness. For the best results, buy the spices whole, store them in airtight containers, and grind small quantities in a food processor or mortar as you need them; the finer the grinding, the better the flavour of the spices. Experiment with different spices to find the mixture you like best; here, the dough is enhanced with a blend of ground cinnamon, ginger, cloves and fennel seeds, grated nutmeg and whole aniseeds.

The spices are sifted together with the flour and a little bicarbonate of soda. During baking, this alkaline substance will react with natural acids in the syrup, producing bubbles of carbon dioxide that raise the dough and lighten the biscuits.

If you like, you can enrich the biscuits and vary their texture by adding grated lemon rind, chopped crystallized peel or chopped nuts—almonds or hazelnuts, for example. These additions can be stirred into the dough or sprinkled over its surface after you have rolled it out.

The sheet of dough can be simply cut into bars or more fancifully shaped with biscuit cutters. After baking, the biscuits can be left plain, or lightly glazed with water icing—here, flavoured with lemon juice. These biscuits are very hard when baked. If you prefer them less hard, store them in a tin for a week or two; they will absorb moisture from the air and consequently soften slightly.

1 Adding the honey. Put butter, sugar—in this case, soft brown sugar—and water into a heavy pan. To weigh the honey, set a jug or other container on kitchen scales, weigh the empty jug, then pour in the required weight of honey. Or measure a tablespoon of honey for each 15 g (1½ oz) required. Add the honey to the other ingredients in the pan (*above*).

2 Melting the ingredients. Over a low heat, stir the mixture with a wooden spoon until the sugar has dissolved and the ingredients are thoroughly blended. Increase the heat and allow the mixture to come to the boil (*above*). Remove the pan from the heat at once and cool to room temperature: do not let it become cold, or it will thicken and form lumps.

6 Rolling out the dough. With your hands or a rolling pin, flatten the ball of dough. Roll the dough out lengthwise (*above*) and then crosswise, into a rectangle about 8 mm (⅓ inch) thick.

7 Cutting and baking. Trim the dough's uneven edges with a knife. Cut the dough lengthwise into strips, then crosswise into bars—here, about 7.5 cm (3 inches) by 2.5 cm (1 inch). Transfer the biscuits to a buttered baking sheet and bake them in a preheated 150°C (300°F or Mark 2) oven for 10 to 15 minutes or until their undersides are lightly browned.

3 **Blending in flour and spices.** Prepare crystallized peel and chop it finely (*page 7*); chop nuts, or use slivered almonds. Reserve the peel and nuts. Sift flour, bicarbonate of soda and spices into a bowl. Gradually add these to the pan, stirring in each addition (*above*).

4 **Stirring in nuts and peel.** Tip the nuts and chopped peel into the mixture, stirring thoroughly to combine the ingredients. The dough will be quite dry and crumbly at this stage, but it will cling together when you knead it (*right*).

5 **Kneading the dough.** Lightly flour a work surface and, because the dough is sticky, flour your hands as well. Transfer the dough from the bowl to the floured surface. Push the dough together with your fingers, gathering it into a ball; then knead the dough lightly until it forms a smooth, compact mass (*above*).

8 **Glazing and serving.** Transfer the bars to a wire rack and leave them to cool. Make a thin icing sugar glaze (*page 9*), flavoured, if you like, with a little strained lemon juice. Brush the surfaces of the biscuits with the glaze (*above*). Allow the glaze to set before arranging the biscuits for serving (*right*).□

Scope for Inventive Shaping

Syrup-based doughs can vary markedly in texture, depending on the amount of syrup and butter in the mixture. A dough containing a relatively small amount of syrup and butter will be firm enough to hold its shape, but sufficiently pliable to roll out thinly. Since it will not spread much during baking, this dough is ideal for cutting into decorative shapes, such as little men (*right; recipe, page 146*).

By contrast, a higher proportion of butter and syrup will produce a dense, sticky dough that is most easily shaped by hand (*box, right, below; recipe page 147*). During baking, the dough will spread slightly and the walnut-sized balls will become hard, domed biscuits.

Both the doughs demonstrated here are made with black treacle, which contributes a deep colour and a strong flavour; if you like, substitute raw cane molasses, light golden cane syrup or honey. The spices can also be varied, from a blend of ground spices (*page 74*) to one distinctive flavouring, such as grated ginger root.

In this instance, the dough that is to be rolled out is lightened in two ways: by adding baking powder—bicarbonate of soda could be used instead—and by stirring in a beaten egg, which also helps to bind the mixture. Any cutters can be used to shape the rolled-out dough, from simple shapes to more complex designs such as animals, trees or figures. If you want to decorate the little men, use raisins for eyes, pressing them into place while the biscuits are still warm and soft. Once cooled, you can pipe royal icing (*page 8*) to form noses, mouths, hats and buttons.

1 Melting the ingredients. Weigh out the sugar; leave it on the scale, make a well in the centre and pour in syrup—in this case, treacle—until you reach the total weight of sugar and syrup. Alternatively, measure one tablespoon of treacle for each 15 g (½ oz) required. Place the sugar, syrup, butter and spices in a heavy pan; stir over a low heat with a wooden spoon.

2 Adding beaten egg. As soon as the mixture comes to the boil, remove the pan from the heat; allow the ingredients to cool to room temperature. Stir in baking powder. In a large bowl, sift flour; make a well in the centre and pour in the melted mixture. Beat an egg lightly and add it to the bowl (*above*).

Golden-Brown Nuggets from a Sticky Dough

1 Shaping the dough. Warm butter, brown sugar and treacle; leave to cool. Stir in spices and flour. Pull off small pieces of dough about the size of walnuts and roll them into balls between your palms (*above*). You may need to flour your hands as you work. Arrange the balls on a lightly buttered baking sheet, spacing them well apart to allow for expansion.

2 Baking and serving. Bake the biscuits in a preheated 170°C (325°F or Mark 3) oven for about 15 minutes. Using a metal spatula, transfer them to a wire rack to cool. Store them in an airtight tin; they will keep well for up to two months.

3 **Mixing the dough.** Using the wooden spoon, stir the ingredients until they are evenly blended. Flour your hand and gather the dough into a ball (*above*); place it on a lightly floured work surface. Knead the dough lightly into a smooth ball, flouring your hands as necessary.

4 **Rolling out the dough.** With a rolling pin, lightly flatten the dough. Roll out the dough, give it a quarter turn and roll it out again. Roll and turn the dough until it is an even round about 3 mm (⅛ inch) thick.

5 **Cutting out shapes.** Firmly press a biscuit cutter on to the rolled-out dough. Vary its position so that you can cut out as many shapes as possible (*above*). The scraps surrounding the shapes will be rolled out and used to make more biscuits.

6 **Baking the biscuits.** Pull the scraps of dough from round the shapes (*above*); gather the scraps into a ball, roll them out and cut them. With a metal spatula, transfer the biscuits to a lightly greased baking sheet. Bake them in a preheated 170°C (325°F or Mark 3) oven for about 10 minutes, until their edges begin to darken. Cool them on a rack (*right*). □

A Blueprint for Building a Gingerbread House

A decorated gingerbread house, with its pitched roof frosted with snowy icing, makes an unusual and festive centre-piece. A firm syrup-based dough (*page 76; recipe, page 146*), baked in broad slabs and cut into shapes, is an ideal building material. The plan shown below will help you cut the precise shapes needed for the house. By drawing the shapes on a sheet of stiff card, you can cut out templates to provide the outlines for the house. The scale may be varied according to the size you want for the finished house—the plan will provide the correct proportions.

The baked slabs must be cut while they are still warm and soft; they will become hard when they cool. The house is built on a board or tray, so that you can move it as you work. Royal icing (*page 8*), which quickly hardens, cements the structure. The same icing can be spread over the roof, and piped to form windows. You can also use it to fix on decorations, such as toasted almonds and crystallized peel (*page 6*) or other light confectionery.

1 **Cutting the pieces.** Cut out templates (*box, below*). Roll out the dough 1 cm (½ inch) thick. Bake it in slabs—here, 45 by 36 cm (18 by 15 inches)—in a preheated 180°C (350°F or Mark 4) oven for 25 minutes. Lay the templates on the warm slabs and cut round them with a sharp knife (*above*); the piece you cut from the front wall (D) will become the door.

2 **Beginning the house.** Make royal icing. Set the base of the house (A) on a board or tray. Lay one side wall (C) on the work surface. With a metal spatula, spread a support (F) with icing, and lay it face downwards parallel with one side of the wall, 1 cm (½ inch) from the edge. Fix a second support on the other side. In the same way, assemble the other side wall.

Cutting Out Templates from an Adaptable Grid

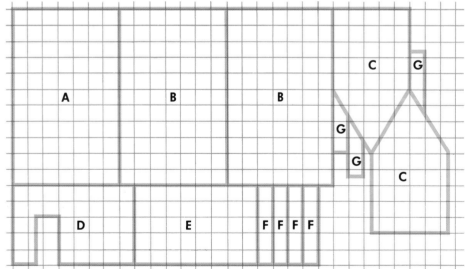
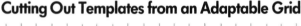

On a sheet of stiff card, draw the shapes shown on the plan with a pencil and ruler; work to a scale—in the demonstration, each square represents 2.5 cm (1 inch). With a trimming knife, and using a metal ruler for a straight edge, cut out the pieces; A represents the base; B, the roof pieces; C, the side walls; D, the front wall; E, the back wall; F, the supports and G, the chimney.

6 **Icing the roof.** Using a metal spatula, ice the roof, applying the icing to a small section of the roof at a time, and swirl the icing with the tip of the spatula to create a rough finish (*above*). Ice both sides of the roof, then ice the chimney, leaving the inner side of the chimney plain, if you like.

3 **Joining the walls.** Ice two adjoining edges of the back wall (E) and two edges of a side wall. Join the two walls to form the corner, pressing the edge of the back wall against the support. Centring the joined walls over the base, lower them into position (*above*). Cement the front wall (D) to the second side wall and fix them into position on the base.

4 **Fastening the door and roof.** Ice one long edge of the door. Working from the inside, secure the door at the opening in the front wall. Spread the top edges of the walls with icing. Gently press one roof piece (B) into position (*above*), holding it in place until it does not slip. Fix on the second roof piece. Ice the central ridge to make a smooth join.

5 **Erecting the chimney.** Join the three chimney pieces (G) together with icing, making sure that their tops and bottoms are parallel. Ice the slanting end of the assembled chimney and press it into place so that it is aligned with the front wall of the house (*above*).

7 **Decorating the exterior.** Prepare a variety of decorations—here, toasted, blanched almonds, strips of angelica and crystallized fruits cut into various shapes. Before the icing hardens, stick almonds on to the roof (*above*). Pipe icing on to the walls to make windows. Use dabs of icing to stick the other decorations on to the walls (*right*).□

A Molten Binding for Fruit and Nuts

By adding only a little flour to a syrup made from sugar, butter and cream, you can make a soft, loose batter that will spread to form thin, candy-like wafers. The batter is used to bind a generous amount of chopped nuts and crystallized peel and fruit to make the florentines on the right (*recipe, page 146*).

In this demonstration, the batter is made with granulated sugar. This forms a syrup when it is dissolved in butter and cream; as an alternative, you could use honey or treacle, diluted with cream or water. After baking, the undersides of the fruit-laden wafers are coated with melted chocolate. Before the chocolate sets, it can be decorated by scoring wavy lines with the prongs of a fork.

Another way to use a soft, syrup-based batter is to omit the fruit and nuts. Spooned on to a baking sheet, the batter will yield wafers with a lacy texture. While they are still warm, these wafers are soft enough to shape round a wooden spoon or a rolling pin (*page 51*); when cool, the biscuits become hard and brittle, and can be filled with a little whipped cream.

1 **Assembling the ingredients.** Put butter and sugar in a heavy pan. Pour in cream (*above*). Warm the pan over a medium heat, stirring the mixture continuously with a wooden spoon, until the butter melts and the sugar dissolves.

2 **Bringing the mixture to the boil.** When the sugar has dissolved, let the mixture come to the boil, stirring it gently to make sure that it does not burn on the bottom of the pan. Remove the pan from the heat, and leave the mixture to cool.

5 **Spreading the batter.** Lightly butter a baking sheet and sprinkle it with flour; tilt and tap the sheet to remove excess flour. Spoon the batter into mounds on the baking sheet, leaving plenty of space between each mound to allow for the batter spreading. Dip a fork in a bowl of water to prevent sticking, and use the fork to spread the mounds into rounds, distributing the nuts and fruit evenly. Bake the florentines in a preheated 180°C (350°F or Mark 4) oven for 12 to 15 minutes, until their edges are browned. With a metal spatula transfer the biscuits to a wire rack to cool.

6 **Spreading the chocolate.** Break or cut plain chocolate into pieces and place them in a small bowl. Boil a pan of water. Remove it from the heat and set the bowl of chocolate over the pan, covering it with a lid to keep in the heat. After a few moments, when the chocolate starts to melt, remove the lid and stir the chocolate until smooth. With a spatula, spread the underside of each biscuit with melted chocolate (*above*); place them on a tray, chocolate side up.

3 **Adding the dry ingredients.** Prepare the flavourings—blanched almonds, slivered and chopped, and finely chopped crystallized fruit and peel are used here. Sift flour. Tip the slivered almonds into the melted ingredients in the pan (*above*), then add the chopped almonds, the crystallized fruit and the sifted flour.

4 **Blending the batter.** Using a wooden spoon, stir the mixture together, so that the nuts, fruit and flour are thoroughly incorporated. Continue stirring until all the flavourings are coated with syrup.

7 **Decorating the biscuits.** Holding the fork at a slight angle (*above*), score parallel sets of wavy lines into the chocolate. To decorate the chocolate while it is still tacky, score the biscuits in the same order in which you coated them. Allow the chocolate to set, before arranging the biscuits on a plate to serve (*right*).□

6
A Miscellany of Methods
Diverse Results from Traditional Techniques

A single baking is not the only way to cook biscuits. For exceptionally crisp, dry or crunchy results, some biscuits may be cooked on a griddle on top of the stove; others are baked twice in the oven instead of once. Sometimes the nature of the dough itself dictates a different cooking method: this is particularly true of yeast dough, which is scalded in boiling water before it is baked in the oven.

The easiest of these variations is griddle cooking. In the past, the flat, cast-iron griddle used to be suspended over an open fire. Although today the griddle is more often placed on a hob, the technique of using it remains the same: shaped pieces of dough are put directly on to its hot surface. The open griddle allows any steam to escape during cooking, ensuring dry, brittle biscuits such as flatbread (*opposite and page 86*). However, the heat comes from one side only and so, to guarantee that the biscuits are evenly cooked throughout, either the dough must be turned over and cooked on the other side, or else the cooking must be completed by another method such as toasting the biscuits under a grill.

Savoury griddle biscuits are often made from coarse flours produced from barley, wheat, oats and rye. Used alone, as for oatcakes (*page 84*), or in combination, these ingredients impart nutty, earthy flavours and a pleasantly grainy texture.

Cooking biscuits twice removes almost all moisture from the dough. A second stage of cooking can be applied to oatcakes that are first cooked on a griddle, as well as to biscuits that are initially baked in the form of cake-like loaves, then sliced for a second baking (*page 88*). This gentle toasting can take place in the oven, under a grill, or in front of an open fire.

A different kind of double cooking is appropriate for biscuits made from yeast-leavened dough (*pages 90-92*). After the dough has been kneaded, left to rise and fashioned into rings, plaits or other shapes, it is plunged into boiling water. This process moistens the surface of the dough, preventing the formation of a hard crust. The scalded dough is then promptly baked, before the yeast can begin its leavening action again, and the result is a firm, chewy biscuit with a compressed crumb.

Crisp rounds of savoury flatbread lie neatly stacked, ready to be snapped into irregular fragments. Made from a mixture of barley and whole wheat flours, the dough was rolled paper thin, and cooked on a griddle (*page 86*).

Cooking an Oatmeal Dough on a Griddle

Oatcakes are savoury biscuits which acquire their distinctively nutty flavour from the oatmeal used to make them. The biscuits owe their exceedingly dry, crisp texture to the technique used for cooking them (*right; recipe, page 160*).

The dough is made by mixing oatmeal, a fine meal produced by grinding the grain of oats, with water; a little melted butter is added to prevent excessive dryness, but the dough will still remain rather dry and may crack. It should be handled as little and as lightly as possible.

The dough is rolled into a sheet and can then be shaped in different ways. It can be formed by hand into a rough disc to fit the griddle on which it is cooked or, for a perfect circle, a plate may be used as a cutting guide, as here. The rounds may be cooked whole or divided into wedge-shaped segments that are easy to handle and will fit neatly on the griddle. If you like, dust the shapes with oatmeal before cooking them, to give the finished biscuits an attractive white surface.

The crisp texture of oatcakes results from double cooking. The dough is first cooked on top of the stove on a flat, iron griddle, which turns it into a firm, mealy biscuit. At this point, the oatcakes may be cooled on racks, then stored in airtight tins before they receive their second cooking. Or they may be toasted immediately.

Traditionally, oatcakes were toasted in front of the fire; nowadays it is more usual to finish them in the oven—as here—or under a grill. The oatcakes are delicious when served still warm from the toasting. If you like, spread them with butter and jam, or serve them with cheese.

1 Adding fat. In a large mixing bowl, combine fine oatmeal and salt. Melt butter in a heavy pan. Make a well in the middle of the oatmeal; pour in the melted butter (*above*). Add a little warm water and stir the mixture.

2 Gathering up the dough. Stir in more water until the mixture forms a soft paste. When the dough comes away cleanly from the sides of the bowl, gather it up into a ball with your hands (*above*).

4 Cutting segments. With a long, sharp knife, cut the circle of dough into equal segments—here, it is divided into six (*above*). Roll out the other ball of dough and cut it in the same way. Transfer the segments to a tray.

5 Cooking the oatcakes. Put a griddle or heavy cast-iron frying pan over medium heat. When the pan is hot, place the segments of dough on it, leaving enough room between (*above*) to lift each one off easily. Cook the oatcakes until the edges begin to curl up—5 to 10 minutes.

3 **Rolling out the dough.** Sprinkle a work surface—here, a marble slab—with fine oatmeal. Divide the ball of dough in two. Roll out one ball into a rough circle about 3 mm ($\frac{1}{8}$ inch) thick (*above, left*). Sprinkle the dough with oatmeal and rub it lightly with the palm of your hand (*above, centre*). Choose a plate either the same size or slightly smaller than the griddle. Invert the plate over the dough and cut round the plate with a sharp knife to form a disc (*above, right*).

6 **Crisping the oatcakes.** Using a metal spatula, transfer the cooked oatcakes to a baking sheet (*above*). Cook the rest of the oatcakes in batches in the same way. Place the baking sheet in a preheated 180°C (350°F or Mark 4) oven. Toast the oatcakes for a few minutes until they are dry and crisp; if you like, serve them in a napkin-lined basket (*right*). □

Flatbread: Brittle Sheets That Snap Apart

An unleavened dough containing only flour, water and a little salt can be cooked on a griddle to make paper-thin flatbread biscuits (*right; recipe, page 160*). The dough can be made with any type of flour; the blend of wholemeal and barley flours used in this instance gives the flatbread a pleasant nutty taste and a grainy texture. You can also vary the flavour of the biscuits by the addition of herbs and spices.

The dough requires kneading in order to develop the moistened protein and starch in the flour. When kneaded, the simple ingredients form a cohesive dough which can be rolled out very thinly.

The dough is rolled into rounds the same size as the griddle, and pricked with a fork so that steam can escape during baking, rather than bubbling within the dough and causing it to buckle. For maximum crispness, flatbread is cooked on both sides. The brittle, nut-brown biscuits will complement the flavours of cheese and savoury spreads.

1 **Mixing the dough.** Put sifted barley and wholemeal flours in a large mixing bowl. Add salt and blend the ingredients together with your hands. Stirring the mixture with a knife, pour in just enough water to bind the flour (*above, left*). When the dough clings together and comes away cleanly from the sides of the bowl, gather it up into a ball with your hand (*above, right*).

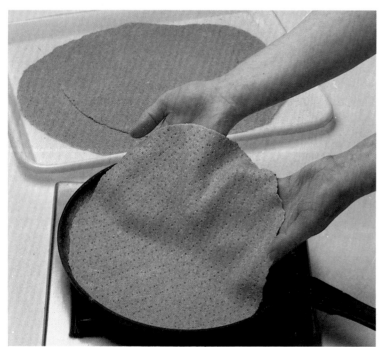

5 **Cooking the flatbread.** Set the griddle over a low heat. Using both hands, carefully transfer a round of dough from the tray to the griddle (*above*). Cook the dough for about 15 minutes, pushing it down with a spatula if it curls up at the edges.

6 **Turning the flatbread.** After about 15 minutes, check whether the underside of the flatbread is cooked by sliding a spatula under the biscuit and lifting it up. When the underside is slightly coloured, turn the flatbread over, lifting it up on the spatula and using your other hand to hold the flatbread steady (*above*).

2 **Kneading the dough.** Transfer the ball of dough to a floured work surface—here, the surface is sprinkled with barley flour. Press down on the dough with the heel of your hand and push it away from you (*above*); fold the dough back over on itself, give it a quarter turn, and repeat. Continue kneading for at least 5 minutes, or until the dough is completely smooth.

3 **Rolling out the dough.** With a knife, divide the dough into portions—in this case, it is cut into quarters to make four flatbread biscuits. With a floured rolling pin, roll out one portion as thinly as possible. To make an even round, roll forwards only, away from yourself from one edge to the other, giving the dough a quarter turn after every few strokes.

4 **Pricking the dough.** Lightly flour the surface of a griddle. Prick the rolled-out dough all over with a fork; transfer the pricked round to a tray. Roll out and prick the other portions in the same way.

7 **Serving the biscuits.** Cook the flatbread for a further 10 to 15 minutes, until it is brown and crisp. Transfer the cooked biscuit to a wire rack. Cook the rest of the biscuits in the same way, and leave them to cool on the rack. Serve the rounds whole—they are so crisp that they can easily be broken into smaller pieces without making crumbs (*right*).□

A Double Baking for Almond Toasts

The kind of soft creamed dough generally used for dropped or piped biscuits can also be shaped into free-form loaves. After baking, the loaves will have a cake-like texture and a soft crust, but if they are cut into slices and baked a second time, the texture will become crunchy and the crust brittle. The result is the lightly toasted biscuits demonstrated here, familiarly known as rusks (*recipe, page 156*).

For the first baking, the dough is formed into long loaves on a baking sheet lined with greaseproof paper. Since this dough is almost as soft as cake batter, it is too sticky to mould by hand. The simplest way to shape it is with a wet metal spatula. After baking, the loaves will be very fragile; the safest way to transfer them to a cooling rack is to slide the paper and loaves together on to the rack. When cool, the loaves are firm enough to be removed intact from the paper and sliced.

Although the rusks are perfectly good plain, you can vary the flavour by substituting 1 to 2 tablespoons of vanilla sugar for plain sugar in the dough, or by adding spices such as grated nutmeg, ground mace, cloves or cinnamon, either separately or blended. Adding saffron will not only flavour the biscuits, but it will also colour them a delicate yellow. Nuts, such as almonds, hazelnuts or walnuts, can be folded into the mixture to enhance the texture. These can be toasted, ground, chopped, or, as in this demonstration, simply blanched and left whole.

1 Starting the dough. Blanch almonds (*page 6*). Set them aside. Stand a mixing bowl on a damp cloth and place soft butter in the bowl. With a wooden spoon, beat the butter until it becomes creamy; add sugar and beat the mixture until it is fluffy and pale. Stir in liquid flavourings. One at a time, beat in the eggs (*above*).

2 Adding the almonds. Sift flour, baking powder and spices into another bowl. Tip the flour and spices into the egg mixture and gradually stir them in. Add the blanched whole almonds (*above*), and fold them into the dough until they are evenly incorporated.

6 Slicing the loaves. Leave the loaves to cool on the wire rack, and then remove them from the paper. Using a sharp knife, cut across the loaves to make slices about 2 cm (¾ inch) wide (*above*).

7 Toasting the biscuits. Place the slices in a single layer on a baking sheet. Dry them out in a preheated 150°C (300°F or Mark 2) oven for 15 minutes. Turn the biscuits over (*above*) and bake the other side for 15 minutes or until brown.

3 **Forming loaves.** Butter the four corners of a baking sheet, then cover the sheet with greaseproof paper. Press down the corners of the paper to stick it to the sheet. With a metal spatula, push the batter off the spoon on to the paper (*above*). Shape the batter into a strip about 25 by 9 cm (10 by 3½ inches). Form a second loaf with the rest of the mixture.

4 **Smoothing the strips.** Dip the spatula into cold water to moisten its blade and thus prevent it sticking to the batter. Smooth the tops and even the sides of the loaves with the spatula (*above*). Wet the spatula between strokes.

5 **Cooling the loaves.** Bake the loaves in a preheated 190°C (375°F or Mark 5) oven for 15 to 20 minutes, until they are pale golden. Remove the sheet from the oven and, holding it over a rack, pull the paper and the loaves on to the rack (*above*).

8 **Serving the rusks.** Place the toasted biscuits on a rack: they will be ready to serve as soon as they are cooled (*right*). If the rusks are stored in an airtight tin, they will keep for about a month.□

Special Handling for a Yeast-Leavened Dough

Yeast dough is most often associated with bread cookery, but it can also be used to make the firm, chewy biscuits known as *gimblettes* (*right and page 92; recipe, page 158*). To make the dough, yeast that has been mixed with water is combined with flour, butter, sugar, salt and flavourings such as citrus peel, nuts, or—as here—aniseeds. Eggs are added to bind the dough, making it moist and sticky.

Like a bread dough, the dough for yeast biscuits is kneaded, then left to rest for a couple of hours before it is shaped. This interval will allow the yeast to ferment, releasing the gases that cause a dough to rise. The dough can then be shaped into different forms: rings, as here, triangles, petals or plaits.

But at this point the resemblance to bread dough ends, for as soon as it is shaped, the dough is plunged into boiling water and briefly poached. This scalding will moisten the dough and seal its surface, limiting expansion and preventing it from crisping as it bakes. The result is a biscuit with a more compressed crumb than bread and a close, even texture.

1 Mixing yeast and water. If you are using fresh yeast, put it in a small bowl with a little tepid water. Mash the yeast with a fork against the side of the bowl to make a thin, smooth paste (*above*). If you are using dried yeast, sprinkle it on to tepid water. Leave the mixture for 15 to 20 minutes until all the liquid has been absorbed, then stir thoroughly.

2 Adding the yeast. Sift flour into a large mixing bowl and make a well in the centre. Cut butter into little cubes and place them in the well. Add sugar, salt and aniseeds, then pour the yeast and water mixture into the well (*above*).

5 Gathering the dough together. Press the dough gradually into a ball with your hand, moving it round the sides of the bowl in order to incorporate all the egg into the dough (*above*). Turn the dough out on to a floured work surface.

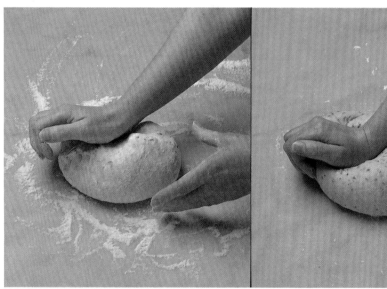

6 Kneading the dough. Holding the dough with one hand, push the dough away from you with the heel of the other hand (*above, left*). Fold the dough back towards yourself and turn it slightly. Continue pushing, folding and turning for 10 to 15 minutes, until the dough becomes smooth and elastic (*above, right*).

3 **Mixing the ingredients.** Steady the bowl with one hand. Between the fingers of the other hand, rub the butter pieces and the yeast into the dry ingredients (*above*). Gradually incorporate the flour from the sides of the well until the mixture has the texture of coarse breadcrumbs.

4 **Adding eggs.** Form a hollow in the centre of the mixture: crack an egg into it (*above, left*). Break the yolk with your fingers and, working from the centre outwards, mix the egg into the other ingredients. One by one, add the rest of the eggs to create a soft, moist dough that sticks to your hand (*right*).

7 **Letting the dough rise.** Place the dough in a clean bowl. Cover it tightly with plastic film and leave the dough to rise until it doubles in bulk—about 2 hours. Remove the plastic film (*above*).

8 **Expelling air.** Tip the bowl over a floured surface and pull out the dough (*above, left*). Use your fingers to scrape away the dough that sticks to the sides of the bowl. Heap all the dough together on the work surface. To expel trapped air, knead the dough lightly, or pummel the entire surface with clenched fists (*above, right*). ▶

9 **Rolling the dough into balls.** Dust your hands lightly with flour to prevent the dough from sticking to them. Pull pieces about the size of walnuts away from the mass of dough. Roll each piece between the palms of your hands to shape them into neat balls (*above*).

10 **Shaping into rings.** Push a floured finger right through the centre of each ball of dough. Then enlarge the hole by gently rotating the ring of dough round your finger (*above*). Place the rings on a floured surface.

11 **Scalding the rings.** Bring a large pan of water to the boil. Fill a bowl with cold water. Butter a baking tray. Plunge a few rings into the boiling water. As they rise to the surface, transfer them to the cold water in the bowl to arrest the cooking. Drain the rings and place them on the baking sheet. Repeat the process with the remaining rings.

12 **Baking the rings.** Preheat an oven to 200°C (400°F or Mark 6). Bake the rings for at least 12 minutes, or until they are evenly brown. Cool them on a wire rack before serving them from a napkin-lined basket (*left*). □

Anthology
of Recipes

In selecting the 230 recipes in the Anthology that follows, the Editors and consultants have drawn upon the cooking literature and traditions of 28 countries. The recipes range from the exquisite confections of the famous 19th-century *pâtissier*, Antonin Carême, to homely regional specialities such as Scottish shortbread; from the spicy, honey-soaked sweetmeats of India and the Middle East to plain biscuits for serving with cheese.

The Anthology spans three centuries and includes recipes from 143 writers. Many have been selected from rare and out-of-print books in private collections; a large number have never before been published in English. Throughout the Anthology the emphasis is on techniques fully accessible to the home cook that do justice to fresh, high-quality ingredients.

Since many early recipe writers did not specify quantities, oven temperatures or cooking times, this information has been judiciously included. Where appropriate, introductory notes in italics have been added by the Editors. Modern terms have been substituted for archaic language, but, to preserve the character of the originals and to create a true anthology, the authors' texts have been changed as little as possible.

Some instructions have been expanded, but in those cases where the description of techniques may seem somewhat abrupt, the reader need only refer to the appropriate demonstration in the front of the book to find the method in question explained more fully in words and pictures. Cooking terms and ingredients that may be unfamiliar are explained in the combined General Index and Glossary at the end of the book.

The recipes in the Anthology are divided into categories according to the method by which the biscuit dough is made. These correspond to the chapters of the techniques section of the book. In addition, there are separate categories for biscuits which are cooked twice and for deep-fried biscuits. There is also a section for savoury biscuit recipes. Standard preparations—basic doughs and fillings—appear at the end.

Recipe ingredients are listed in order of use, but the main ingredient is always placed first. Metric and imperial measurements for each ingredient are given in separate columns. The two sets of figures are not exact equivalents, but are consistent for each recipe. Working from either metric or imperial weights and measures will produce equally good results, but the two systems should not be mixed. All spoon measures are level.

Pastry Dough Biscuits

Shortbread

If the dough becomes rather soft in the making, it will be well to allow the shortbread to stand until quite cool before baking, otherwise it is apt to lose its form.

A strip of candied peel may be put on the top, if wished, or any other decoration that is desired.

To make 1

125 g	flour	4 oz
60 g	rice flour	2 oz
60 g	castor sugar	2 oz
125 g	butter	4 oz
½ tsp	vanilla or almond extract	½ tsp

Sift all the dry ingredients into a basin and rub in the butter. Add the flavouring and then knead all into one lump without using any liquid. Turn out on to a board sprinkled with rice flour and form into a smooth round, 20 cm (8 inches) in diameter. If a shortbread mould is obtainable, shape the cake in that; if not, pinch round the edges with the fingers or mark it with a knife. Then place the shortbread on a greased baking sheet and prick it all over with a fork. Bake in a preheated 180°C (350°F or Mark 4) oven for 20 to 30 minutes, or until the shortbread is of a uniform brown colour and feels firm to the touch. Allow to cool before removing from the baking sheet.

FLORENCE B. JACK
COOKERY FOR EVERY HOUSEHOLD

Balmoral Shortbread

Queen Victoria was very fond of this shortbread and is said to have enjoyed a piece regularly with her afternoon tea.

To make 36

350 g	flour	12 oz
	salt	
125 g	sugar	4 oz
250 g	butter	8 oz

Sift the flour on to a board with a pinch of salt. Put the sugar into a separate pile and, using both hands, work all the sugar into the butter. Now start kneading in the flour a little at a time. When all the flour is worked in, you should have a firm ball of dough. Sprinkle a little flour on the board and roll out very thinly to between 3 and 5 mm (⅛ and ¼ inch). Cut into circles about 6 cm (2½ inches) in diameter and prick with a fork in domino fashion with three pricks.

Bake on a greased baking sheet in a preheated 180°C (350°F or Mark 4) oven for 30 minutes.

CATHERINE BROWN
SCOTTISH REGIONAL RECIPES

Dorset Shortbread

To make about 36

350 g	flour	12 oz
125 g	icing sugar, sifted	4 oz
250 g	butter, softened	8 oz
60 g	Demerara sugar	2 oz

Mix all ingredients except the Demerara sugar together. Roll into a sausage shape with your hands. Roll this in Demerara sugar to coat thinly. Chop into 5 mm (¼ inch) slices and place on a baking sheet. Bake in a preheated 180°C (350°F or Mark 4) oven for 10 to 15 minutes or until pale golden-brown.

DORSET FEDERATION OF WOMEN'S INSTITUTES
WHAT'S COOKING IN DORSET

Ayrshire Shortbread

It is perhaps significant, in a milk-producing area, that this shortbread should use cream. It seems to be the only area where this is common.

To make about 36

250 g	flour	8 oz
1 tbsp	rice flour	1 tbsp
125 g	butter	4 oz
125 g	castor sugar	4 oz
1	egg yolk	1
2 tbsp	cream	2 tbsp

Sift the flour and rice flour together into a bowl. Rub in the butter and add the sugar. Make a well in the centre and add the egg yolk and cream. Knead together lightly to make a fairly stiff dough. Divide into three pieces and roll each piece into a sausage shape about 4 cm (1½ inches) in diameter. Put into a cool place and leave for several hours or overnight. Cut each sausage shape into rounds 5 mm (¼ inch) thick, place on a greased baking sheet and bake in a preheated 180°C (350°F or Mark 4) oven for 10 to 15 minutes.

CATHERINE BROWN
SCOTTISH REGIONAL RECIPES

Four Species

Firespecier

The Danes are famous bakers. Many of their biscuits and small cakes are reminiscent of Scottish biscuits and cakes. This delicious biscuit, a species of shortbread, has the curious name of 'Four Species'.

To make about 80

500 g	flour	1 lb
500 g	butter	1 lb
500 g	castor sugar	1 lb
60 g	almonds, blanched and grated	2 oz

Sift the flour into a basin. Rub in the butter. When blended, combine the sugar and almonds, and gradually knead into the flour and butter. Chill. Roll out very thinly. Stamp out in rounds about 4 to 4.5 cm (1½ to 1¾ inches) across. Arrange a little apart on a very lightly greased baking sheet. Bake in a preheated 190°C (375°F or Mark 5) oven until golden, about 10 minutes. Cool on a wire rack.

ELIZABETH CRAIG
SCANDINAVIAN COOKING

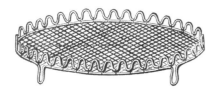

Walnut Shortbread

To make 18

40 g	walnuts, chopped	1½ oz
250 g	flour	8 oz
60 g	cornflour	2 oz
90 g	castor sugar	3 oz
	vanilla extract	
250 g	butter, cut into small pieces	8 oz

Place the flour, cornflour and castor sugar in a bowl. Add a few drops of vanilla extract and the butter. Crumb the butter with the fingers and gradually work all into one piece. Towards the end of this process, add the chopped walnuts.

Finally, turn the mixture on to a floured board and shape in three round cakes 18 cm (7 inches) in diameter. Place in greased sandwich tins. Cut into triangular pieces, prick and bake in a preheated 180°C (350°F or Mark 4) oven for 20 minutes or until just beginning to brown. Dust with castor sugar while still hot and in the tin.

MARGARET BATES
TALKING ABOUT CAKES WITH AN IRISH AND SCOTTISH ACCENT

Coconut Shortbread

To make about 24

60 g	coconut, grated	2 oz
125 g	flour	4 oz
½ tsp	baking powder	½ tsp
	salt	
60 g	butter	2 oz
60 g	sugar	2 oz
1	egg yolk	1
1 tbsp	milk	1 tbsp

Sift the flour, baking powder and a pinch of salt into a mixing bowl, and rub in the butter. Add the sugar and coconut, and the egg yolk and milk mixed together. Knead lightly. Roll out the dough and cut into squares. Bake in a preheated 180°C (350°F or Mark 4) oven for 20 minutes.

THE GIRL GUIDES' ASSOCIATION OF FIJI (EDITORS)
SOUTH SEA ISLANDS RECIPES

Pitcaithly Bannock

A rich festive shortbread made into a thick, round bannock.

To make 1 or 2

225 g	flour	8 oz
100 g	cornflour	4 oz
50 g	icing sugar	2 oz
50 g	castor sugar	2 oz
225 g	butter	8 oz
50 g	almonds, flaked	2 oz
30 g	candied citron peel, finely chopped	1 oz

Sift the flours and sugars on to a board and knead into the butter gradually. This is the traditional method which takes a little longer than the creaming method.

If you use the creaming method, just beat the sugars and butter together until creamy, then add the flours and mix in. Add almost all the almonds to the mixture and roll out into one large round about 2 cm (1 inch) thick or two smaller ones. Sprinkle the remaining flaked almonds and the citron peel on top and press them in by rolling over gently with a rolling pin. Now decorate the edge by pinching with finger and thumb.

Put on a greased baking sheet and bake for 45 minutes to 1 hour in a preheated 170°C (325°F or Mark 3) oven. If you have made two smaller ones, they will not take quite so long. They should be a pale golden colour.

CATHERINE BROWN
SCOTTISH REGIONAL RECIPES

Rich Biscuits

Sablés

The authors suggest varying this basic rich biscuit mixture by flavouring it with jam, almonds or chocolate.

To make about 16

250 g	flour	8 oz
100 g	icing sugar	3½ oz
½ tsp	salt	½ tsp
½ tsp	baking powder (optional)	½ tsp
125 g	butter, cubed	4 oz
1	egg	1
1	egg yolk	1
1 tsp	vanilla extract or grated lemon rind (optional)	1 tsp
	egg and caramel glaze (*page 9*)	

Put the flour, icing sugar, salt, baking powder (if using) and butter into a mixing bowl. With your fingertips, rub the butter into the dry ingredients until it is evenly distributed and the consistency of the mixture is crumbly. Add the egg, the egg yolk and the flavouring, if using. Mix, then knead and shape into a ball. Place in the refrigerator to chill.

Flatten the ball with your hand to make a thick disc. Roll the dough out to a thickness of about 3 mm (⅛ inch), using a steady stroke and turning the dough. Flour the dough and the surrounding surface lightly and often.

With a round biscuit cutter, 10 cm (4 inches) in diameter (or a triangular, heart-shaped or square one), cut out 10 to 12 biscuits, leaving as few dough scraps as possible. It is often necessary to roll the central part of the dough once more, as this is always a bit thicker.

Gather the dough scraps gently and place them one on another without overhandling them. Flour the work surface and dough scraps, and roll out to the same thickness as before. Cut out the remaining four or five biscuits.

Using a palette knife, transfer each biscuit to a lightly buttered and moistened baking sheet, in staggered rows. Take care not to distort them.

Prepare the egg and caramel glaze, and paint each biscuit with it, taking care to keep the glaze off the baking sheet. When finished, glaze them a second time. Then, with the tines of a fork, scratch marks on the biscuits in squares, diamonds or triangles.

Bake in a preheated 200°C (400°F or Mark 6) oven for about 15 minutes. Do not judge whether the biscuits are done by the colour of the tops, which will be dark from the glaze and will give a false impression. Instead, check the undersides which should be golden at the end of cooking. Arrange the biscuits on a rack as soon as they come out of the oven.

B. DESCHAMPS AND J.-CL. DESCHAINTRE
PÂTISSERIE, CONFISERIE, GLACERIE: TRAVAUX PRATIQUES

Salers Squares

Carrés de Salers

To make about 50

300 g	flour	10 oz
300 g	sugar	10 oz
5	eggs, lightly beaten	5
300 g	butter	10 oz
	icing sugar	

Mix together all the ingredients except the icing sugar to make a smooth dough. Roll to a thickness of about 2 mm (1/15 to ⅛ inch). Cut in 8 cm (3 inch) squares. Place on a greased baking sheet and cook in a preheated 230°C (450°F or Mark 8) oven for 10 minutes. Keep a close eye on the cooking and sprinkle icing sugar over the squares at least twice during the cooking to give a perfect glaze. These squares will keep well if stored in a closed box in a dry place.

AMICALE DES CUISINIERS ET PÂTISSIERS AUVERGNATS DE PARIS
CUISINE D'AUVERGNE

Alice's Cookies

To make about 40

About 250 g flour		About 8 oz
150 g	icing sugar	5 oz
1	vanilla pod	1
600 g	butter	1¼ lb
6	egg yolks	6

Sift the flour on to a board. Pound 125 g (4 oz) of the icing sugar with the vanilla pod and sift the mixture.

With the tips of the fingers, very lightly work in one-sixth of the flour, vanilla sugar, butter and egg yolks, and continue until all the ingredients have been worked in. It may take more flour, depending upon the size of the yolks of the eggs and the quality of the butter. Only add enough flour to roll.

Roll out the dough about 5 mm (¼ inch) thick. Cut it with a round biscuit cutter of any size that suits, but not more than 6 cm (2½ inches) in diameter. Place on baking sheets and bake in a preheated 150°C (300°F or Mark 2) oven for about 15 minutes. The biscuits should not be coloured.

When done, remove very carefully from the baking sheets with a metal spatula. They are as fragile as they are exquisite. Cover generously with the remaining icing sugar. Do not put in a tin box until cold. If the box has a cover that closes hermetically, the biscuits will keep for two weeks or more.

ALICE B. TOKLAS
THE ALICE B. TOKLAS COOK BOOK

Sand Biscuits from Caen

Sablés de Caen

These biscuits should be light-coloured, so it is not necessary to glaze them with egg.

To make about 40

1	orange, rind grated	1
250 g	flour	8 oz
125 g	sugar	4 oz
	salt	
3	hard-boiled egg yolks, crumbled	3
250 g	butter, softened	8 oz

Blanch the orange rind for 3 minutes in boiling water and drain it. In a bowl, mix the flour and sugar, a pinch of salt, the orange rind and the crumbled, hard-boiled egg yolks. Little by little, incorporate the butter. Form the dough into a ball, cover the bowl with a cloth, and leave to rest for 1 to 2 hours.

Roll out the dough to a thickness of 5 mm ($\frac{1}{4}$ inch); cut it into rounds with a biscuit cutter or a glass. Place the rounds on a lightly moistened baking sheet; with the point of a knife, make criss-cross lines on the top of each biscuit. Bake in a preheated 180°C (350°F or Mark 4) oven for 8 to 10 minutes.

CÉLINE VENCE
ENCYCLOPÉDIE HACHETTE DE LA CUISINE RÉGIONALE

Quick Economical Biscuits

Biscotti Economici e Spicci

These biscuits can be made quickly and at a very low cost. They are really tasty and light and can be kept in an airtight tin for quite a long time. Lemon rind may be substituted for the vanilla extract.

To make about 48

500 g	flour	1 lb
150 g	sugar	5 oz
	salt	
	vanilla extract	
1 tsp	baking powder	1 tsp
125 g	butter, melted	4 oz
$\frac{1}{4}$ litre	milk	8 fl oz

Put the flour, sugar, a pinch of salt, a drop of vanilla extract and the baking powder on a board or work surface. Mix together and make a well in the centre. Into this pour the butter and 20 cl (7 fl oz) of the milk. Mix well and knead energetically. Roll the dough out into a sheet 5 mm ($\frac{1}{4}$ inch) thick. Cut into sticks about 6 cm ($2\frac{1}{2}$ inches) long and 1 cm ($\frac{1}{2}$ inch) wide. Oil a baking sheet and line the biscuits on the sheet, leaving about 2 cm (1 inch) between them. Brush with the rest of the milk to give a glaze. Bake in a preheated 200°C (400°F or Mark 6) oven for about 20 minutes or until golden.

STELLA DONATI (EDITOR)
LE FAMOSE ECONOMICHE RICETTE DI PETRONILLA

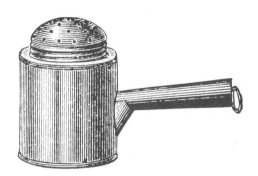

Crisp Biscuits from Mauriac

Croquants de Mauriac

These biscuits, more or less dry according to the proportions used of milk, flour and eggs, will keep for a long time.

To make about 100

1 kg	flour	2 to $2\frac{1}{2}$ lb
500 g	sugar	1 lb
3	eggs	3
80 g	butter, softened	$2\frac{1}{2}$ oz
17.5 cl	milk	6 fl oz
1	egg yolk	1
1 tbsp	clear honey	1 tbsp

Place the flour in a bowl, make a well in the centre, and put in the sugar, whole eggs and butter. Mix with the fingers until well blended, adding the milk gradually to make a stiff dough that can be gathered into a ball. Leave to rest for 30 minutes.

Roll out the dough, in two or three batches if necessary, to a thickness of about 5 mm ($\frac{1}{4}$ inch). Cut out the dough with cutters in the shape of hearts, diamonds, squares and circles with scalloped or plain edges.

Mix the egg yolk and honey, and brush the biscuits with this mixture. Place on a floured baking sheet and bake in a preheated 170°C (325°F or Mark 3) oven for about 30 minutes, or until golden.

LA CUISINE AUVERGNATE

Rum Butter Biscuits

Vajas Piskóta

To make 15 to 20

2 tsp	rum	2 tsp
125 g	butter	4 oz
125 g	flour, sifted	4 oz
½ tsp	salt	½ tsp
3	egg yolks	3

Cut the butter into the flour until there are granules the size of peas. Combine the rum, salt and two of the egg yolks. Stir into the flour mixture. Knead lightly, then chill well. Roll out 5 mm (¼ inch) thick and cut into 5 cm (2 inch) rounds. Beat the remaining egg yolk slightly and brush the biscuits with it. Bake in a preheated 180°C (350°F or Mark 4) oven for about 10 minutes or until golden.

INGE KRAMARZ
THE BALKAN COOKBOOK

Candlemas Biscuits

Les Navettes

These boat-shaped biscuits—thought to represent the boat of the Holy Marys—are traditionally eaten in Marseilles at Candlemas (February 2).

To make 30

1.5 kg	flour	3 lb
750 g	castor sugar	1½ lb
130 g	butter, softened	4½ oz
17.5 cl	water	6 fl oz
6	eggs	6

Pour the flour on to a marble working surface, make a well in the centre, add the sugar, butter, water and eggs and mix well to form a smooth dough. Divide the dough into 10 pieces and roll each piece into a sausage shape on the floured marble slab. Cut each sausage again into three pieces, crosswise. Roll them in the flour again, making them thinner and rounded at each end. Place them, a little apart, on a buttered baking sheet and then make a small cut in the middle of each biscuit with the tip of a knife. Leave for 2 hours in a warm place. Bake in a preheated 180°C (350°F or Mark 4) oven for 30 minutes.

C. CHANOT-BULLIER
VIEILLES RECETTES DE CUISINE PROVENÇALE

Candlemas Biscuits from Saint Victor

Navettes de Saint Victor

To make about 30

750 g	flour	1½ lb
75 g	butter, softened	2½ oz
375 g	castor sugar	13 oz
1	lemon, rind grated	1
2 tbsp	orange-flower water	2 tbsp
2	eggs	2
¼ litre	water	8 fl oz

Put the flour on a work surface, make a well in the centre, and in the well put the butter, sugar, lemon rind, orange-flower water, eggs and water. Knead everything together.

Flour the work surface and roll the dough into sausage shapes. Cut the dough and make the pieces into boat shapes, pointed at either end. Place on a greased baking sheet, set aside and leave to rest for 2 hours.

Bake in a preheated 200°C (400°F or Mark 6) oven for 15 minutes. These biscuits keep for a long time in a biscuit tin.

FLORENCE DE ANDREIS
LA CUISINE PROVENÇALE D'AUJOURD'HUI

Orange Loaves

Pains d'Orange

To make about 20

1 tsp	grated orange rind	1 tsp
50 g	candied orange peel, diced	2 oz
250 g	flour	8 oz
190 g	sugar	7 oz
50 g	butter	2 oz
1	egg	1
⅛ tsp	salt	⅛ tsp
1	egg white, lightly beaten	1
30 g	sugar crystals	1 oz

Work together the flour, sugar, butter, egg, salt and grated rind with your fingers to form a smooth dough. Add the candied peel. Form the dough into loaf shapes about 5 cm (2 inches) long and place them on a buttered baking sheet. Brush with the egg white and sprinkle with the sugar crystals. Bake in a preheated 180°C (350°F or Mark 4) oven for 20 minutes.

MADAME ELISABETH
500 NOUVELLES RECETTES DE CUISINE

Czech Cinnamon Biscuits

Zimtkekse

To make about 72

1 tsp	ground cinnamon	1 tsp
500 g	flour	1 lb
250 g	icing sugar	8 oz
300 g	butter, diced and softened	10 oz
2 tbsp	milk	2 tbsp
1	egg	1
3 to 4 tbsp	white wine	3 to 4 tbsp

Sift the flour, icing sugar and cinnamon on to a board. Add the butter, milk, egg and white wine and knead into a dough. Roll out thinly and cut into small squares or triangles. Transfer to a greased baking sheet and bake in a preheated 190°C (375°F or Mark 5) oven until golden-brown, about 15 minutes.

JOZA BŘÍZOVÁ AND MARYNA KLIMENTOVÁ
TSCHECHISCHE KÜCHE

Star-Shaped Biscuits from Ca's Català

Crespells de Ca's Català

Ca's Català is a Majorcan village now a suburb of Palma.

To make about 24

165 g	flour	5½ oz
100 g	lard	3½ oz
2	egg yolks	2
80 g	sugar	2¾ oz
½ tsp	ground cinnamon	½ tsp
½	lemon, juice strained	½
½	egg white	½

Beat together the flour, lard, egg yolks, 65 g (2¼ oz) of the sugar, the cinnamon and lemon juice. Roll out the dough and cut out star shapes (or other traditional shapes such as hearts or rectangles). Place the biscuits on greased baking sheets

and bake them in a preheated 180°C (350°F or Mark 4) oven for 20 minutes or until just beginning to brown. When they are cooked, let them cool, then paint them with the egg white beaten with the rest of the sugar.

LUIS RIPOLL
NUESTRA COCINA

Cinnamon Biscuits

Zimt-Pitte

Zimt-pitte are a cinnamon-flavoured shortbread. This recipe comes from Chur, in Graubünden, a Romansh-speaking district where many terms are borrowed from the Italian, as for instance 'pitte' from the Italian *pizza*.

To make about 72

60 g	ground cinnamon	2 oz
45 g	sugar	1½ oz
400 g	unblanched almonds, grated	14 oz
275 g	butter	9 oz
300 g	plain flour	10 oz
3	egg yolks, lightly beaten	3
1	egg, lightly beaten	1
	Topping	
3	egg whites, stiffly beaten	3
150 g	castor sugar	5 oz
150 g	almonds, blanched and cut into strips	5 oz

Quickly and thoroughly knead together the ingredients for the paste; roll out not too thinly and place over a buttered and well-floured baking sheet.

Mix the topping ingredients and spread over the paste. Cut into diamond-shaped pieces and bake in a preheated 200°C (400°F or Mark 6) oven for 20 minutes, until lightly browned. Lift the biscuits off the baking sheet while still warm.

EVA MARIA BORER
TANTE HEIDI'S SWISS KITCHEN

Dutch Cinnamon Biscuits

Janhagel

To make about 20

1 tsp	ground cinnamon	1 tsp
160 g	flour	5 oz
100 g	butter	$3\frac{1}{2}$ oz
80 g	castor sugar	$2\frac{1}{2}$ oz
$\frac{1}{4}$ tsp	salt	$\frac{1}{4}$ tsp
$\frac{1}{2}$	egg, beaten with $\frac{1}{2}$ tbsp milk	$\frac{1}{2}$
40 g	granulated sugar	$1\frac{1}{2}$ oz
20 g	almonds, slivered (optional)	$\frac{1}{2}$ oz

Sift the flour, rub in the butter and add the castor sugar, salt and cinnamon. Roll the dough out into a rectangle just under 5 mm ($\frac{1}{4}$ inch) thick. Butter a baking sheet and place the dough on it. Brush the dough with the egg and milk. Sprinkle on the granulated sugar and the almonds, if using, and press them in lightly with a rolling pin. Place the baking sheet in the centre of a preheated 180°C (350°F or Mark 4) oven and bake until cooked and golden-brown, about 20 minutes.

While it is still on the baking sheet, quickly cut the warm cake into rectangles about 4 by 8 cm ($1\frac{1}{2}$ by 3 inches). Remove the biscuits from the baking sheet and lay them flat to cool.

H. H. F. HENDERSON, H. TOORS AND H. M. CALLENBACH
HET NIEUWE KOOKBOEK

Vercelli Spice Sticks

Bicciolani di Vercelli

To make about 60

1 tsp	ground coriander seeds	1 tsp
$\frac{1}{2}$ tsp	ground cinnamon	$\frac{1}{2}$ tsp
	ground cloves, grated nutmeg and ground white pepper	
400 g	flour	14 oz
100 g	maize flour	$3\frac{1}{2}$ oz
1	lemon, rind grated	1
175 g	sugar	6 oz
5	eggs, lightly beaten	5
350 g	butter, melted	12 oz

Mix together the flours, lemon rind, sugar, coriander, cinnamon and a pinch each of the cloves, nutmeg and pepper. Make a well in the centre and add the eggs and melted butter. Combine the ingredients to make a smooth dough. Leave it for 6 hours in a cool place.

Divide the dough into eight to 10 pieces and press them one by one into a piping bag fitted with a rectangular nozzle. Pipe out strips of dough about 10 cm (4 inches) long directly on to a buttered and floured baking sheet. Leave some space between the sticks as they will swell during cooking. Bake in a preheated 220°C (425°F or Mark 7) oven for 10 minutes.

LAURA GRAS PORTINARI
CUCINA E VINI DEL PIEMONTE E DELLA VALLE D'AOSTA

Chinese Almond Biscuits

Sablés aux Amandes

These can be kept for several weeks in a tightly closed tin at room temperature. Nearly all the Chinese and Vietnamese restaurants in France serve these biscuits.

To make about 36

100 g	almonds, blanched	$3\frac{1}{2}$ oz
1 tsp	almond extract	1 tsp
2 tsp	baking powder	2 tsp
$\frac{1}{2}$ tsp	bicarbonate of soda (optional)	$\frac{1}{2}$ tsp
	water	
75 g	lard or butter, melted	$2\frac{1}{2}$ oz
1	egg, lightly beaten	1
$\frac{1}{2}$ tsp	salt	$\frac{1}{2}$ tsp
100 g	soft brown sugar	$3\frac{1}{2}$ oz
200 g	flour, sifted	7 oz
1	egg yolk, lightly beaten	1

Dissolve the baking powder and the bicarbonate of soda (if used) in a tablespoon of water. In a large bowl, mix together thoroughly the lard or butter, the egg, the salt, the diluted baking powder and the almond extract. Gradually stir in the sugar and the flour. Knead the dough well. If it is too dry, add a little water, but it should be fairly firm.

Roll the dough into two or three cylinders about 4 cm ($1\frac{3}{4}$ inches) in diameter on a lightly floured board. Wrap each cylinder in plastic film or aluminium foil and leave for 30 minutes in the freezer (or at least 3 hours in the refrigerator).

Take out the cylinders, unwrap them and cut them into rounds about 5 mm ($\frac{1}{4}$ inch) thick, using a knife which you should flour lightly from time to time.

Arrange the rounds on an oiled baking sheet, leaving about 2 cm ($\frac{3}{4}$ inch) between each round. Place one or two blanched almonds horizontally on each round and press them into the dough gently. Then use a brush to coat each round lightly with the beaten egg yolk.

Bake the biscuits in a preheated 180°C (350°F or Mark 4) oven for about 25 minutes or until they are golden-brown.

NGUYEN NGOC RAO
LA CUISINE CHINOISE À L'USAGE DES FRANÇAIS

Tea Cakes

Zoete Koekies

To render mutton or lamb fat, cut it into 2.5 cm (1 inch) cubes and place in a heavy pan. Pour cold water in to cover the bottom of the pan and set it over a low heat. Do not cover the pan. Cook for about 4 hours until the liquid becomes completely clear. Stir frequently to prevent the fat from sticking to the pan and to help it melt thoroughly and evenly. Pour the fat through a strainer lined with several layers of muslin, and allow to cool.

This is a very old Dutch recipe. The old Dutch people put a small piece of citron preserve in the centre of each little cake.

To make about 120

2 kg	flour	4 lb
1.5 kg	brown sugar	3 lb
500 g	butter	1 lb
250 g	rendered mutton or lamb fat, or lard	8 oz
1 tbsp	ground cloves	1 tbsp
2 tbsp	ground cinnamon	2 tbsp
1 tbsp	bicarbonate of soda	1 tbsp
500 g	unblanched almonds, ground	1 lb
4	eggs, lightly beaten	4
17.5 cl	claret	6 fl oz

First, rub the flour, sugar, butter, mutton or lamb fat, spices and bicarbonate of soda well together. Mix in the almonds and the eggs, adding the eggs one by one. Lastly, add the wine; knead all well together. Roll the dough out with a rolling pin. Make into shapes with a wine glass or any thin shape. Bake on buttered baking sheets in a preheated 180°C (350°F or Mark 4) oven for 20 minutes.

HILDAGONDA J. DUCKITT
HILDA'S "WHERE IS IT?" OF RECIPES

Bride's Cookies

Pastelitos de Boda

These are the best known of all the *polvorones*, Mexican sugar biscuits, but there are many variations. Other kinds of nuts can be used—almonds, hazelnuts or peanuts—or they can be replaced with a teaspoon of ground cinnamon mixed with 30 g (1 oz) of flour to make cinnamon biscuits. These are rolled twice in 300 g (10 oz) of icing sugar mixed with 2 teaspoons of ground cinnamon: once while still warm from the oven and again when cold. To make the basic *polvorones*, the nuts are replaced by an extra 60 g (2 oz) of flour.

To make 24

250 g	flour	8 oz
125 g	icing sugar, sifted	4 oz
125 g	pecan nuts, finely chopped	4 oz
	salt	
1 tsp	vanilla extract	1 tsp
250 g	butter, softened	8 oz

Mix the flour, 60 g (2 oz) of the sugar and the nuts together with a pinch of salt. Stir in the vanilla extract. Work the butter into the mixture until it forms a ball and shape the dough into 24 patties. Lightly oil a baking sheet and place the patties on it. Bake them in a preheated 180°C (350°F or Mark 4) oven for 30 minutes or until they are delicately brown.

Lift the cookies off the baking sheet and cool them slightly on a wire rack. Dust with the remaining icing sugar.

ELISABETH LAMBERT ORTIZ
THE COMPLETE BOOK OF MEXICAN COOKING

Caraway Seed Biscuits

To make about 72

15 g	caraway seeds	½ oz
125 g	butter	4 oz
500 g	flour	1 lb
125 g	castor sugar	4 oz
1	egg, beaten	1
About 30 cl	ale	About ½ pint

Work the butter into the flour with your fingers, mix in the sugar and caraway seeds, and then stir in the beaten egg and enough of the ale to make a fairly stiff paste. Roll the dough out as thin as possible, prick it all over with a fork and cut into rounds with a biscuit cutter. Place the rounds on baking sheets. Bake in a preheated 190°C (375°F or Mark 5) oven for 5 to 10 minutes or until golden.

MRS. AUBREY DOWSON (EDITOR)
THE WOMEN'S SUFFRAGE COOKERY BOOK

Derbyshire Wakes Cakes

To make about 40

350 g	flour	12 oz
250 g	butter	8 oz
250 g	sugar	8 oz
60 g	currants	2 oz
1 to 2 tsp	caraway seeds	1 to 2 tsp
1	lemon, rind grated	1
½ tsp	baking powder	½ tsp
1	egg, beaten	1

Rub the flour and butter together until thoroughly blended; add 175 g (6 oz) of the sugar, the currants, caraway seeds (whose quantity must be judged according to taste, lest the distinctive, somewhat astringent flavour dominates), lemon rind and baking powder. Make into a strong paste by beating in the egg. Roll out the dough and cut into rounds about the size of your palm. Scatter one surface with the remaining sugar and bake in a preheated 200°C (400°F or Mark 6) oven for about 20 minutes, so that the cakes become crisp after the fashion of biscuits.

JOYCE DOUGLAS
OLD DERBYSHIRE RECIPES AND CUSTOMS

Aniseed Shells

Coques à l'Anis

To make about 20

15 g	aniseeds	½ oz
250 g	flour	8 oz
250 g	castor sugar	8 oz
2	egg whites, lightly beaten	2
	salt	

In a large bowl, mix together the flour, sugar, egg whites, aniseeds and a pinch of salt. Work all the ingredients together well to obtain a smooth dough. Flour a pastry board or work surface and roll out the dough to a thickness of 7 to 8 mm (about ⅓ inch). Use a biscuit cutter, 10 cm (4 inches) in diameter, to cut out the biscuits, then place them on a greased and floured baking sheet. Bake the biscuits in a preheated 170°C (325°F or Mark 3) oven for about 20 minutes.

LUCETTE REY-BILLETON
LES BONNES RECETTES DU SOLEIL

Easter Cakes

Fugazzi

These cakes are a speciality of Bonifacio, in Corsica, and are traditionally eaten on Good Friday.

To make about 80

1 kg	flour	2 to 2½ lb
350 g	sugar	12 oz
12.5 cl	oil	4 fl oz
8 cl	white wine	3 fl oz
8 cl	pastis	3 fl oz
	salt	

Mix together the flour, sugar, oil, wine, pastis and a pinch of salt. Knead the mixture for a few moments until smooth and uniform in consistency. Roll out the dough to about 5 mm (¼ inch) thick. Cut out rounds with a tea cup. Nick the edges of the cakes with a knife. Prick the dough with a fork and sprinkle with sugar.

Arrange the cakes on a floured baking sheet and bake in a preheated 180°C (350°F or Mark 4) oven for 20 to 30 minutes.

MARIE CECCALDI
CUISINE DE CORSE

Currant Biscuits

To make about 50

175 g	currants	6 oz
250 g	butter	8 oz
350 g	flour	12 oz
175 g	castor sugar	6 oz
¼ tsp	grated nutmeg	¼ tsp
3	egg yolks, beaten	3

Rub the butter into the flour, add the sugar, currants and nutmeg, and bind the mixture with the egg yolks. Roll the dough out and cut it into shapes with a biscuit cutter or a glass. Place on baking sheets and bake in a preheated 180°C (350°F or Mark 4) oven for 10 to 15 minutes or until very pale brown.

MRS. AUBREY DOWSON (EDITOR)
THE WOMEN'S SUFFRAGE COOKERY BOOK

Always Fresh Biscuits

Biscotti Sempre Freschi

These are quick to make, inexpensive, delicious and keep fresh for a long time. There is only one thing wrong with them: they must be kept locked up if you want them to last.

To make about 48

500 g	flour	1 lb
100 g	sugar	3½ oz
10 cl	olive oil	3½ fl oz
2	eggs	2
2 tsp	baking powder	2 tsp
About 4 tbsp	milk	About 4 tbsp
50 g	sultanas, soaked in warm water, drained and dried (optional)	2 oz

Work together the flour, sugar, olive oil, eggs, baking powder and enough milk to make the mixture malleable. Knead well for about 10 minutes. Now, if you like, you can add the sultanas to make the biscuits that little bit more delicious. Cut the dough into half and divide each half into three. Roll these into cylinders the thickness of your finger. Cut each cylinder into eight small ones about 7 cm (3 inches) long. Line them up on ungreased baking sheets and bake in a preheated 200°C (400°F or Mark 6) oven for 15 minutes or until golden.

STELLA DONATI (EDITOR)
LE FAMOSE ECONOMICHE RICETTE DI PETRONILLA

Cherry Biscuits

These biscuits can be made very elegant by being iced over with an icing sugar glaze (*page 9*) coloured with one or two drops of food colouring and decorated with half a glacé cherry.

Those who like caraway seeds can substitute a few for the cherries. If neither cherries nor currants nor caraway seeds are used, two of the plain biscuits are very nice sandwiched together with a little jam. These make a very pretty dish if the tops are iced in different colours. In Kent, biscuits sandwiched together in this way are called "sweethearts".

To make about 60

90 g	glacé cherries, cut up into pieces about the size of currants	3 oz
250 g	butter	8 oz
350 g	flour	12 oz
150 g	castor sugar	5 oz
	salt	
1 to 1½	eggs, lightly beaten	1 to 1½

Rub the butter quickly and lightly into the flour, add the sugar, pieces of cherries and a pinch of salt. Bind with the beaten egg, using a knife to mix all together. Gather into one piece, turn on to a floured board and roll out 3 mm (⅛ inch) thick. Cut out with a round fluted cutter 5 cm (2 inches) in diameter. Lay on a greased baking sheet and bake in a preheated 180°C (350°F or Mark 4) oven for 10 to 15 minutes.

FLORENCE WHITE
GOOD ENGLISH FOOD

Beautiful Biscuits

Gâteaux Jolis

To make about 60

500 g	flour	1 lb
8	eggs	8
350 g	castor sugar, dissolved in 10 cl (3½ fl oz) water	12 oz
500 g	butter, softened	1 lb
1	lime, rind grated, or 30 g (1 oz) crystallized lemon peel, finely chopped	1
30 g	caramelized orange flowers, crushed	1 oz
	icing sugar glaze (*page 9*)	

Work together the flour, eggs, dissolved sugar and butter to form a smooth dough. Add the rind or peel and the orange flowers. Roll out the dough and cut it into biscuits. Bake in a preheated 180°C (350°F or Mark 4) oven for 12 to 15 minutes. Brush with icing sugar glaze and serve hot or cold.

LE MANUEL DE LA FRIANDISE

Moroccan Sesame-Seed Biscuits

Ghoriba dial Jeljlane

To make about 40

300 g	sesame seeds, washed and drained	10 oz
200 g	flour, sifted	7 oz
300 g	castor sugar	10 oz
1 tbsp	baking powder	1 tbsp
1	lemon, rind grated	1
5	eggs	5
	icing sugar	

Toast the sesame seeds in a heavy frying pan with no fat over a medium heat. Stir them frequently so that they brown evenly. Toast the flour in the same way. Mix the sesame seeds and flour with the castor sugar, baking powder and lemon rind. Place the mixture on a working surface, form a well and break the eggs into it. Blend all the ingredients together and knead vigorously to form a fairly soft dough that is just malleable.

Grease your hands with oil. Take a ball of dough the size of a walnut and flatten it on one side by pressing it down in the icing sugar. Continue in the same way until all the dough is used up. Place the balls of dough on a lightly oiled baking sheet with the sugared side facing upwards. Bake in a preheated 180°C (350°F or Mark 4) oven for about 20 minutes.

AHMED LAASRI
240 RECETTES DE CUISINE MAROCAINE

Sesame Roundels

Petits Fours au Sésame

These biscuits can be kept for several weeks in a tightly closed tin at room temperature.

To make about 36

100 g	sesame seeds	3½ oz
2 tsp	baking powder	2 tsp
½ tsp	bicarbonate of soda (optional)	½ tsp
75 g	lard or butter, melted	2½ oz
1	egg, lightly beaten	1
½ tsp	salt	½ tsp
100 g	soft brown sugar	3½ oz
200 g	flour, sifted	7 oz

Toast the sesame seeds in a dry frying pan over a moderate heat, stirring all the time, until they are lightly browned.

Dissolve the baking powder and bicarbonate of soda, if using, in a tablespoon of water.

In a large bowl, mix together thoroughly the lard or butter,

the egg, the salt and the dissolved baking powder. Gradually stir in the sugar, the flour and, finally, the sesame seeds. Mix everything together, preferably with an electric beater with spiral whisks, then knead the dough by hand. If the dough is too dry, add a little water.

On a lightly floured board, form the dough into two or three cylinders about 4 cm (1½ inches) in diameter. Wrap these in plastic film or aluminium foil and leave them to rest for 30 minutes in the freezer (or at least 3 hours in the refrigerator).

Take out the cylinders, unwrap them and cut them crosswise into rounds about 5 mm (¼ inch) thick, using a knife which you should flour lightly from time to time. Arrange the rounds of dough on an oiled baking sheet, leaving about 2 cm (¾ inch) between them.

Bake in a preheated 180°C (350°F or Mark 4) oven for about 20 minutes or until the biscuits are light golden.

NGUYEN NGOC RAO
LA CUISINE CHINOISE À L'USAGE DES FRANÇAIS

Poppy Seed Biscuits

Ciastka Makowe

To make about 48

60 g	poppy seeds	2 oz
250 g	flour	8 oz
100 g	butter	3½ oz
80 g	icing sugar	3 oz
2	egg yolks	2
About 3 tbsp	soured cream	About 3 tbsp
1	egg, beaten	1

Parboil the poppy seeds for 5 minutes and leave them to soak in the cooking water until they swell and become soft enough to crush between the fingers, about 2 hours. Drain the seeds and leave them in a sieve.

Sift the flour on to a pastry board, setting a little aside to use when rolling out the dough. Add the butter to the flour, chop finely with a knife and mix in the sugar and poppy seeds. Add the egg yolks and enough soured cream to make a dough that does not stick to the board. Leave in a cool place for 1 hour. Divide the dough into thirds and roll each third into a thin sheet. Cut out the biscuits with a glass or a cutter. Transfer to a buttered baking sheet, spacing them well apart, and brush each biscuit with the beaten egg. Bake in a preheated 200°C (400°F or Mark 6) oven for 12 minutes or until golden-brown.

ZOFIA CZERNY AND MARIA STRASBURGER
ŻYWIENIE RODZINY

Karen's Oat Macaroons

Karens Havremakroner

To make about 24

250 g	fine oatmeal	8 oz
250 g	castor sugar	8 oz
1 tsp each	ground cloves and cinnamon	1 tsp each
1 tsp	baking powder	1 tsp
150 g	flour	5 oz
250 g	butter, melted	8 oz
About 5 tbsp	cream	About 5 tbsp
150 g	sultanas or chopped raisins	5 oz

Mix the oatmeal with the sugar. Sift the spices and baking powder with the flour. Stir into the oatmeal mixture, then gradually beat in the butter and cream. Add the sultanas or raisins. Roll out on a lightly floured board into a round about 5 mm (¼ inch) thick. Cut into plain or fluted rounds. Bake the rounds on a greased baking sheet, placed a little apart, in a preheated 190°C (375°F or Mark 5) oven for 12 to 15 minutes, until golden-brown.

ELIZABETH CRAIG
SCANDINAVIAN COOKING

Carolina Oatmeal Cookies

To make 72

200 g	rolled oats	7 oz
500 g	sugar	1 lb
250 g	flour	8 oz
2	eggs, beaten	2
1 tsp	ground cinnamon	1 tsp
1 tsp	baking powder	1 tsp
300 g	raisins	10 oz
½ tsp	salt	½ tsp
1 tsp	bicarbonate of soda	1 tsp
125 g	butter, melted	4 oz
4 tbsp	milk	4 tbsp

Mix all the ingredients together, adding the rolled oats last. Drop teaspoonfuls on to greased baking sheets, some distance apart because the batter spreads during baking. Bake in a preheated 190°C (375°F or Mark 5) oven for 15 minutes.

MRS. DON RICHARDSON (EDITOR)
CAROLINA LOW COUNTRY COOK BOOK OF GEORGETOWN,
SOUTH CAROLINA

Flapjacks

These may be stored in an airtight tin for up to one week.

To make 12

100 g	rolled oats	4 oz
75 g	Demerara sugar	3 oz
75 g	butter, creamed	3 oz

Grease a shallow 19 cm (7½ inch) square tin. Mix together the sugar and oats, and gradually work them into the butter until thoroughly blended. Press evenly into the prepared tin with a round-bladed knife. Bake in a preheated 220°C (425°F or Mark 7) oven for about 15 minutes until golden-brown; turn the tin half way through, to ensure even baking. Cool slightly in the tin, mark into fingers with a sharp knife and loosen round the edge; when firm, break into fingers.

THE GOOD HOUSEKEEPING INSTITUTE (EDITOR)
GOOD HOUSEKEEPING COOKERY BOOK

Chick-Pea Flour Squares

Bereshtook Nokhochi

You can prepare chick-pea flour by putting dried chick peas through an electric blender.

To make about 30

500 g	chick-pea flour	1 lb
250 g	butter	8 oz
250 g	icing sugar	8 oz
1 tbsp	ground cardamom	1 tbsp
2 to 3 tbsp	ground or slivered pistachio nuts or almonds (optional)	2 to 3 tbsp

Melt the butter in a frying pan. Turn the heat very low and sift the chick-pea flour in gradually, stirring it constantly with a wire whisk. Remove the pan from the heat and allow the flour to cool slightly. Stir in the icing sugar and cardamom. Oil a baking sheet and spread the dough out on it about 5 mm (¼ inch) thick, smoothing the top with a spatula. Sprinkle on the pistachio nuts or almonds, if using.

Bake the dough in a preheated 150°C (300°F or Mark 2) oven for about 1 hour. When cool, cut it into tiny squares.

NESTA RAMAZANI
PERSIAN COOKING

Almond Sponge Slices

Spongata

You can buy amaretti *from Italian delicatessens or make them yourself, using one of the recipes on pages 129-130.*

La spongata is typical of towns in the Piacenza and Parma areas such as Busseto, Cortemaggiore, Monticelli, etc. In the last century, these were places inhabited by Jewish communities, and this type of sweet may have been introduced and handed on by these groups.

	To make about 20	
100 g	almonds, chopped	3½ oz
250 g	honey	8 oz
150 g	sugar	5 oz
17.5 cl	white wine	6 fl oz
200 g	walnuts, chopped	7 oz
75 g	breadcrumbs	2½ oz
75 g	*amaretti*, crumbled	2½ oz
50 g	pine-nuts	2 oz
50 g	sultanas	2 oz
¼ tsp	ground cloves	¼ tsp
¼ tsp	grated nutmeg	¼ tsp
1 tsp	ground cinnamon	1 tsp
1	orange, rind grated	1
	Dough	
600 g	flour	1¼ lb
150 g	sugar	5 oz
1 tbsp	oil	1 tbsp
150 g	butter, softened	5 oz
15 cl	milk	¼ pint
15 cl	white wine	¼ pint

Melt the honey in a large pan over a low heat. Add the sugar and the wine and, stirring continuously, the almonds, walnuts, breadcrumbs and *amaretti*. Add the remaining filling ingredients, mix well and keep warm.

For the dough, mix together the flour and sugar, work in the oil and butter, and moisten with the milk and wine. Roll out 5 mm (¼ inch) thick on a floured board. Use two-thirds of the dough to line the bottom and sides of a buttered 25 cm (10 inch) square baking tin. Pour in the filling and spread it out evenly. Cover with the remaining dough and press the edges together. Bake in a preheated 180°C (350°F or Mark 4) oven for 30 minutes. Cut into slices and turn out when cool.

CARMEN ARTOCCHINI
400 RICETTE DELLA CUCINA PIACENTINA

Nut-Filled Pastries

Bubana

Rosolio *is an Italian liqueur; you can use rum or brandy, or another flavoured liqueur instead.*

This sweet is something similar to the Greek *baklava*.

	To make about 30	
500 g	rough-puff dough (*page 165*)	1 lb
	Filling	
125 g	blanched almonds	4 oz
125 g	pine-nuts	4 oz
125 g	walnuts	4 oz
60 g	pistachio nuts	2 oz
60 g each	candied lemon and orange peel	2 oz each
2	egg whites	2
90 g	honey, melted	3 oz
60 g	sugar	2 oz
2 tbsp	*rosolio*	2 tbsp
125 g	sultanas	4 oz
1 tsp	ground cinnamon	1 tsp
½ tsp	ground mace	½ tsp
	Glaze	
2	egg yolks, lightly beaten	2
2 tbsp	granulated sugar	2 tbsp

Pass the almonds, pine-nuts, walnuts, pistachio nuts and candied lemon and orange peel through a grinder with a medium or coarse disc, or pound them in a mortar, to make a thick paste. Bind the paste with the egg white, honey, sugar and *rosolio*, and add the sultanas, cinnamon and mace. Roll out the rough-puff dough into three sheets and, on a buttered baking sheet, make alternate layers of dough and filling. Brush the top layer of dough with the egg yolks and sprinkle with the sugar. Bake in a preheated 180°C (350°F or Mark 4) oven for about 30 minutes or until the pastry is crisp and golden. Cut into squares when cool.

GIUSEPPE MAFFIOLI
CUCINA E VINI DELLE TRE VENEZIE

Walnut Turnovers

Bourak'r-râna

To make about 40

750 g	flour	1½ lb
1 tbsp	sugar	1 tbsp
	salt	
500 g	butter, melted	1 lb
	Walnut paste	
500 g	walnuts, finely chopped	1 lb
500 g	castor sugar	1 lb
About 20 cl	orange-flower water	About 7 fl oz

To prepare the dough, sift the flour on to a board and make a well in the centre. Sprinkle in the sugar and a pinch of salt, and then pour in the melted butter. Mix and knead, adding water if necessary to make a manageable dough. Shape the dough into a ball, cover and set aside.

To prepare the walnut paste, stir together the walnuts and sugar. Add just enough orange-flower water to make the paste cohere. Roll out the dough about 2 mm ($\frac{1}{16}$ inch) thick. Cut into strips 10 to 12 cm (4 to 5 inches) wide. Lay a rope of walnut paste crosswise along the edge of each strip. Roll the dough over on itself to form a cigar enclosing the walnut paste. Cut off the rest of the strip with a pastry wheel. Flatten the two ends of the cigar to seal in the paste, and cut off the two ends close to the paste with the pastry wheel. Repeat with the remaining dough and paste.

Place the turnovers on an oiled baking sheet and bake in a preheated 170°C (325°F or Mark 3) oven for about 25 minutes or until just turning golden-brown.

FATIMA-ZOHRA BOUAYED
LA CUISINE ALGÉRIENNE

Easter Biscuits

Ma'moul

These are, above all others, the Easter speciality of the Lebanon. The flour may be replaced by semolina, or half of each may be used.

To make about 15

250 g	butter, melted	8 oz
500 g	flour	1 lb
3 tbsp	orange-flower water	3 tbsp
3 tbsp	rose-water	3 tbsp
2 to 4 tbsp	water (optional)	2 to 4 tbsp
	icing sugar	

	Filling	
200 g	walnuts, almonds or pistachio nuts, chopped	7 oz
200 g	castor sugar	7 oz
3 tbsp	orange-flower water or rose-water	3 tbsp

Add the melted butter to the flour with the orange-flower water and the rose-water. Then add a little water, if necessary, to make a firm dough with the consistency of shortcrust. Set aside and leave to rest for 2 hours.

To make the filling, mix the nuts with the castor sugar and orange-flower water. Take pieces of dough the size of an egg, and shape each into a hollow cone. Place a bit of the filling in the cone, close the base and flatten it. Stamp a design on the surface of the cone with a special mould (or stamp with lines, using a fork). Place on a lightly oiled baking sheet and bake in a preheated 180°C (350°F or Mark 4) oven for 20 minutes. Take from the oven and sprinkle with icing sugar.

FAYEZ AOUN
280 RECETTES DE CUISINE FAMILIALE LIBANAISE

Puff Pastry Slices with Almond Topping

Condé Grand Four

You can vary this recipe by sprinkling coarse sugar crystals or finely chopped pistachio nuts over the almond topping.

To make about 40

500 g	rough-puff dough, turned and rolled six times (*page 165*)	1 lb
	Topping	
175 g	almonds, blanched and cut into very fine slivers	6 oz
3	eggs, beaten	3
125 g	sugar, sifted	4 oz

Place the eggs, 100 g (3½ oz) sugar and almonds in a mixing bowl. Mix together to form a well-blended paste that is easy to spread. If the paste is too thick, add a little more beaten egg.

Roll out the rough-puff dough in a sheet 1 cm (½ inch) thick. Cut into strips 8 by 3 cm (3¼ by 1¼ inches). Spread a layer of almond topping on each of the strips and sprinkle with the remaining sugar. Bake in a preheated 220°C (425°F or Mark 7) oven for 15 minutes or until golden.

MME. ROSALIE BLANQUET
LE PÂTISSIER DES MÉNAGES

Exquisite Cakes

Gâteaux Exquis

To make about 30

500 g	rough-puff dough (page 165)	1 lb
2	egg yolks, beaten with 1 tbsp water	2
30 g	caramelized orange flowers, crushed	1 oz
1	lime, rind grated	1
60 g	macaroons, finely chopped	2 oz
30 g	almonds, blanched and slivered	1 oz

Roll out the dough and cut it into lozenge-shaped biscuits about 5 cm (2 inches) long. Brush the tops with the beaten egg yolks. Mix the orange flowers, grated rind, macaroons and almonds, and sprinkle the tops of the biscuits with this mixture. Chill for about 1 hour. Place in a preheated 230°C (450°F or Mark 8) oven for 2 minutes, then reduce the temperature to 200°C (400°F or Mark 6) and continue to cook for 10 minutes. Cover the tops with a piece of greaseproof paper if they brown before the pastry is cooked.

LE MANUEL DE LA FRIANDISE

Linz Nut Biscuits

Linzer Nußgebäck

To make about 48

200 g	ground almonds or hazelnuts	7 oz
400 g	flour	14 oz
250 g	butter	8 oz
400 g	sugar	14 oz
5	eggs, yolks separated from whites	5
250 g	plain chocolate, grated	8 oz

Work the flour, butter, 150 g (5 oz) of the sugar and the egg yolks into a dough and knead well. Roll out the dough to a thickness of 5 mm (¼ inch); place on a greased baking sheet and bake in a preheated 180°C (350°F or Mark 4) oven for 10 minutes until half done. Meanwhile, stir the remaining sugar, egg whites, ground nuts and chocolate over a low heat until the mixture is thick and creamy. When the half-cooked pastry has cooled down, coat it with this mixture. Bake again in a preheated 180°C (350°F or Mark 4) oven until the surface layer has dried out, about 10 minutes. Remove from the oven and allow to cool before cutting into pieces.

ELEK MAGYAR
KOCHBUCH FÜR FEINSCHMECKER

Frazer's Cheaters (Nut Squares)

These squares are also good if you omit the coconut and increase the quantity of chopped pecan nuts to 175 g (6 oz). A creamed dough (recipe, page 166) can be used as the base for these biscuits, instead of the shortcrust base given here.

To make 64

125 g	flour	4 oz
2 tbsp	granulated sugar	2 tbsp
1 tsp	salt	1 tsp
125 g	butter	4 oz
	Topping	
125 g	pecan nuts, coarsely chopped	4 oz
90 g	grated coconut	3 oz
450 g	light brown sugar	15 oz
2	eggs	2
2 tbsp	flour	2 tbsp

To make the dough, combine the flour, granulated sugar and salt in a mixing bowl. Using a pastry blender, cut in the butter. Mix with the hands and press the dough over the bottom of a 20 cm (8 inch) square baking tin. Bake in a preheated 180°C (350°F or Mark 4) oven for 10 minutes, then remove from the oven.

Increase the oven temperature to 190°C (375°F or Mark 5).

Make the topping by mixing together the nuts, coconut, brown sugar, eggs and flour. Spread this mixture over the bottom crust. Bake for 20 minutes. Cool, cut into 2.5 cm (1 inch) squares and remove from the pan with a narrow spatula.

JEAN HEWITT
THE NEW YORK TIMES NEW ENGLAND HERITAGE COOKBOOK

Almond-Date Bars

Horikhivnyk

To make about 24

125 g	flour	4 oz
2 tbsp	sugar	2 tbsp
	salt	
60 g	butter	2 oz
2	egg yolks	2
1 tbsp	double cream	1 tbsp
½ tsp	vanilla extract	½ tsp

Almond and date filling

250 g	almonds, blanched and chopped	8 oz
250 g	stoned dates, finely chopped	8 oz
250 g	icing sugar	8 oz
6	egg whites, stiffly beaten	6
250 g	chocolate, grated	8 oz

Sift the flour with the sugar and a pinch of salt. Cut in the butter. Combine the egg yolks, cream and vanilla. Add to the flour and mix until the dough holds together. Pat evenly into a buttered 22 by 30 cm (9 by 12 inch) tin. Bake in a preheated 180°C (350°F or Mark 4) oven for 10 to 15 minutes.

While the crust is baking, prepare the filling. Add the icing sugar gradually to the beaten egg whites and continue beating. Fold in the almonds, dates and chocolate. Spread the filling over the partially baked crust. Reduce the oven temperature to 170°C (325°F or Mark 3) and continue baking for about 40 minutes or until the filling is set. Remove from the oven and cool in the tin. Cut into bars.

SAVELLA STECHISHIN
TRADITIONAL UKRAINIAN COOKERY

Spicy Speculaas

Gevulde Speculaas

Speculaas *spice, which is sold ready packaged in the Netherlands, can be made with ground spices in the following proportions: 3½ tablespoons of cinnamon, 1 tablespoon of nutmeg, 1 tablespoon of cloves, 2 teaspoons of ginger, 1 teaspoon of cardamom and 1 teaspoon of white pepper.*

Instead of being used to sandwich the marzipan filling, the dough can be rolled round the filling, as shown in the demonstration on page 24.

To make about 80

1 tbsp	*speculaas* spice	1 tbsp
1 kg	flour	2¼ lb
1 tbsp	baking powder	1 tbsp
	salt	
600 g	butter	1¼ lb
500 g	castor sugar	1 lb
1	lemon, rind grated	1
3	eggs, beaten	3
	marzipan (*page 167*)	
1	egg yolk, beaten with 1 tbsp water	1
	blanched and halved almonds	

Put the flour, baking powder and salt into a bowl and rub in the butter until the texture resembles breadcrumbs. Mix in the sugar, lemon rind and *speculaas* spice. Add the beaten eggs and mix the dough with a fork or knife until it is smooth and elastic. Leave it to rest in a cool place for a few hours.

Roll out half the dough 3 mm (⅛ inch) thick and lay it on a baking sheet. Roll out the marzipan to a thickness of 2 mm (¹⁄₁₆ inch), then place it on top of the dough. Roll the rest of the dough to 3 mm (⅛ inch) thickness and cover the marzipan with it. Brush with some of the egg yolk, cover well with halved almonds and brush with the rest of the egg yolk. Bake in a preheated 180°C (350°F or Mark 4) oven for 25 to 30 minutes. When cool, cut it into slices.

WILFRED J. FANCE (EDITOR)
THE NEW INTERNATIONAL CONFECTIONER

Small Redcurrant Cakes

Kleine Johannisbeer-Kuchen

To make a redcurrant purée, stew 500 g (1 lb) of redcurrants very gently with a tablespoon of water and 60 g (2 oz) of sugar until the fruit has disintegrated—about 15 minutes. Pass the mixture through a sieve. Alternatively, you can use blackcurrant purée or sieved jam.

To make about 80

30 cl	redcurrant purée	½ pint
500 g	flour	1 lb
300 g	butter	10 oz
70 g	sugar	2½ oz
2	sugar lumps, rubbed over the rind of 1 lemon, then crushed	2
9	hard-boiled egg yolks, sieved	9
3	egg whites, stiffly beaten	3
	icing sugar	

Place the flour in a bowl, add the butter and cut in until the mixture has the texture of coarse meal. Add the sugar, lemon-flavoured sugar and hard-boiled egg yolks, and work until the dough coheres. Roll out fairly thickly. Cut out rounds 7.5 cm (3 inches) in diameter or ovals, as preferred. Transfer to a baking sheet, prick here and there with the point of a knife, and bake in a preheated 190°C (375°F or Mark 5) oven for 15 minutes or until well coloured.

Combine the egg whites and 3 tablespoons of icing sugar. Fill a piping bag with the mixture and pipe a delicate lattice-work on to the biscuits. Pipe a rim round the edges. Sprinkle with a little more icing sugar and bake in a 150°C (300°F or Mark 2) oven for 15 minutes or until the meringue is golden. Allow the meringue to cool, then fill the gaps in the lattice-work with redcurrant purée.

SOPHIE WILHELMINE SCHEIBLER
ALLGEMEINES DEUTSCHES KOCHBUCH
FÜR ALLE STÄNDE

Choux Biscuits from Albi

Gimblettes d'Albi

To make 40 to 50

¼ litre	milk	8 fl oz
100 g	butter	3½ oz
1 tbsp	granulated sugar	1 tbsp
125 g	flour	4 oz
2 tsp	salt	2 tsp
5	eggs	5
60 g	almonds, blanched and chopped	2 oz

Put the milk into a heavy saucepan over a low heat; add the butter and sugar. Sift the flour and salt on to greaseproof paper. When the butter has melted, increase the heat to bring the milk to the boil. Turn off the heat immediately and slide all the flour off the paper into the liquid. Stir the mixture until thoroughly combined, then stir over a medium heat until it forms a solid mass that comes away cleanly from the sides of the pan. Remove the pan from the heat and cool the mixture for a few minutes.

Break one egg into a bowl and add it to the contents of the pan, beating with a spoon to incorporate the egg thoroughly. Repeat with three more eggs, adding them one at a time. Continue beating until the ingredients are smoothly blended.

Place the mixture in a piping bag with a round nozzle 1 cm (½ inch) in diameter. On a lightly buttered baking sheet, form little balls the size of an apricot. Arrange the balls in staggered rows, well spaced out.

Beat the remaining egg and paint the surface of each bun with a brush, taking care not to let any egg drop on to the baking sheet. Press each one lightly with a finger to spread it out slightly without squashing it, then scatter chopped almonds over the top.

Bake at once, so that the dough does not have time to cool down, in a preheated 230°C (450°F or Mark 8) oven for 10 minutes. Then reduce the heat to 220°C (425°F or Mark 7) and let the biscuits cook for another 10 minutes, with the oven door propped open with a spoon, so that they dry out. Allow the biscuits to cool on a rack.

DOMINIQUE WEBER
LES BONNES RECETTES DES PROVINCES DE FRANCE

Apricot Slices

Herminenschnitten

To make the apricot purée, halve and stone 250 g (8 oz) fresh apricots. Over a gentle heat, dissolve 90 g (3 oz) of sugar in 10 cl (3½ fl oz) of water, then boil the sugar syrup for 1 minute. Cook the apricots for 10 minutes in the sugar syrup. Rub the apricots only through a sieve or purée in a blender. Measure the amount and, if necessary, make it up to 15 cl (¼ pint) with the syrup.

Alternatively, place 125 g (4 oz) dried apricots in 15 cl (¼ pint) hot water and leave them to soak for 4 hours. Then rub through a sieve or purée in a blender.

To make 36

15 cl	apricot purée	¼ pint
500 g	flour	1 lb
350 g	butter	12 oz
250 g	sugar	8 oz
350 g	unblanched almonds, ground	12 oz
2	eggs	2
1	egg yolk	1
	ground cinnamon	
10 cl	milk	4 fl oz
	Glaze	
1	egg, lightly beaten	1

Prepare a dough from the flour, butter, sugar, almonds, eggs, egg yolk, a little cinnamon and the milk. Work the dough thoroughly and divide into two. Roll out one half into a square, 5 mm (¼ inch) thick. Coat with apricot purée. Roll out the remaining dough, cut into long thin strips and place them over the apricot purée in a lattice pattern. Brush the latticework with the egg. Bake in a preheated 200°C (400°F or Mark 6) oven for about 25 minutes or until golden. When cooked, cut into squares.

ELEK MAGYAR
KOCHBUCH FÜR FEINSCHMECKER

Fingers of Zénobie

Les Doigts de Zénobie

To make about 80

1 kg	semolina	2 to 2½ lb
500 g	butter	1 lb
15 g	fresh yeast or 2 tsp dried yeast, dissolved in 2 tbsp warm water	½ oz
15 g	ground cinnamon	½ oz
500 g	honey	1 lb

Knead the semolina with the butter and add the yeast. When the dough becomes firm, place in a warm place for 12 hours. At the end of this time, pull off small pieces of dough and shape them into sticks the length of a finger. Roll them over the surface of a drum sieve and place them on a dry cloth.

Bake in a preheated 150°C (300°F or Mark 2) oven for 30 minutes or until cooked, that is, until the biscuits have a very crumbly texture when bitten. Arrange the fingers in a pyramid on a plate. Sprinkle with the cinnamon. Heat the honey and pour over the pile of biscuits.

RENÉ R. KHAWAM
LA CUISINE ARABE

Easter Milk Biscuits

Kâk bi Halîb

Mahlab *is a Middle-Eastern flavouring made from the kernels of black cherries. If this is unavailable, a few drops of almond extract can be substituted.*

These biscuits are traditionally prepared at Easter and are offered to visitors during the holiday.

Once the biscuits are cooked, you can dissolve 2 tablespoons of sugar in 6 tablespoons of milk and soak the surface of the biscuits in the mixture, then sprinkle them with sugar. Let the biscuits dry a bit before serving them.

To make about 24

About 17.5 cl	milk	About 6 fl oz
500 g	flour	1 lb
$\frac{1}{3}$ tsp each	ground *mahlab*, dried marjoram leaves and ground aniseeds	$\frac{1}{3}$ tsp each
1 tsp	dried yeast	1 tsp
2 tbsp	olive oil	2 tbsp
100 g	butter, melted	$3\frac{1}{2}$ oz
200 g	sugar	7 oz

Make a well in the flour and add the *mahlab*, marjoram leaves and aniseeds, the yeast and, a little at a time, the olive oil and butter. Dissolve the sugar in the milk and add to the mixture. Work the dough well with the fingertips, as you would bread dough. Let rest for about 2 hours.

Make the dough into flat biscuits about 7 cm (3 inches) in diameter and 1 to 1.5 cm ($\frac{1}{2}$ to $\frac{3}{4}$ inch) thick. (You can stamp a design on them with a wooden mould.) The biscuits may also be made in bracelet shapes the thickness of a finger. Place in a preheated 200°C (400°F or Mark 6) oven, then lower the heat to 180°C (350°F or Mark 4) for 15 minutes or until nicely browned. Eat these biscuits warm or cold.

FAYEZ AOUN
280 RECETTES DE CUISINE FAMILIALE LIBANAISE

Creamed Dough Biscuits

Cigarettes

To help the mixture spread as thinly as possible during baking, 1 to 2 tablespoons of cooled, melted butter may be added after the flour has been incorporated.

Cigarettes may be eaten plain or with a piped filling of praline butter (*recipe, page 166*), the two ends dipped in chopped, toasted almonds or chocolate vermicelli.

To make 90 to 100

250 g	butter	8 oz
400 g	icing sugar	14 oz
1 tsp	vanilla extract	1 tsp
11	egg whites	11
300 g	flour, sifted	10 oz

Cream the butter, add the sugar and beat well. Add the vanilla extract, then gradually add the egg whites. Stir in the flour. Using a piping bag with a medium-sized plain round nozzle, pipe small balls of dough spaced well apart on lightly greased baking sheets. Bake in a preheated 220°C (425°F or Mark 7) oven for 8 to 10 minutes. While the biscuits are still warm, remove them one by one from the baking sheet and roll them round the handle of a wooden spoon, pressing where they overlap so that they will harden into closed cylinders.

M. VITALIS
LES BASES DE LA PÂTISSERIE, CONFISERIE, GLACERIE

Cat's Tongues

Langues de Chat

The method of making these biscuits is shown on page 48.

To make 90 to 100

250 g	butter	8 oz
400 g	icing sugar	14 oz
1 tsp	vanilla extract	1 tsp
10	egg whites	10
400 g	flour, sifted	14 oz

Cream the butter, add the sugar and beat the mixture well. Add the vanilla. Little by little, add the egg whites, then fold in the flour. Using a piping bag with a small plain round nozzle, pipe strips of dough 7 cm (2¾ inches) long on to ungreased baking sheets. Bake in a preheated 220°C (425°F or Mark 7) oven for about 8 minutes.

M. VITALIS
LES BASES DE LA PÂTISSERIE, CONFISERIE, GLACERIE

Small Cornets

Petits Cornets

To shape biscuits around a cream horn mould, see the demonstration on page 52. The author suggests filling the cornets with chocolate ganache or butter cream (page 12).

To make about 40

125 g	butter	4 oz
125 g	castor or icing sugar	4 oz
	vanilla extract	
5	egg whites	5
125 g	flour	4 oz

Cream the butter and sugar together, then add two to three drops of vanilla extract. Gradually beat in the egg whites. The mixture usually curdles at this stage but becomes smooth once the flour is added. Fold in the flour. Using a 5 mm (¼ inch) plain nozzle, pipe very small mounds of the mixture on to well greased baking sheets. Leave ample room between each mound for them to spread into rounds of about 3.5 to 5 cm (1½ to 2 inches) across. Bake in a preheated 200°C (400°F or Mark 6) oven for 10 minutes, until light golden-brown. Remove the rounds from the sheets one at a time whilst they are still hot and shape them quickly round a cream horn mould.

When made in advance the cornets should be kept dry and crisp in a closed biscuit tin.

WILLIAM BARKER
THE MODERN PÂTISSIER

Piped Cookies, Sweet Thumbs and Sand Rosettes

Sprits, Zoete Duimpjes, Zandrozetten

A typical *sprits* pipe is a metal pipe with a wooden nozzle; a strong piping bag with a 1 cm (½ inch) serrated nozzle may also be used successfully.

To make about 36

125 g	butter	4 oz
125 g	soft brown sugar, sifted	4 oz
1	vanilla pod, seeds removed and reserved, or 1 lemon, rind grated	1
½ tsp	salt	½ tsp
1	egg white	1
200 g	flour	7 oz
1 tsp	baking powder	1 tsp

Cream the butter with the sugar, vanilla seeds or grated lemon rind, and salt. Add the egg white, beat until smooth and then add the flour and baking powder. Put the dough into a *sprits* pipe or piping bag.

Pipe the dough on to a greased baking sheet in straight or wavy ribbons, small rosettes or ribbed waves about 4 cm (1½ inches) long and 2 cm (¾ inch) apart. Bake in a preheated 170°C (325°F or Mark 3) oven for 20 to 25 minutes. Remove the biscuits immediately from the baking sheet (they soon become brittle) and lay them on a flat surface.

F. M. STOLL AND W. H. DE GROOT
HET HAAGSE KOOKBOEK

Sighs from Cudillero

Suspiros de Cudillero

Sighs or suspiros *is the generic name for this kind of confectionery, which is as light as a sigh or a breath. Cudillero is à town in Oviedo, in north-west Spain.*

To make about 48

250 g	butter, softened	8 oz
200 g	sugar	7 oz
2	egg whites	2
500 g	flour	1 lb

Put the butter in a bowl and add the sugar, little by little, beating until the mixture is creamy. Then add the egg whites and stir in the flour, a little at a time, mixing all the ingredients thoroughly. Shape the mixture into balls about the size of walnuts. Flatten them a little and place on a lightly greased baking sheet. Bake in a preheated 170°C (325°F or Mark 3) oven for about 12 minutes or until firm. Remove from the oven and sprinkle with sugar.

MARIA LUISA GARCÍA
EL ARTE DE COCINAR

Ladies' Wafers

Palets de Dame

To make currant wafers (*page 38*), stick some currants on each biscuit before baking. Ice the biscuits as below.

To make 80 to 90

250 g	butter	8 oz
250 g	icing sugar	8 oz
6	eggs	6
1 tsp	vanilla extract	1 tsp
300 g	flour	10 oz
	apricot glaze (*page 9*)	
	icing sugar glaze with rum (*page 9*)	

Cream the butter, add the sugar and beat until fluffy. Beat in the eggs one by one, then the vanilla, then the flour. Pipe small balls of the mixture on to greased and lightly floured baking sheets, spacing them well apart. Bake in a preheated 180°C (350°F or Mark 4) oven for 12 to 15 minutes.

Heat the apricot glaze and brush the biscuits with it, then cover them with the icing sugar glaze flavoured with rum. Return to the oven for a moment to fix the glaze.

M. VITALIS
LES BASES DE LA PÂTISSERIE, CONFISERIE, GLACERIE

Rum Biscuits

Palais de Dames

To make rum and currant biscuits, simply add 120 g (4 oz) of currants to the dough.

To make about 80

8 cl	rum	3 fl oz
5	eggs	5
250 g	unsalted butter, softened	8 oz
300 g	castor sugar	10 oz
250 g	flour, sifted	8 oz
2	egg yolks, beaten with 1 tbsp water	2

Place all the ingredients except the beaten egg yolks into a mixing bowl and beat well until thoroughly blended. Put the dough in a piping bag and pipe small round biscuits on to

a buttered baking sheet. Allow the dough to stand for 1 hour.

Brush the biscuits lightly with the egg yolk mixture and bake in a preheated 150°C (300°F or Mark 2) oven for 25 minutes or until browned.

MME. ROSALIE BLANQUET
LE PÂTISSIER DES MÉNAGES

Raisin Cakes

"Galetes" aux Raisins

To make about 50

40 g	raisins	1½ oz
60 g	butter	2 oz
60 g	castor sugar	2 oz
1	egg	1
75 g	flour	2½ oz
1 tsp	rum	1 tsp

Place the butter in a bowl and work with a fork until soft. Stir in the sugar and beat the mixture for 3 to 4 minutes. Break in the egg and continue to work the mixture until it is smooth. Add the flour a spoonful at a time, and then mix in the raisins and the rum. Arrange spoonfuls of the dough on a buttered baking sheet, a fair distance apart. Bake in a preheated 220°C (425°F or Mark 7) oven for 4 to 6 minutes. Keep a careful watch over the cooking.

ÉLIANE THIBAUT COMELADE
LA CUISINE CATALANE

Tea Crackers

These are fine for tea—not so rich as to destroy the dinner appetite. Nuts, currants, raisins, peel or pieces of dried fruit may be used for decoration.

To make about 24

60 g	butter	2 oz
60 g	sugar	2 oz
½ tsp	vanilla or almond extract, or lemon juice	½ tsp
1	egg, well beaten	1
¼ tsp	salt	¼ tsp
60 g	flour	2 oz

Cream the butter; add the sugar, then cream again. Add the flavouring, egg, salt and flour. Drop teaspoonfuls of the mixture, well spaced, on a greased baking sheet and bake in a preheated 180°C (350°F or Mark 4) oven for 13 to 15 minutes. Do not let them get too brown.

LOIS LINTNER SUMPTION AND MARGUERITE LINTNER ASHBROOK
AROUND-THE-WORLD COOKY BOOK

Black and White Biscuits

Marmorplätzchen

To make about 90

250 g	butter	8 oz
250 g	sugar	8 oz
1 tbsp	vanilla sugar	1 tbsp
2	eggs	2
2 tbsp	rum	2 tbsp
½ tsp	baking powder	½ tsp
500 g	flour	1 lb
3 tbsp	cocoa powder	3 tbsp
1	egg white, lightly beaten	1

Cream the butter, sugar and vanilla sugar until fluffy. Beat in the eggs, and add the rum. Mix the baking powder with the flour and work into the butter and sugar mixture quickly. Divide the mixture in half and colour one half with the cocoa powder. Chill both portions.

For spirals, roll out the light and dark mixtures separately into equal, thin rectangles. Brush the light mixture with egg white and place the dark mixture on top. Brush the dark mixture with egg white, and roll the two rectangles up together, starting at one of the long sides.

For chequerboards, form each mixture into two long, thin rolls, reserving about a quarter of the light mixture. Coat all the thin rolls with egg white. Place a dark roll beside a light roll. Place the other two rolls on top, reversing the colours. Press them all together. Roll out the remaining light mixture into a thin rectangle, coat it with egg white, and roll it round the four thin rolls.

For tree-trunk slices, roll out the light mixture thinly. Form the dark mixture into a roll, coat with egg white, and roll up in the light mixture.

Wrap the shaped roll in foil, and chill in the refrigerator. Cut the roll into 5 mm (¼ inch) thick slices. Bake in a preheated 190°C (375°F or Mark 5) oven for 8 to 10 minutes.

HEDWIG MARIA STUBER
ICH HELF DIR KOCHEN

Mother's White Christmas Cakes

Muttis Weiße Weihnachtskuchen

To make 150 to 200

500 g	butter	1 lb
500 g	sugar	1 lb
1.2 kg	flour	2½ lb
15 g	baking powder	½ oz
2 tbsp	double cream	2 tbsp
2 tbsp	rose-water	2 tbsp
	almonds, blanched and halved (optional)	

Cream the butter and sugar together. Add the flour, baking powder, cream and rose-water. Knead until you have a smooth dough which no longer sticks to your hands. Roll the dough out and cut into squares or use shaped biscuit cutters. Decorate the cakes with halved almonds, if desired. Bake in a preheated 180°C (350°F or Mark 4) oven for 10 to 15 minutes or until firm but not coloured.

JUTTA KÜRTZ
DAS KOCHBUCH AUS SCHLESWIG-HOLSTEIN

Little Alberts

Albertle

To make about 60

100 g	butter, beaten until fluffy	3½ oz
4	eggs	4
200 g	sugar	7 oz
1 tbsp	vanilla sugar	1 tbsp
200 g	flour	7 oz
200 g	cornflour	7 oz
2 tbsp	double cream	2 tbsp
2 tsp	baking powder	2 tsp

Put the butter in a bowl and alternately beat in the eggs and sugar; then beat in all the other ingredients. Mix well. Leave the resulting dough to rest in a cool place for 1 hour. Roll out the dough thinly and make a pattern on the surface by pressing down with a grater. Cut out round biscuits and bake in a preheated 180°C (350°F or Mark 4) oven until pale gold, 12 to 15 minutes.

HANS KARL ADAM
DAS KOCHBUCH AUS SCHWABEN

Butter Biscuits

Mantecadas

To make about 50

200 g	butter or lard	7 oz
70 g	castor sugar	2½ oz
8 cl	sweet sherry	3 fl oz
400 g	flour	14 oz

Cream together the butter or lard and the sugar, adding the sherry little by little. Mix in the flour, a bit at a time, stirring well but not too much. Roll out the dough to a thickness of 1 cm (½ inch) and cut out rounds with a biscuit cutter. Place on a greased baking sheet and bake in a preheated 180°C (350°F or Mark 4) oven for 15 to 20 minutes.

MARIA DEL CARMEN CASCANTE
150 RECETAS DE DULCES DE FACIL PREPARACION

Browned Butter Biscuits

Heidesand

To make about 60

200 g	butter	7 oz
150 g	sugar	5 oz
1 tbsp	vanilla sugar	1 tbsp
About 1 tbsp	milk	About 1 tbsp
250 g	flour	8 oz

Heat the butter in a pan until it browns. Pour it into a bowl and leave to cool. When the butter has set again, beat it until it is fluffy. Add the sugar and the vanilla sugar, and continue to beat until the mixture is very white and frothy. Gradually stir in the milk and flour. Knead briefly. Form the mixture into rolls 3 cm (1¼ inches) thick and chill. Cut the rolls into slices 5 mm (¼ inch) thick. Bake in a preheated 180°C (350°F or Mark 4) oven for 12 to 15 minutes.

HEDWIG MARIA STUBER
ICH HELF DIR KOCHEN

Sand Tarts

To make about 50

125 g	butter	4 oz
250 g	sugar	8 oz
1	egg, well beaten	1
1 tsp	grated orange or lemon rind	1 tsp
200 g	flour	7 oz
2 tsp	baking powder	2 tsp
½ tsp	salt	½ tsp

Topping		
1	egg white, lightly beaten with 2 tsp water	1
1 tbsp	sugar	1 tbsp
¼ tsp	ground cinnamon	¼ tsp
	blanched almonds, raisins or cherries	

Cream the butter. Add the sugar gradually and then the egg. Add the flavouring and the dry ingredients. Chill the dough. Toss on a floured board and roll out 3 mm (⅛ inch) thick. Cut with a round biscuit cutter or in long narrow strips. Brush with the egg white and water. Mix the sugar and cinnamon and sprinkle over the tarts. Decorate with almonds, raisins or cherries. Place on a buttered baking sheet and bake in a preheated 180°C (350°F or Mark 4) oven for 8 to 10 minutes.

LADIES AUXILIARY OF THE LUNENBURG HOSPITAL SOCIETY
DUTCH OVEN

Russian Sugar Cookies

To make about 72

125 g	sugar	4 oz
250 g	butter, softened	8 oz
¼ tsp	salt	¼ tsp
3	eggs, beaten	3
3 tbsp	soured cream	3 tbsp
½ tsp	grated lemon rind	½ tsp
1 tsp	lemon juice	1 tsp
400 g	flour	14 oz
⅛ tsp	bicarbonate of soda	⅛ tsp
	coarse sugar or crushed lump sugar	

Beat the butter, sugar and salt until fluffy. Beat in the eggs, a little at a time. Mix in the soured cream and lemon rind and juice. Gradually mix in the flour and soda with a wooden spoon. On a floured board, roll out the dough 5 mm (¼ inch) thick. Sprinkle with coarse sugar. Cut into diamonds. Place on a buttered and floured baking sheet. Bake in a preheated 230°C (450°F or Mark 8) oven for 8 minutes or until barely gold. Watch the biscuits don't brown.

VIOLETA AUTUMN
A RUSSIAN JEW COOKS IN PERÚ

Orange Juice Cookies

To make about 72

17.5 cl	orange juice, strained	6 fl oz
300 g	flour	10 oz
½ tsp	bicarbonate of soda	½ tsp
¼ tsp	salt	¼ tsp
175 g	butter	6 oz
250 g	sugar	8 oz
2	eggs, lightly beaten	2
75 g	desiccated coconut	2½ oz

Sift together the flour, bicarbonate of soda and salt; set it aside. Cream the butter and sugar together, add the eggs and continue creaming. Add the flour alternately with the orange juice, and then the coconut. Lightly butter a baking sheet and drop teaspoons of the mixture on to it. If desired, sprinkle the cookies with additional coconut. Bake in a preheated 200°C (400°F or Mark 6) oven for 10 to 12 minutes.

NEW JERSEY RECIPES, OLDE AND NEW

Bottle Cakes

To make about 48

250 g	butter	8 oz
250 g	sugar, sifted	8 oz
2	eggs, beaten	2
250 g	flour	8 oz
½	lemon, rind grated, juice strained	½

Cream the butter. Add the sugar. Add the eggs with the rest of the ingredients, beating all thoroughly. Grease a baking sheet and drop on it teaspoonfuls of the mixture. Bake for about 5 minutes in a preheated 180°C (350°F or Mark 4) oven. Slip the cakes off the sheet with a knife. Lay a number of bottles on their sides on a table. Lay the cakes on the bottles to cool and press the cakes gently down on the bottles in order to give them a rounded shape. These cakes should be very thin and richly coloured round the edges.

ELIZABETH DOUGLAS
THE CAKE AND BISCUIT BOOK

Orange Jumbles

To make about 36

2	oranges, rind grated, juice strained	2
125 g	sugar	4 oz
90 g	butter	3 oz
125 g	almonds, shredded	4 oz
60 g	flour	2 oz
	cochineal	

Beat together the sugar and butter, and add the almonds, flour, orange rind and juice, and a soupçon of cochineal to colour all. Mix and put on a slightly greased baking sheet in quantities of about 1 teaspoon to each jumble, allowing room to spread, and bake in a preheated 180°C (350°F or Mark 4) oven for about 15 minutes. They will be the size of teacup rims, and should curl their crisp edges, faintly pink as the underneath of a young mushroom.

LADY JEKYLL
KITCHEN ESSAYS

Orange Pipes

Cannoli all'Arancia

To make about 30

2	oranges, rind grated	2
150 g	butter, softened and cut into small pieces	5 oz
150 g	icing sugar, sifted	5 oz
1 tbsp	vanilla sugar	1 tbsp
1½ tbsp	orange liqueur	1½ tbsp
275 g	flour	9 oz
3	egg whites, stiffly beaten	3

Butter one or two baking sheets and sprinkle them with flour, shaking off the surplus. Place the butter in a bowl and work it with a wooden spoon until it is like cream. Add the icing sugar, orange rind, vanilla sugar and liqueur. When these ingredients are thoroughly mixed together, sift in the flour. Finally, add the stiffly beaten egg whites.

Put the mixture into a piping bag with a plain nozzle about 1 cm (½ inch) across. Squeeze it on to the baking sheets to form small ovals or discs, about 6 cm (2½ inches) long. Leave about 5 cm (2 inches) between them so they do not stick together while cooking, as they will spread out considerably. When you have used up all the mixture, put the sheets into a preheated 240°C (475°F or Mark 9) oven for a few minutes. As soon as the biscuits start to colour at the edges (but are still white in the centre), take the sheets out of the oven. Keep them on top of the oven so that they stay hot. Lift each biscuit off in turn with a knife and press it over the handle of a wooden spoon into the shape of a brandy snap. Cool the biscuits on a wire rack.

FERNANDA GOSETTI
IN CUCINA CON FERNANDA GOSETTI

Italian Roof Tiles

Tegoline

The technique of shaping tiles is shown on page 50.

To make about 40

50 g	almonds, blanched and dried	2 oz
200 g	castor sugar	7 oz
130 g	butter, softened and cut into small pieces	4 oz
2	eggs	2
2	egg whites	2
1	orange, rind grated	1
130 g	flour	4 oz
	vegetable oil	

Pound the almonds in a mortar with about 1 tablespoon of the sugar until you have a very fine powder.

Line one or two baking sheets with greaseproof paper. Butter the paper and flour it, shaking off the excess.

Put the butter into a bowl and work it with a wooden spoon until it is like cream. Add the rest of the sugar and work the mixture again for a few more minutes. Now add the eggs, egg whites, powdered almonds, orange rind and flour, making sure that each ingredient is well blended before adding the next. Pour some of the mixture into a piping bag with a plain nozzle about 1 cm ($\frac{1}{2}$ inch) in diameter. Squeeze the bag lightly and form strips on the baking sheet about 8 cm (3 inches) long. When you have used up all the mixture, put the baking sheet or sheets into a preheated 220°C (425°F or Mark 7) oven and leave for a few minutes.

Rub a little vegetable oil on to a rolling pin. When the edges of the biscuits start to colour but the centres are still white, and before they are set, take the baking sheet out of the oven. Keeping the sheet on top of the warm oven so that the biscuits do not cool, lift them off one by one with a knife and press them on the rolling pin so that they curve. Cool before serving.

FERNANDA GOSETTI
IN CUCINA CON FERNANDA GOSETTI

Cat's Tongues with Almonds

Langues-de-Chat aux Amandes

To make about 40

80 g	sugar	2$\frac{1}{2}$ oz
2 tbsp	vanilla sugar	2 tbsp
80 g	butter, beaten until creamy	2$\frac{1}{2}$ oz
2	eggs, lightly beaten	2
80 g	flour	2$\frac{1}{2}$ oz
50 g	almonds, chopped	2 oz

Add the sugars to the butter and beat together very thoroughly until light and fluffy. Add the eggs, one by one, beating continuously. Finish the dough by adding the flour and stir until the mixture is quite smooth. Using a piping bag with a 5 mm ($\frac{1}{4}$ inch) nozzle, form the mixture into small sticks, spaced well apart on a buttered and floured baking sheet. Sprinkle the sticks with the chopped almonds.

Bake in a preheated 180°C (350°F or Mark 4) oven for 5 to 6 minutes or until firm. As soon as they are cooked, take from the baking sheet and leave to cool, preferably on a rack. When the biscuits are cold, store them in an airtight tin box or jar.

JACQUELINE GÉRARD
BONNES RECETTES D'AUTREFOIS

Hussar's Kisses

Huszárcsók

To make 20 to 30

175 g	butter, softened	6 oz
125 g	sugar	4 oz
175 g	flour	6 oz
1	lemon, rind grated	1
1	egg, yolk separated from white, white lightly beaten	1
60 g	almonds, finely chopped	2 oz
175 g	thick jam	6 oz

Blend the butter and sugar together, then the flour, lemon rind and egg yolk. Make into small balls. Dip each in egg white and roll in almonds. Place on a greased baking sheet. Make a depression in each ball and bake in a preheated 190°C (375°F or Mark 5) oven until lightly browned. Fill with jam.

INGE KRAMARZ
THE BALKAN COOKBOOK

Genoese Biscuits

Dolcetti di Genova

To make about 48

75 g	butter, melted	2½ oz
150 g	sugar	5 oz
3	eggs	3
40 g	flour	1½ oz
125 g	almonds, blanched and finely chopped	4 oz
12.5 cl	kirsch	4 fl oz
	castor or vanilla sugar	

Put the butter in a bowl with the sugar and beat well until light and fluffy. Add the eggs, then the flour and the almonds, stirring continuously. Lastly, add the kirsch. Butter and flour an 18 cm (7 inch) square baking tin and pour in the mixture. Bake in a preheated 180°C (350°F or Mark 4) oven for 20 to 25 minutes. Allow the biscuit to cool before cutting it into 2.5 cm (1 inch) squares. Arrange these in a serving dish and sprinkle them with castor or vanilla sugar.

ERINA GAVOTTI (EDITOR)
MILLERICETTE

Butter Leaves

To make about 80

250 g	unsalted butter	8 oz
125 g	sugar	4 oz
1	egg yolk	1
4	bitter almonds, blanched and finely chopped	4
300 g	flour	10 oz
1	egg white, lightly beaten	1
25	almonds, chopped	25
4 tbsp	sugar	4 tbsp

Work the butter and sugar until creamy and fluffy. Add the egg yolk, bitter almonds and flour and mix thoroughly. Chill. Roll out thin on a floured pastry board and cut into shapes with a biscuit cutter. Brush with the beaten egg white and sprinkle with the almonds and sugar mixed together. Place on a buttered baking sheet and bake in a preheated 180°C (350°F or Mark 4) oven for 8 to 10 minutes or until golden yellow.

SELMA WIFSTRAND (EDITOR)
FAVORITE SWEDISH RECIPES

Dead Men's Bones

Totenbeinli

A somewhat macabre name—and in a tin with a well-fitting lid, these "bones" keep for a long time!

To make about 72

90 g	butter, softened	3 oz
275 g	castor sugar	9 oz
3	eggs	3
275 g	almonds, blanched and chopped	9 oz
½ tbsp	ground cinnamon	½ tbsp
	salt	
350 g	flour, sifted	12 oz
1	egg yolk, lightly beaten	1

Beat the butter with the sugar until white and creamy. Add one egg at a time, beating well, then the almonds, cinnamon, a pinch of salt and finally the flour. Knead the paste well and shape it into a long roll about 4 cm (1½ inches) thick and 7 cm (2¾ inches) wide. Leave in a cold place until quite firm. Cut the paste into 5 mm (¼ inch) slices, place them on a baking sheet and brush with the egg yolk. Bake in a preheated 200°C (400°F or Mark 6) oven for 20 minutes until just golden.

EVA MARIA BORER
TANTE HEIDI'S SWISS KITCHEN

Soured Cream Cookies

Sugar mixed with a little flour may be sifted over the dough before cutting. Raisins may also be pressed on to each cooky.

To make about 36

12.5 cl	soured cream or soured milk	4 fl oz
125 g	butter, or half butter and half lard	4 oz
250 g	sugar	8 oz
2	eggs, well beaten	2
300 g	flour	10 oz
½ tsp	bicarbonate of soda	½ tsp
½ tsp	salt	½ tsp
2 tsp	grated nutmeg	2 tsp

Cream the butter, add the sugar, and cream again. Add the eggs and the soured cream or milk. Sift 125 g (4 oz) of the flour with the remaining ingredients and stir in. Add the rest of the flour. Work to a smooth dough.

Roll out the dough 8 mm ($\frac{1}{3}$ inch) thick and cut out the desired shape. Place the shapes on a baking sheet and bake in a preheated 180°C (350°F or Mark 4) oven for 15 minutes or until the biscuits are lightly browned.

LOUISE BENNETT WEAVER AND HELEN COWLES LECRON
A THOUSAND WAYS TO PLEASE A HUSBAND

Cardamom Butter Cookies

To make about 96

1 tsp	ground cardamom	1 tsp
250 g	butter	8 oz
300 g	sugar	10 oz
2	eggs, lightly beaten	2
1 tsp	vanilla extract	1 tsp
350 g	flour	12 oz
1 tsp	baking powder	1 tsp
$\frac{1}{2}$ tsp	salt	$\frac{1}{2}$ tsp
$\frac{1}{2}$ tsp	ground cinnamon	$\frac{1}{2}$ tsp
$\frac{1}{4}$ tsp	ground allspice	$\frac{1}{4}$ tsp

Cream the butter and sugar until light and fluffy. Add the eggs a little at a time and the vanilla, and beat well. Sift together the remaining ingredients; stir into the creamed mixture and mix well. Chill the dough, roll it out and cut it with a biscuit cutter. Or, if you prefer, shape the dough into two rolls and wrap in greaseproof paper. Chill the rolls, then cut into thin slices. Place on baking sheets and bake in a preheated 180°C (350°F or Mark 4) oven for 8 to 10 minutes, depending on the thickness of the cookies.

THE McCORMICK SPICES OF THE WORLD COOKBOOK

Karlsbad Biscuits

Karlsbader Plätzchen

To make about 40

150 g	butter	5 oz
80 g	castor sugar	3 oz
4	hard-boiled egg yolks	4
	ground cloves, allspice and cinnamon	
180 g	flour	6 oz
1	egg, beaten	1
	coarse sugar or crushed lump sugar	

Beat the butter and castor sugar together until fluffy. Press the egg yolks through a sieve and add to the mixture. Stir in a pinch each of the spices and lastly the flour. Work into a dough. Roll out and cut with a biscuit cutter. Brush with the beaten egg and sprinkle with coarse sugar. Place the biscuits on a greased baking sheet and bake in a preheated 180°C (350°F or Mark 4) oven for 20 minutes.

JOZA BŘÍZOVÁ AND MARYNA KLIMENTOVÁ
TSCHECHISCHE KÜCHE

Peppernuts

Pfeffernüsse

To make about 48

30 g	butter	1 oz
150 g	icing sugar, sifted	5 oz
3	eggs, yolks separated from whites, yolks well beaten, whites stiffly beaten	3
1 tsp	grated lemon rind	1 tsp
250 g	flour	8 oz
$\frac{1}{2}$ tsp	bicarbonate of soda	$\frac{1}{2}$ tsp
$\frac{1}{2}$ tsp	salt	$\frac{1}{2}$ tsp
2 tsp	ground cinnamon	2 tsp
$\frac{1}{2}$ tsp	ground cloves	$\frac{1}{2}$ tsp
$\frac{1}{2}$ tsp	grated nutmeg	$\frac{1}{2}$ tsp
$\frac{1}{8}$ tsp	ground black pepper	$\frac{1}{8}$ tsp
250 g	candied citron, finely chopped	8 oz
2 tsp	crushed cardamom seeds	2 tsp
$\frac{1}{2}$ tsp	aniseeds	$\frac{1}{2}$ tsp
	Glaze	
175 g	icing sugar, sifted	6 oz
3 tbsp	milk	3 tbsp

Cream the butter. Add the icing sugar, then the egg yolks and lemon rind. Sift the dry ingredients together three times and mix them with the citron, cardamom and aniseeds. Add the flour mixture to the creamed ingredients. Fold in the egg whites. Chill for 1 hour. Form the mixture into small balls, place on greaseproof paper and let stand overnight.

Mix together the glaze ingredients and brush the biscuits all over the top and sides with the glaze. Place the balls on a greased baking sheet. Bake in a preheated 190°C (375°F or Mark 5) oven for 15 minutes.

ANNETTE LASLETT ROSS AND JEAN ADAMS DISNEY
GOOD COOKIES

Shrewsbury Cakes

To make about 30

250 g	butter	8 oz
175 g	castor sugar, sifted	6 oz
250 g	flour	8 oz
1 tsp	ground cinnamon	1 tsp
2 tsp	caraway seeds	2 tsp
2	eggs	2
$\frac{1}{4}$ tsp	rose-water	$\frac{1}{4}$ tsp

Beat the butter to a cream and mix it with the sugar, flour, cinnamon, caraway seeds, eggs and rose-water. Roll the paste out 5 mm ($\frac{1}{4}$ inch) thick, cut the cakes into shapes and place on baking sheets. Bake in a preheated 170°C (325°F or Mark 3) oven for 20 minutes.

ANNE COBBETT
THE ENGLISH HOUSEKEEPER

Rosa Flexner's Butter Cookies

The dough for this cookie is so easy to handle that it can be cut into any desired shape, and it can be varied by garnishings of nuts, fruits, etc. It stays fresh for a long time, too.

The cookies are crisp and crunchy, and keep indefinitely in a tightly closed container.

To make about 75

250 g	butter	8 oz
250 g	sugar	8 oz
2	eggs, yolk and white of one separated	2
1 tsp	vanilla extract	1 tsp
1	lemon, juice strained	1
500 g	flour, sifted	1 lb
1 tbsp	cold water	1 tbsp

Nut topping (optional)

2 tbsp	sugar	2 tbsp
1 tsp	ground cinnamon	1 tsp
2 tbsp	finely chopped almonds or pecan nuts	2 tbsp

Filling (optional)

1 tbsp	flour	1 tbsp
4 tbsp	water	4 tbsp
4 tbsp	sugar	4 tbsp
125 g	dates or raisins, chopped	4 oz
1 tbsp	lemon juice	1 tbsp
$\frac{1}{2}$	lemon, rind grated	$\frac{1}{2}$
4 tbsp	chopped nuts	4 tbsp

Cream the butter and sugar until light. Add the whole egg and the yolk, vanilla and lemon juice. Add just enough flour to make the dough firm enough to roll out thin.

For plain cookies, pinch off small amounts of dough and roll as thin as possible with a floured rolling pin. Cut out with fancy biscuit cutters, or make into squares or rectangles with a pastry wheel. Place side by side on greased baking sheets. Lightly beat the reserved egg white with the water and brush each cookie with the mixture. Leave plain or combine the topping ingredients and sprinkle this over the cookies.

Bake the cookies in a preheated 190°C (375°F or Mark 5) oven for about 10 minutes or until golden-brown. Watch them to see they do not burn.

For filled cookies, make the dough as above and set it aside while you make the filling. Mix the flour with the water and beat it until it becomes a smooth paste. Add the sugar and chopped dates or raisins and the lemon juice. Cook until thick in a saucepan. Add the grated rind and chopped nuts.

Roll the dough out thin and cut out rounds with a biscuit cutter about 5 cm (2 inches) in diameter, or use the top of a glass tumbler. Spread half of each round with a little of the filling mixture, not letting it come to the edge. Fold the other half over and press the edges together with a fork, being careful that the filling is sealed in. Brush the cookies with the egg white and water, and bake according to the directions for plain cookies, above. These filled cookies may take a few minutes longer to bake.

Mincemeat cookies: Mincemeat laced with brandy also makes a good winter filling for these cookies. Substitute it for the filling given above, if you wish.

MARION FLEXNER
OUT OF KENTUCKY KITCHENS

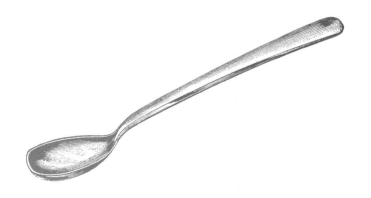

Apple Sauce Gems

To make about 60

250 g	apple sauce or apple purée	8 oz
250 g	butter, softened	8 oz
400 g	brown sugar	14 oz
12.5 cl	cold black coffee	4 fl oz
400 g	flour, sifted	14 oz
½ tsp	bicarbonate of soda	½ tsp
1 tsp	baking powder	1 tsp
1 tsp	salt	1 tsp
1 tsp	grated nutmeg	1 tsp
1 tsp	ground cinnamon	1 tsp
175 g	sultanas or diced candied fruit	6 oz
175 g	currants or seedless raisins	6 oz

Cream the butter and sugar well. Add the coffee and apple sauce or purée. Sift together the dry ingredients and blend in, adding the fruits last. Drop spoonfuls of the mixture on to a lightly greased baking sheet and bake in a preheated 190°C (375°F or Mark 5) oven for about 10 minutes. To keep these richly moist cookies soft, store in airtight containers.

ANNETTE LASLETT ROSS AND JEAN ADAMS DISNEY
GOOD COOKIES

Fig Newtons

For the child of any age who has wondered how the filling gets into a fig bar, here's one way that doesn't require a factory full of machinery. The sweet, figgy filling tunnels through tender pillows of dough to make a generously overstuffed version of a sweet that's been a favourite for generations.

To make about 20

75 g	unsalted butter, at room temperature	2½ oz
2 tbsp	soured cream	2 tbsp
150 g	dark brown sugar, sifted through a coarse sieve	5 oz
2	eggs	2
1 tsp	vanilla extract	1 tsp
250 g	flour	8 oz
2 tsp	baking powder	2 tsp
½ tsp	bicarbonate of soda	½ tsp
¼ tsp	ground cinnamon	¼ tsp
½ tsp	salt	½ tsp

Filling		
500 g	dried figs, preferably moist-pack black figs, heavy stems removed	1 lb
40 cl	water	14 fl oz
90 g	sugar	3 oz
2 tsp	grated lemon rind	2 tsp
¼ tsp	salt	¼ tsp

In a small bowl, beat the butter and soured cream until light. Gradually add the brown sugar, beating until the mixture is very light and thick. Incorporate the eggs one at a time; beat in the vanilla extract.

Sift together the flour, baking powder, bicarbonate of soda, cinnamon and salt. Add to the creamed mixture, beating with an electric mixer on a low speed or by hand. Mix well and turn out on to a sheet of floured plastic film; wrap, then refrigerate for at least 2 hours.

For the filling, combine the figs and water in a heavy saucepan and simmer, covered, for 30 minutes, or until the fruit is soft. Add the sugar, lemon rind and salt, and simmer, covered, for 15 minutes longer. Press the mixture through the coarse disc of a food mill, then cool.

Lightly grease a large baking sheet or cover it with grease-proof paper. Divide the chilled dough into thirds and refrigerate two parts. Roll the remaining piece on a well-floured board to form a rectangle about 12 by 28 cm (5 by 11 inches).

Spread one-third of the fig filling slightly to one side of centre, along the length of the dough, covering an area roughly 5 cm (2 inches) wide and 25 cm (10 inches) long and leaving a 1 cm (½ inch) margin on the three sides of the filling away from the centre. Mound the filling slightly in the centre along its whole length, then moisten the exposed margin with water. Very gently, lift the uncovered dough with a spatula and fold it over the filling. Press the upper dough against the lower to seal it. Trim the edges and shape the roll into a neat half-cylinder form about 28 cm (11 inches) long and 5 to 6 cm (2 to 2½ inches) wide. Place on the prepared baking sheet.

Repeat the filling operation with the remaining two-thirds of the dough and filling, then bake the three rolls in a preheated 180°C (350°F or Mark 4) oven for 25 minutes or until they are slightly browned.

Cool the rolls somewhat on a rack, then trim off the ends and, with a sharp, serrated knife, cut each one into slices 4 cm (1½ inches) wide. Replace the slices on the rack. When the fig bars are completely cool, store them in airtight containers.

HELEN WITTY AND ELIZABETH SCHNEIDER COLCHIE
BETTER THAN STORE-BOUGHT

Pecan Cookies

To make 30

500 g	pecan nuts, halved	1 lb
250 g	butter	8 oz
250 g	sugar	8 oz
1	egg, yolk separated from white, white lightly beaten	1
250 g	flour	8 oz
½ tsp	ground cinnamon	½ tsp

Cream the butter and sugar, then add the egg yolk, flour and cinnamon. Spread out very thin on a large, greased baking sheet and smear egg white over the top. Then place a layer of pecan nuts over the top and bake in a preheated 180°C (350°F or Mark 4) oven for 15 minutes or until golden-brown. Cut into squares while still hot, making certain there is a pecan nut on each cookie.

JUNIOR LEAGUE OF MEMPHIS, INC. (EDITORS)
THE MEMPHIS COOK BOOK

Refrigerator Cookies

Black walnuts are only available in America. Ordinary walnuts can be substituted.

To make about 72

350 g	butter, melted	12 oz
250 g	sugar	8 oz
250 g	dark brown sugar	8 oz
3	eggs, well beaten	3
125 g	black walnuts, finely chopped	4 oz
550 g	flour	1 lb 2 oz
2 tsp	bicarbonate of soda	2 tsp
1 tsp	salt	1 tsp
½ tsp	grated nutmeg	½ tsp
½ tsp	ground cloves	½ tsp
1 tsp	ground cinnamon	1 tsp

In a large bowl, cream the butter and sugars. Add the eggs one at a time, mixing thoroughly. Stir in the nuts. Sift together the remaining ingredients and blend them into the mixture. Shape the dough into a roll 5 cm (2 inches) in diameter and refrigerate it overnight.

The next morning, cut the dough into 5 mm (¼ inch) thick slices and place on buttered baking sheets. Bake the biscuits in a preheated 220°C (425°F or Mark 7) oven for 8 minutes.

DOROTHY C. FRANK
COOKING WITH NUTS

Cherokee Date Rocks

These cookies keep well if wrapped, when cold, in waxed paper and stored in a tin with a tight-fitting lid.

To make about 50

250 g	dates, stoned and chopped	8 oz
350 g	butter	12 oz
350 g	brown sugar	12 oz
3	eggs, yolks separated from whites, whites stiffly beaten	3
1 tsp	bicarbonate of soda, dissolved in 2 tsp water	1 tsp
500 g	flour, sifted with 1 tsp ground allspice and 1 tbsp ground cinnamon	1 lb
250 g	pecan nuts or walnuts, coarsely chopped	8 oz
	castor sugar	

Cream the butter and brown sugar, and add the egg yolks and bicarbonate of soda. Combine the sifted flour mixture with the butter and egg yolk mixture. Fold the egg whites into the batter and, last of all, fold in the dates and nuts. Drop by teaspoonfuls on to a well-greased baking sheet, leaving about 7.5 cm (3 inches) between each "rock". Bake in a preheated 190°C (375°F or Mark 5) oven for 15 to 18 minutes or until the cookies are done in the centre. Do not cook too long, or they will be as hard as their name implies. Remove from the baking sheet with a spatula and dust with castor sugar.

MARION FLEXNER
OUT OF KENTUCKY KITCHENS

Toffee Squares

These cookies will keep fresh for two weeks in a tin.

To make about 30

250 g	butter	8 oz
250 g	sugar	8 oz
1	egg, yolk separated from white, white lightly beaten	1
250 g	flour, sifted	8 oz
⅛ tsp	salt	⅛ tsp
1 tbsp	ground cinnamon	1 tbsp
175 g	pecan nuts, finely chopped	6 oz

Cream the butter and sugar. Add the egg yolk, flour, salt and cinnamon. Mix until the mixture resembles coarse meal. Flour a baking sheet and spread the mixture into place with your fingers or a spatula. It should be evenly distributed over the sheet and the dough should not be more than 5 mm (¼ inch) thick. Pour the egg white over the surface of the dough and with a brush smooth the whole surface. Cover the dough with the nuts. Bake in a preheated 190°C (375°F or Mark 5) oven for 5 minutes and then increase the heat to 200°C (400°F or Mark 6) and bake for 15 to 20 minutes more. Remove the baking sheet from the oven and, while the dough is still hot, cut it into 5 cm (2 inch) squares. Do not try to remove the cookies from the sheet until they are cold.

MARION FLEXNER
OUT OF KENTUCKY KITCHENS

Parson's Hats

Pfaffenhütchen

To make about 24

90 g	butter	3 oz
90 g	sugar	3 oz
1	egg	1
$\frac{1}{4}$	lemon, rind grated	$\frac{1}{4}$
125 g	ground almonds	4 oz
200 g	flour	7 oz
$\frac{1}{2}$ tsp	baking powder	$\frac{1}{2}$ tsp
1	egg yolk	1
	Hazelnut filling	
100 g	hazelnuts, lightly roasted and ground	$3\frac{1}{2}$ oz
80 g	sugar	3 oz

For the dough, cream the butter and sugar and beat in the egg, lemon rind and ground almonds. Sift together the flour and baking powder and fold in.

For the filling, mix together the hazelnuts and sugar and add enough water to make a creamy mixture.

Roll out the dough and cut it into 7.5 cm (3 inch) rounds. Place a small amount of hazelnut filling in the centre of each round, draw the edges up and pinch them together to form a pyramid. Brush with the egg yolk and bake in a preheated 200°C (400°F or Mark 6) oven for 15 minutes or until the biscuits are browned.

ELIZABETH SCHULER
MEIN KOCHBUCH

Sweet Potato Cookies

To make about 60

300 g	sweet potatoes, mashed	10 oz
250 g	flour	8 oz
4 tsp	baking powder	4 tsp
1 tsp	grated nutmeg	1 tsp
125 g	butter	4 oz
300 g	soft brown sugar	10 oz
2	eggs	2
1 tsp	vanilla extract	1 tsp
1 tsp	grated lemon rind	1 tsp
75 g	desiccated coconut	$2\frac{1}{2}$ oz
60 g	crystallized ginger, chopped	2 oz
60 g	hazelnuts, chopped	2 oz

Sift together the flour, baking powder and nutmeg; set it aside. Cream the butter and sugar and beat in the eggs, sweet potatoes, vanilla extract and lemon rind. Add the sifted ingredients and mix in the coconut, ginger and nuts. Lightly oil two baking sheets and drop tablespoons of the mixture on to them 4 cm (1½ inches) apart. Bake the cookies in a preheated 200°C (400°F or Mark 6) oven for 12 to 15 minutes.

NEW JERSEY RECIPES, OLDE AND NEW

Brown Sugar Squares

To make 24

500 g	soft brown sugar	1 lb
175 g	butter, softened	6 oz
3 tbsp	sugar	3 tbsp
175 g	flour	6 oz
3	eggs, yolks separated from whites, whites stiffly beaten	3
	salt	
60 g	desiccated coconut	2 oz
125 g	mixed nuts, chopped	4 oz

Cream the butter and white sugar together and fold in the flour. Pat the mixture into a 30 by 20 cm (12 by 8 inch) greased baking tin and bake in a preheated 170°C (325°F or Mark 3) oven for 15 minutes.

Mix the egg yolks with the brown sugar, a pinch of salt, the coconut and nuts. Fold in the egg whites and pour on top of the biscuit base. Raise the oven temperature to 180°C (350°F or Mark 4) and bake for about 1 hour. Cool and cut into squares.

MRS. DON RICHARDSON (EDITOR)
CAROLINA LOW COUNTRY COOK BOOK OF GEORGETOWN,
SOUTH CAROLINA

Ice Box Cookies

To make about 130

250 g	butter	8 oz
500 g	brown sugar	1 lb
2	eggs	2
400 g	flour	14 oz
125 g	nuts, chopped	4 oz
½ tsp	salt	½ tsp
1 tsp	bicarbonate of soda	1 tsp

Cream the butter and sugar. Add the eggs and mix well. Sift the flour, add the nuts to this, then mix in the salt and soda. Combine with the creamed mixture. Make into a rectangular shape and place in a refrigerator overnight or until good and cold. Slice thin and bake in a preheated 180°C (350°F or Mark 4) oven for about 8 minutes.

JUNIOR LEAGUE OF SPARTANBURG, INC. (EDITORS)
SPARTANBURG SECRETS II

Chocolate Chip Cookies

To make about 72

175 g	chocolate chips	6 oz
175 g	butter	6 oz
250 g	brown sugar	8 oz
125 g	sugar	4 oz
2	eggs, beaten	2
275 g	flour, sifted	9 oz
½ tsp	salt	½ tsp
1 tsp	bicarbonate of soda	1 tsp
1½ tsp	vanilla extract	1½ tsp
125 g	nuts, chopped	4 oz

Cream the butter and sugars together. Add the beaten eggs. Sift together the dry ingredients and add, then add the vanilla, nuts and chocolate chips. Drop the mixture by spoonfuls on an ungreased baking sheet. Bake in a preheated 190°C (375°F or Mark 5) oven for 10 to 12 minutes.

ANNETTE LASLETT ROSS AND JEAN ADAMS DISNEY
GOOD COOKIES

Chocolate Walnut Wheels

To make 24

60 g	chocolate, melted	2 oz
250 g	walnuts, 24 halves reserved, the remainder finely chopped	8 oz
90 g	butter	3 oz
250 g	sugar	8 oz
1	egg, lightly beaten	1
¼ tsp	vanilla extract	¼ tsp
75 g	flour, sifted	2½ oz
¼ tsp	salt	¼ tsp

Cream the butter and add the sugar gradually. Add the egg, a little at a time, then the chocolate and vanilla. Add the flour, salt and chopped nuts, and beat well. Drop the batter from a spoon into mounds 2.5 cm (1 inch) apart on a greased baking sheet. Garnish each mound with a walnut half. Bake in a preheated 180°C (350°F or Mark 4) oven for 10 minutes.

JOSH GASPERO (EDITOR)
HERSHEY'S 1934 COOKBOOK

Toffee Treats

To make about 30

250 g	butter	8 oz
250 g	soft brown sugar	8 oz
1	egg yolk	1
1 tsp	vanilla extract	1 tsp
¼ tsp	salt	¼ tsp
250 g	flour, sifted	8 oz
175 g	plain chocolate, melted	6 oz
90 g	nuts, finely chopped	3 oz

Cream the butter and sugar until fluffy; beat in the egg yolk and vanilla. Blend in the salt and flour. Pat the dough evenly into a greased 25 by 38 cm (10 by 15½ inch) Swiss roll tin. Cover with the melted chocolate; sprinkle with the nuts. Bake for 15 to 20 minutes in a preheated 190°C (375°F or Mark 5) oven. Cut into bars while still warm.

THE JUNIOR CHARITY LEAGUE OF MONROE, LOUISIANA (EDITORS)
THE COTTON COUNTRY COLLECTION

Chocolate Fleck Rings

This dough may also be used for apricot or raspberry jam filled biscuits. Cut as many biscuit rounds as rings. Brush the rounds thinly with jam and cover with the rings. Bake as below. While still hot, fill the ring holes with more apricot or raspberry jam. Dust the ring only with a mixture of equal quantities of cocoa and icing sugar.

To make about 36 rings

60 g	chocolate, grated	2 oz
125 g	unsalted butter	4 oz
250 g	sugar	8 oz
250 g	flour	8 oz
⅛ tsp	salt	⅛ tsp
3 tbsp	finely chopped almonds	3 tbsp
4	egg yolks	4
1	lemon, rind grated	1
1 tbsp	cinnamon	1 tbsp
1	egg white, lightly beaten	1

Cream together the butter and sugar. Add the flour, salt, almonds, egg yolks and chocolate, and mix to make a smooth and soft dough. Add the grated rind and cinnamon.

Roll out the dough 3 mm (⅛ inch) thick on a floured pastry board. Cut out rounds with a 5 cm (2 inch) biscuit cutter and cut out the centres with a 2.5 cm (1 inch) biscuit cutter. Place the rings on a buttered baking sheet and brush with the egg white. Bake in a preheated 180°C (350°F or Mark 4) oven for 10 to 15 minutes.

JULIETTE ELKON
THE CHOCOLATE COOKBOOK

Chocolate Oatmeal Cookies

To make about 48

125 g	plain chocolate, chopped	4 oz
175 g	rolled oats	6 oz
125 g	unsalted butter, softened	4 oz
90 g	sugar	3 oz
90 g	brown sugar	3 oz
1	egg, well beaten	1
½ tsp	vanilla extract	½ tsp
90 g	flour	3 oz
½ tsp	salt	½ tsp
1 tsp	baking powder	1 tsp
4 tbsp	milk	4 tbsp
60 g	nuts, chopped	2 oz

Cream together the butter and sugars. Mix in the egg and vanilla. Sift together the flour, salt and baking powder, and add to the butter mixture alternately with the milk. Stir in the nuts, oats and chocolate.

Drop teaspoonfuls of the mixture on to a lightly greased baking sheet. Bake in a preheated 190°C (375°F or Mark 5) oven for 10 to 12 minutes or until lightly browned.

JULIETTE ELKON
THE CHOCOLATE COOKBOOK

Oatmeal Cookies

The dough may be chilled, rolled into cookie-sized balls and frozen on a baking sheet until firm. These may then be kept in small containers in the freezer to cook a few at a time.

To make about 48

300 g	oatmeal	10 oz
250 g	butter	8 oz
250 g	soft brown sugar	8 oz
250 g	sugar	8 oz
2	eggs	2
175 g	flour	6 oz
1 tsp	salt	1 tsp
1 tsp	bicarbonate of soda	1 tsp
1 tsp	vanilla extract	1 tsp
125 g	pecan nuts, chopped	4 oz

Cream the butter and sugars together. Add the eggs and beat until fluffy. Sift together the dry ingredients and slowly add to the mixture. Add the vanilla. Fold in the pecan nuts and oatmeal. Drop spoonfuls of the batter on to a greased baking sheet. Bake in a preheated 180°C (350°F or Mark 4) oven for 10 to 15 minutes or until lightly browned.

THE JUNIOR CHARITY LEAGUE OF MONROE, LOUISIANA (EDITORS)
THE COTTON COUNTRY COLLECTION

Gipsy Creams

To make about 24

60 g	butter	2 oz
60 g	lard	2 oz
60 g	sugar	2 oz
125 g	flour	4 oz
1 tsp	bicarbonate of soda	1 tsp
125 g	porridge oats	4 oz
3 tbsp	water	3 tbsp
1 tsp	golden syrup or jam	1 tsp
125 g	chocolate butter cream (*page 166*)	4 oz

Cream the butter and lard with the sugar until fluffy; mix in the flour, bicarbonate of soda and oats and gather to a stiff dough with the water and syrup or jam.

Knead the dough lightly and shape into small balls; set on greased baking sheets, allowing room for spreading, and bake in a preheated 180°C (350°F or Mark 4) oven for 30 minutes. When cold, sandwich the biscuits in two with the icing.

LIZZIE BOYD (EDITOR)
BRITISH COOKERY

Peanut Butter and Chocolate Cookies

To make 48

125 g	smooth or chunky peanut butter	4 oz
100 g	flour	3½ oz
½ tsp	bicarbonate of soda	½ tsp
125 g	butter, softened	4 oz
125 g	light brown sugar	4 oz
125 g	granulated sugar	4 oz
1	egg, lightly beaten	1
1 tsp	vanilla extract	1 tsp
75 g	salted Spanish peanuts, red skins left on	2½ oz
75 g	plain chocolate, chopped	2½ oz

On greaseproof paper, thoroughly stir together the flour and soda. In a medium-sized bowl, cream the butter and peanut butter; beat in, one ingredient at a time, the brown sugar, granulated sugar, egg and vanilla. Add the flour mixture; mix well with a spoon. Stir in the peanuts and chocolate.

Drop the batter by heaping teaspoonfuls about 5 cm (2 inches) apart on ungreased baking sheets. Press down with a floured fork to make a criss-cross pattern; reflour the fork for each biscuit. (Marking will not show after baking.)

Bake in a preheated 180°C (350°F or Mark 4) oven until lightly browned, about 10 minutes. Leave the biscuits on the sheets for about 1 minute, then use a wide metal spatula to transfer them to racks to cool. Store in a tightly covered tin.

CECILY BROWNSTONE
CECILY BROWNSTONE'S ASSOCIATED PRESS COOK BOOK

Best Peanut Butter Cookies

To make 60

250 g	peanut butter	8 oz
125 g	dark brown sugar	4 oz
125 g	sugar	4 oz
125 g	butter	4 oz
1	egg	1
½ tsp	salt	½ tsp
½ tsp	bicarbonate of soda	½ tsp
175 g	flour, sifted	6 oz
½ tsp	vanilla extract	½ tsp

Cream the sugars and butter together. Beat in the egg, peanut butter, salt and soda. Blend in the flour. Add the vanilla extract. Roll the dough into small balls and place them on a greased baking sheet. Flatten them with a fork. Bake in a preheated 180°C (350°F or Mark 4) oven for 12 to 15 minutes or until slightly brown on the edges.

THE JUNIOR CHARITY LEAGUE OF MONROE, LOUISIANA (EDITORS)
THE COTTON COUNTRY COLLECTION

Peanut Butter Cookies

To make about 24

125 g	peanut butter	4 oz
125 g	butter	4 oz
125 g	sugar	4 oz
125 g	soft brown sugar	4 oz
1	egg, well beaten	1
150 g	flour, sifted	5 oz
¼ tsp	salt	¼ tsp
½ tsp	baking powder	½ tsp
¼ tsp	bicarbonate of soda	¼ tsp

Cream the peanut butter and butter; add the sugars gradually, add the egg and mix well. Sift together the flour, salt, baking powder and bicarbonate of soda, and add. Mix well. Chill the dough. Roll out, cut out cookies, and bake for 10 to 15 minutes in a preheated 180°C (350°F or Mark 4) oven.

IMOGENE WOLCOTT (EDITOR)
THE YANKEE COOK BOOK

Egg White Biscuits and Nut Pastes

Ladyfingers

Doigts de Dame

The technique of making these biscuits, using puréed straw-berries, is shown on page 62.

To test the hardness of sugar syrup, dip the saucepan in which the syrup is cooking in cold water to prevent further cooking. Drop a small amount of syrup into a bowl of iced water. If the syrup has reached the hard-ball stage, you will be able to mould it easily with your fingers into a ball which holds its shape and is resistant to pressure. The hard-crack stage has been reached when the solidified syrup snaps easily when it is removed from the water and bent between the fingers.

To make strawberry or raspberry ladyfingers, cook the sugar syrup to the hard-crack stage, 150°C (300°F). Add about 60 g (2 oz) of puréed strawberries or raspberries to bring the temperature of the syrup down to the hard-ball stage before combining it with the egg whites. Omit any other flavouring.

To make 50 to 60

250 g	sugar	8 oz
8 cl	water	3 fl oz
4	egg whites, stiffly beaten	4
1 tbsp	finely grated chocolate, or 1 tsp coffee extract or vanilla extract	1 tbsp

Dissolve the sugar in the water and boil the syrup to the hard-ball stage, 121°C (250°F). Pour the syrup on to the stiffly beaten egg whites, whisking continuously. When the mixture is again at the stiff peak stage, whisk in the chocolate, coffee or vanilla flavouring.

Using a piping bag with a small tip, pipe strips of the meringue about 7 cm (3 inches) long on to greased and floured baking sheets. Bake in a preheated 130°C (250°F or Mark ½) oven for about 3 hours, or until thoroughly dried.

M. VITALIS
LES BASES DE LA PÂTISSERIE, CONFISERIE, GLACERIE

Dutch Meringue Biscuits

Schuimpje

To make about 48

375 g	castor sugar	13 oz
9 cl	water	3½ fl oz
4	egg whites	4
1 tbsp	vanilla sugar	1 tbsp
	red food colouring	
1 tbsp	raspberry jam, sieved	1 tbsp
2 tsp	coffee extract	2 tsp
2 tsp	cocoa powder	2 tsp

Dissolve 300 g (10 oz) of the sugar in the water and bring it to the boil. When the liquid is perfectly clear, boil until the syrup reaches 115°C (239°F), the soft-ball stage. Beat the egg whites with the remaining sugar until they form stiff peaks. Add a thin trickle of the syrup and continue beating. Repeat until all the syrup is used and the mixture is smooth and firm.

Divide the meringue into four parts. Leave one uncoloured and mix in the vanilla sugar. Colour the second pink with two drops of red food colouring and flavour with the raspberry jam. Flavour the third with the coffee extract and the fourth with the cocoa powder.

Using a piping bag with a serrated edge nozzle, pipe small, pointed rosettes of meringue on to a buttered and floured baking sheet. Place in a preheated 100°C (200°F or Mark ¼) oven for 1 hour to dry out.

C. A. H. HAITSMA MULIER-VAN BEUSEKOM
CULINAIRE ENCYCLOPÉDIE

Crispy Meringue Drops

Croquignoles Fins

To make about 30

125 g	castor or vanilla sugar	4 oz
2	egg whites	2

Whisk the sugar and egg whites together. Continue whisking until the mixture thickens and is of such a consistency that it can be placed on paper without running. Using a small coffee spoon, form very small mounds of the paste on a sheet of greaseproof paper. Place immediately in a preheated 140°C (275°F or Mark 1) oven and leave until the insides of the *croquignoles* are quite dry. Check by breaking one of them open. Remove from the oven and leave to cool. Store in a very dry place. *Croquignoles* do not keep for very long.

MME. ROSALIE BLANQUET
LE PÂTISSIER DES MÉNAGES

Rose Puffs

Petits Soufflés à la Rose

To make about 20

	rose-water	
	red food colouring	
250 g	castor sugar	8 oz
1	egg white	1

Mix together the castor sugar and egg white to make a fairly firm paste; work the paste for 10 minutes, adding a few drops of rose-water and enough red food colouring to make the mixture bright pink.

On a board sprinkled with castor sugar, roll out the paste into strips the width of a finger. Cut these strips into small dice. Moisten your hands with water and roll each die into a small ball. Place each one in a small round paper case about 2.5 cm (1 inch) in diameter and 1 cm (½ inch) deep. Moisten the top of each biscuit with your index finger dipped in water; this will make the biscuits shiny and glaze them during baking.

Place the biscuits in a preheated 150°C (300°F or Mark 2) oven. They will rise about 2 cm (¾ inch) above the paper cases. After 15 minutes, remove them from the oven, making sure that the tops are quite dry; if they are not, cook them for a few minutes more. Watch carefully that their original colour does not change too much.

Coarse sugar, pistachio nuts and currant puffs: These are the same as the rose puffs already described, with one difference: when the rose puffs are ready for baking, dip their tops gently into coarse sugar (or crushed lump sugar) before they go into the oven. For rose-pistachio nut puffs, add only the rose-water, leaving out the red food colouring, and dip the tops into finely chopped pistachio nuts before baking them.

The other kinds of puffs may also be dipped into coarse sugar, or coarse sugar mixed with chopped pistachio nuts, or coarse sugar mixed with currants.

Orange-flower puffs: Make these in the same way as rose puffs, substituting 8 g (¼ oz) of caramelized orange flowers for the rose-water and red food colouring.

Saffron puffs: Simmer a pinch of saffron threads in 10 cl (3½ fl oz) of water until only 1 tablespoon is left. Cool. Mix the castor sugar with the egg white; add enough of the saffron infusion to colour the mixture lemon-yellow. Add a little more sugar if necessary to make a paste that will roll out easily, and then finish as for rose puffs.

Springtime puffs: Mix the castor sugar with the egg white and ¼ teaspoon of spinach extract, to colour the paste a nice pistachio-nut green. Add the candied peel of half a citron, finely chopped, and finish as above.

Hazelnut puffs: Toast and grate 90 g (3 oz) of hazelnuts; mix with the castor sugar and the egg white, adding more egg white if necessary. Finish as above.

Bitter almond puffs are made the same way, with 15 g (½ oz) of bitter almonds pounded with the sugar.

Vanilla puffs: Pound a vanilla pod with the castor sugar and sieve the mixture before combining it with the egg white and finishing as above.

Lemon puffs: Rub the surface of a lemon with a sugar lump; when it has absorbed all the flavour from the rind, crush it with a rolling pin, add it to the sugar and the egg white, and then finish as for rose puffs.

Orange, citron and Seville orange puffs may be made in the same way as lemon puffs.

Chocolate puffs: Substitute 125 g (4 oz) of grated chocolate for the rose-water and colouring and allow it to melt slowly over hot water. Add the tepid chocolate to the sugar and egg paste, using 175 g (6 oz) of sugar, and mix as above. The mixture will become very stiff; you may have to add a little more egg white to be able to roll it out. Finish as above.

ANTONIN CARÊME
LE PÂTISSIER ROYAL PARISIEN

Date Cookies

To make about 24

175 g	dates, chopped	6 oz
250 g	castor sugar	8 oz
125 g	walnuts, chopped	4 oz
2	egg whites, stiffly beaten	2

Cut the castor sugar, dates and nuts into the beaten egg whites. Do not stir. Drop spoonfuls of the mixture on to a buttered baking sheet and bake in a preheated 150°C (300°F or Mark 2) oven for 45 minutes.

MRS. DON RICHARDSON (EDITOR)
CAROLINA LOW COUNTRY COOK BOOK OF GEORGETOWN,
SOUTH CAROLINA

Chocolate Snaps

To make 24 to 36

60 g	plain chocolate, grated	2 oz
125 g	flour	4 oz
1 tsp	baking powder	1 tsp
250 g	icing sugar	8 oz
8	egg whites, stiffly beaten	8
2 tsp	grated orange rind	2 tsp

Sift together the flour and baking powder. Gradually beat the icing sugar into the egg whites to make a stiff meringue. Fold in the grated chocolate, the sifted flour mixture and the grated orange rind.

Drop teaspoonfuls of the batter 5 cm (2 inches) apart on a buttered baking sheet. Bake for 8 to 10 minutes in a preheated 180°C (350°F or Mark 4) oven.

JULIETTE ELKON
THE CHOCOLATE COOKBOOK

Macaroons from Nice

Macarons ou Amaretti Niçois

Add a teaspoonful of egg white to the almonds when pounding them in a mortar. This will prevent too much oil from being extracted. If bitter almonds are not available, you can substitute ¼ teaspoon of almond extract.

To make about 36

200 g	sweet almonds, blanched	7 oz
4 or 5	bitter almonds, blanched	4 or 5
300 g	sugar	10 oz
1 to 1½	egg whites, lightly beaten	1 to 1½
	pine-nuts	
	icing sugar	

Pound the sweet almonds in a mortar together with the bitter almonds. When the almonds are well pounded, add half the sugar and mix with the pestle. Take one egg white and pour half of it into the mortar. Continue to mix. Blend in the remaining sugar, continue to stir and add the other half egg white. If the mixture is a little too sticky, add a further half egg white. Mix thoroughly once again. Place some grease-proof paper on a baking sheet and spoon the mixture on to it in piles, equivalent to about 2 teaspoons, carefully spaced apart so that the macaroons do not stick to one another during cooking. Bake in a preheated 220°C (425°F or Mark 7) oven for 10 minutes or until set. Remove from the oven. Decorate with pine-nuts and sprinkle with icing sugar. Return to the oven for a moment to set the icing sugar; then take them out.

JOSÉPHINE BESSON
LA MÈRE BESSON "MA CUISINE PROVENÇALE"

Bitter Almond Macaroons

Macarons Soufflés aux Amandes Amères

To make about 80

125 g	bitter almonds, blanched	4 oz
350 g	almonds, blanched	12 oz
750 g	castor sugar	1½ lb
2¼	egg whites	2¼

Slice the almonds thinly crosswise. Mix them with 125 g (4 oz) of the sugar and quarter of an egg white; spread them out on a large baking sheet and place in a preheated 130°C (250°F or Mark ½) oven for 30 minutes or until dry and pale golden.

While the almonds are cooling, beat the remaining sugar and egg whites together in a bowl for 15 minutes; stir in the almonds and mix until they are completely coated with the egg white mixture.

To test the mixture, place a spoonful on a baking sheet and bake in the preheated oven for 20 minutes. If the surface collapses, add a little sugar to the mixture; if the surface is too hard and the macaroon is too stiff, add a little egg white. If the test macaroon keeps its shape, you can go ahead with the rest of the mixture. Dampen your hands and roll spoonfuls of the mixture between your palms to form biscuits the size of a nutmeg. Place them on a greased baking sheet. When they are all shaped, dip your fingertips in water and touch the surface of each macaroon lightly.

Place the baking sheet in the oven and do not open the door for 20 minutes. When the macaroons are a beautiful light golden colour and firm to the touch, remove them from the oven. When cold, remove them from the baking sheet.

ANTONIN CARÊME
LE PÂTISSIER ROYAL PARISIEN

Spilamberto Macaroons

Amaretti di Spilamberto

To make about 120

500 g	almonds, blanched	1 lb
60 g	bitter almonds, blanched	2 oz
600 g	castor sugar	1¼ lb
5	egg whites, stiffly beaten	5

Crush the almonds finely in a mortar, adding 15 g (½ oz) of the sugar. Fold the almonds into the egg whites with 485 g (15½ oz) of the sugar. Cut long ribbons of greaseproof paper 5 cm (2 inches) wide. Put teaspoonfuls of the dough on to the strips at regular intervals. Place the strips on baking sheets and sprinkle the biscuits with the rest of the sugar. Bake in a preheated 180°C (350°F or Mark 4) oven for 20 minutes.

GIORGIO GIUSTI (EDITOR)
CENTONOVANTADUE RICETTE DELL' 800 PADANO

Macaroons

Macarons

These macaroons will keep well in tightly closed tins.

To make 12

125 g	ground almonds	4 oz
250 g	sugar	8 oz
¼ tsp	powdered vanilla or 1 or 2 drops vanilla extract	¼ tsp
2	egg whites	2
	icing sugar	

Place the ground almonds in a bowl. Pound them with a wooden pestle, adding the sugar little by little. It is not enough simply to mix the sugar and almonds: some of the oil from the almonds must be extracted by the pounding.

Add the vanilla and, little by little, the egg whites. The dough should be firm enough to be kneaded by hand. Divide into 12 balls of equal size.

Oil a sheet of greaseproof paper placed on a baking sheet. Place the balls on the paper and flatten them a little (they spread out during cooking).

Brush the surface of the macaroons with water. Sprinkle with a pinch of icing sugar. Bake in a preheated 180°C (350°F or Mark 4) oven for 15 to 18 minutes, with the baking sheet fairly high up in the oven.

To remove the biscuits, slide the sheet of paper on to a well-dampened tea towel. As soon as the paper is moist, remove the biscuits without letting them absorb any moisture.

JACQUELINE GÉRARD
BONNES RECETTES D'AUTREFOIS

Dutch Macaroons

The distinctive feature of Dutch macaroons is the lovely smile down the centre of each one. This is obtained by an interesting trick. After shaping, the macaroons are left in a warm place until they form a thick skin. This is then cut through from end to end with a sharp knife. When the macaroons are in the oven, the centre mixture bubbles through giving them a most attractive and appetizing appearance.

To make about 15

175 g	icing sugar, sifted	6 oz
60 g	ground almonds	2 oz
	almond extract	
1 to 1½	egg whites, lightly beaten	1 to 1½

Combine the icing sugar with the ground almonds. Flavour with a few drops of almond extract and mix to a thick, creamy consistency with the whites of egg. The mixture, if correct, should flow level without spreading. Place in a large piping bag, fitted with a 5 mm (¼ inch) plain nozzle, and pipe small oval shapes on to sheets of rice paper. Put aside in a warm place for one to two days until a thick skin has formed. Then, using a sharp knife, make a clean cut from end to end of each biscuit. Bake in a preheated 180°C (350°F or Mark 4) oven for 15 minutes or until golden.

MARGARET BATES
TALKING ABOUT CAKES WITH AN IRISH AND SCOTTISH ACCENT

Sienese Almond Wafer Biscuits

Ricciarelli di Siena

The almonds should be ground in an electric food processor or coffee grinder. Large white wafers can be bought at wholesale bakery suppliers and some specialist shops. Rice paper, cut to the size of the biscuits, may be used if wafers are unobtainable.

To make about 50

500 g	almonds, blanched, dried and ground	1 lb
500 g	castor sugar	1 lb
2	egg whites, very lightly beaten	2
	icing sugar	
½ tsp	vanilla extract	½ tsp
About 50	large white wafers	About 50

Add the sugar to the ground almonds, mix well and put through a sieve. If any pieces of almond remain, grind them again. The resulting mixture of ground almonds and sugar must be fine and uniform.

Add the egg whites to the almond sugar mixture, then add 75 g (2½ oz) of icing sugar and the vanilla extract. Blend well to obtain a soft, smooth paste.

Sprinkle a work surface with icing sugar, then put a tablespoon of the mixture on it and flatten it out with your hand and the flat side of a wide knife dipped in icing sugar. You should obtain a longish diamond about 7.5 cm (3 inches) long and 4 cm (1½ inches) wide.

Continue until all the *ricciarelli* are made, then place each one on a wafer and place the wafers on one or more baking sheets. Leave overnight.

Next morning, place the *ricciarelli* in a preheated 130°C (250°F or Mark ½) oven for about 15 minutes in order to dry them. They should emerge soft and white. Trim off any excess wafer and allow to cool. Then sprinkle the biscuits generously with icing sugar, serve or store.

WILMA PEZZINI
THE TUSCAN COOKBOOK

Almond Petits Fours

Petits Fours aux Amandes

For a demonstration of piping techniques, see page 44.

The biscuits of each shape should be as uniform as possible so that they bake evenly and an attractive platter can be arranged. They can be stored for one to two weeks in an airtight container, or they can be frozen.

To make 12 to 14

200 g	almonds, blanched and ground	7 oz
150 g	sugar	5 oz
1 tsp	apricot jam (optional)	1 tsp
2	egg whites, lightly beaten	2
½ tsp	vanilla extract	½ tsp

Decoration

	blanched, split almonds and/or candied cherries or candied orange peel, cut in pieces of exactly the same size, and/or small diamonds of angelica, and/or raisins	

Glaze

1 tbsp	icing sugar	1 tbsp
2 tbsp	milk or water	2 tbsp

Line a baking sheet with greaseproof paper.

Mix the ground almonds and sugar, add the apricot jam, if using, and stir in enough egg white to make a mixture that is soft enough to pipe but still holds its shape. Beat in the vanilla. Using a piping bag fitted with a large star nozzle, pipe the mixture in flowers, rosettes or figures-of-eight on to the prepared baking sheet. Decorate with one or more of the decorations and bake in a preheated 180°C (350°F or Mark 4) oven for 15 to 20 minutes or until they begin to brown. Leave on the baking sheet.

To prepare the glaze, heat the sugar with the milk until dissolved and brush over the petits fours while still hot. Lift one end of the greaseproof paper slightly, immediately pour a glass of water under the paper and stand back: the hot baking sheet will turn the water into steam, making it easy to remove the petits fours. Leave them for a few moments; then remove them from the paper and transfer to a rack to cool.

FAYE LEVY
LA VARENNE TOUR BOOK

Mirrors

Miroirs

To make about 30

300 g	almonds, blanched, 50 g (2 oz) finely chopped	10 oz
300 g	lump sugar	10 oz
6	egg whites, stiffly beaten	6

Cream filling

100 g	almonds, blanched and pounded	3½ oz
3	eggs	3
100 g	sugar	3½ oz
100 g	butter, softened	3½ oz
4 tbsp	rum	4 tbsp

Grind the whole almonds and lump sugar together in a food processor until they are completely crushed, and sieve the mixture. Fold in the egg whites. Using a piping bag with a medium-sized plain nozzle, pipe oval frames about 4 cm (1½ inches) long on to a buttered and floured baking sheet. Then sprinkle these outlines with the finely chopped almonds in order to give a granite effect.

Whisk together all the filling ingredients. Fill the centres of the frames with this mixture. Bake in a preheated 170°C (325°F or Mark 3) oven for 15 minutes.

MANUEL PRATIQUE DE CUISINE PROVENÇALE

Cinnamon Stars

Zimtsterne

To make about 20

2 tsp	ground cinnamon	2 tsp
6	egg whites, stiffly beaten	6
500 g	castor sugar	1 lb
1	lemon, rind grated	1
500 g	unblanched almonds, ground	1 lb

Combine the egg whites, sugar and lemon rind, and beat continuously for 15 minutes (7 minutes with an electric beater). Add the cinnamon. Divide the mixture in half and mix the almonds thoroughly into one half to make a dough. Roll out the almond dough on a floured board and use a biscuit cutter to cut out stars or other shapes. Coat the biscuits with the remaining egg white mixture. Place on a greased baking sheet and bake in a preheated 170°C (325°F or Mark 3) oven for 15 minutes or until lightly browned.

HENRIETTE DAVIDIS
PRAKTISCHES KOCHBUCH

Tiles

Tuiles

The technique of shaping tiles is shown on page 51.

To make about 30

150 g	almonds, chopped or slivered	5 oz
150 g	icing sugar	5 oz
60 g	flour	2 oz
1	egg (optional)	1
½ tsp	vanilla extract	½ tsp
2 to 3	egg whites	2 to 3

Mix the almonds with the sugar and flour. Add the egg, if using, the vanilla extract, then two egg whites. Mix, then allow the batter to rest for 10 minutes. The batter should be quite runny; if it is too stiff, add a little extra egg white.

With a spoon or piping bag, drop small amounts of the mixture on to a buttered baking sheet. Spread the biscuits into round shapes by pressing down on them with a wet fork.

Bake the biscuits in a preheated 240°C (475°F or Mark 9) oven for 5 minutes or until they are just beginning to brown. Take the biscuits from the oven, remove them at once from the baking sheet and place them round a rolling pin to give them their curved shape.

B. DESCHAMPS AND J.-CL. DESCHAINTRE
LE LIVRE DE L'APPRENTI PÂTISSIER

Roof Tiles

Tejas

For a demonstration of shaping curved biscuits, see page 51.

To make about 24

125 g	sugar	4 oz
125 g	flour	4 oz
2	egg whites, stiffly beaten	2
17.5 cl	double cream	6 fl oz

In a bowl, mix the sugar and flour. Fold the egg whites into the mixture together with the cream. Stir until all the ingredients are thoroughly mixed. Grease a baking sheet and place spoonfuls of the mixture on it. Bake in a preheated 180°C (350°F or Mark 4) oven for 2 minutes, then raise the heat to 200°C (400°F or Mark 6) and continue to cook for 8 minutes more. The biscuits should be beginning to brown. Remove from the oven and, while still hot, bend into curved shapes resembling Spanish roof tiles.

MARIA DEL CARMEN CASCANTE
MANUAL MODERNO DE PASTELERIA CASERA

Wood Shavings

Copeaux

These biscuits keep for a long time in a dry place.

To make about 36

130 g	almonds, blanched and chopped	4 oz
280 g	castor sugar	9 oz
250 g	flour	8 oz
½ tsp	vanilla extract	½ tsp
About 6	egg whites	About 6

Pound the almonds in a mortar, adding the sugar gradually. Stir in the flour and vanilla, and enough egg whites to make a fairly liquid dough.

Oil a baking sheet, or butter it with clarified butter. With a piping bag, pipe strips of dough about 10 cm (4 inches) long and 1 cm (½ inch) wide on to the sheet. Bake in a preheated 200°C (400°F or Mark 6) oven for 8 to 10 minutes, or until the edges are lightly browned.

Keeping the baking sheet warm beside the oven, detach the biscuits one by one and roll them round a small stick to give them a corkscrew shape.

MANUEL PRATIQUE DE CUISINE PROVENÇALE

French Puffs

Petits Soufflés à la Française

These biscuits may be coloured pink, green or yellow with the appropriate food colouring.

To make about 24

175 g	castor sugar	6 oz
2	egg whites	2
125 g	flour, sifted	4 oz
	rose-water	

In a small bowl, work together 125 g (4 oz) of the sugar and the two egg whites for 10 minutes. Stir in the flour and knead together for several minutes more. Add a little rose-water and the remaining sugar, and knead for a few more minutes. The mixture should be fairly firm, very supple and shiny.

With a teaspoon, place mounds of the mixture the size of a large olive on a baking sheet. Place the baking sheet in a warm place such as an oven with the heat turned off, and leave for 5 to 6 hours to dry the surface of the biscuits. Then place the biscuits in a preheated 140°C (275°F or Mark 1) oven. The biscuits will keep their original shape, but rise about 1.5 cm ($\frac{2}{3}$ inch). Take them out when they are a barely noticeable pinkish-gold, after about 10 minutes; even after baking, they will stay quite pale.

ANTONIN CARÊME
LE PÂTISSIER ROYAL PARISIEN

Small Biscuits

Biscotins

To make about 20

125 g	flour	4 oz
3 tbsp	castor sugar	3 tbsp
3 tbsp	fruit jam or puréed fruit	3 tbsp
About 3	egg whites	About 3
	icing sugar glaze (optional) (*page 9*)	

Mix together the flour and sugar, and add the jam and enough egg white to make a smooth dough. Knead the dough lightly, roll it out, and cut it into shapes with biscuit cutters. Bake in a preheated 190°C (375°F or Mark 5) oven for 10 minutes. If you wish, brush the biscuits with an icing sugar glaze.

LE MANUEL DE LA FRIANDISE

Mariette's Biscuits

Biscuits de Mariette

To make about 50

125 g	flour	4 oz
125 g	castor sugar	4 oz
12.5 cl	double cream	4 fl oz
3	egg whites, stiffly beaten	3

Put the flour and sugar in a large bowl. Add the cream and mix together well. Gently fold in the egg whites. Butter a baking sheet. Using a teaspoon, place little heaps of the dough on it, spaced well apart. Cook the biscuits in a preheated 230°C (450°F or Mark 8) oven until brown (less than 5 minutes). Watch them carefully, as they cook very quickly.

ÉLIANE AND JACQUETTE DE RIVOYRE
LA CUISINE LANDAISE

Almond Crescents from Provence

Croissants de Provence

To make about 24

175 g	ground almonds	6 oz
175 g	sugar	6 oz
1 tbsp	apricot jam, sieved	1 tbsp
	vanilla extract	
2	egg whites, lightly beaten	2
75 g	blanched almonds, chopped or slivered	$2\frac{1}{2}$ oz
3 tbsp	milk	3 tbsp

Mix together the ground almonds and 150 g (5 oz) of the sugar in a bowl. Add the jam and a drop or two of vanilla extract. Stir this together, incorporating, little by little, two-thirds of the egg white. You should obtain a fairly thick dough which can be worked by hand.

Divide the dough into pieces the size of a walnut and roll each piece out on a floured work surface to form a stick about 8 cm (3 inches) long. Using a brush, paint the surface of each stick with the remaining egg white, then roll it in the chopped or slivered almonds. Place the sticks on a buttered baking sheet, bending the ends round to form crescents. Bake in a preheated 190°C (375°F or Mark 5) oven for 10 minutes.

Dissolve the remaining sugar in the milk. When the crescents are cooked, take them from the oven and paint them with the sugared milk to give them a beautiful shiny appearance. Leave them to cool.

DOMINIQUE WEBER
LES BONNES RECETTES DES PROVINCES DE FRANCE

Almond Bites

Ossa da Mordere

To make 50 to 60

200 g	almonds, blanched and dried	7 oz
6	egg whites	6
200 g	castor sugar	7 oz
700 g	flour	1½ lb
1 tsp	grated lemon rind	1 tsp

Crush 100 g (3½ oz) of the almonds in a mortar. Cut the rest in halves and set them aside. In a bowl, beat the egg whites and sugar until very firm; add the flour, finely crushed almonds and grated lemon rind. Work the ingredients together to obtain a smooth consistency. Divide the dough into small balls, flatten them, put half an almond on top of each one and place on greased baking sheets.

Bake in a preheated 180°C (350°F or Mark 4) oven until the biscuits start to turn brown, about 20 minutes. Leave to cool and lift them from the baking sheets with a knife.

LAURA GRAS PORTINARI
CUCINA E VINI DEL PIEMONTE E DELLA VALLE D'AOSTA

Little Horns

Cachitos

Brazil nuts and a few drops of almond extract may be used instead of almonds. You can use a blender to crush the nuts.

To make about 24

500 g	almonds, blanched and crushed	1 lb
250 g	icing sugar	8 oz
2	egg whites	2
1 tbsp	apricot jam	1 tbsp
½ tsp	vanilla extract	½ tsp
	salt	
30 g	walnuts, crushed	1 oz

Mix all the ingredients together, except 2 teaspoons of the egg whites and all the walnuts. Working on a floured board, make sculptures as follows: form the mixture into balls 3.5 cm (1½ inches) in diameter, roll them into cigar shapes, then curve them to make horns. Brush on the reserved whites and sprinkle on the walnuts. Arrange the biscuits on a buttered and floured baking sheet. Bake in a preheated 180°C (350°F or Mark 4) oven for 18 minutes or until light brown.

VIOLETA AUTUMN
A RUSSIAN JEW COOKS IN PERÚ

Almond and Pine-Nut Crescents

Pignoulat

To make about 40

150 g	almonds	5 oz
350 g	pine-nuts	12 oz
500 g	flour	1 lb
3	egg whites, lightly beaten	3
4 tbsp	orange-flower water	4 tbsp
500 g	castor sugar	1 lb
15 cl	water	¼ pint

Toast the almonds and 150 g (5 oz) of the pine-nuts, then grind them in a food processor or electric grinder to reduce them to a powder. In a bowl, mix the flour, powdered nuts, two egg whites and the orange-flower water. Work with a wooden spoon to obtain a homogeneous dough.

In a copper pan or heavy metal saucepan, dissolve the sugar in the water over a gentle heat. Stir the dough into the syrup and let it cook on a very low heat for a few minutes, stirring all the time with a wooden spoon. When the dough is firm, turn it out on to an oiled marble slab. Shape pieces of the dough into crescents, dip them one by one into the remaining egg white, then roll them in the rest of the pine-nuts. Place the crescents on a buttered baking sheet and bake them in a preheated 170°C (325°F or Mark 3) oven for about 5 minutes.

LUCETTE REY-BILLETON
LES BONNES RECETTES DU SOLEIL

Crescents with Pine-Nuts

Croissants aux Pignons

If possible, use almonds and pine-nuts from Provence; they are a bit more expensive but have more flavour.

To make about 24

175 g	pine-nuts	6 oz
250 g	ground almonds	8 oz
250 g	castor sugar	8 oz
3	egg whites	3

Mix together the almonds and sugar in a bowl; gradually work in the egg whites. Knead until you have a firm dough. Form into small balls the size of a walnut and roll the balls in the pine-nuts, pressing so that the pine-nuts adhere to the dough. Form each ball into a crescent and arrange them on a buttered baking sheet. Bake in a preheated 130°C (250°F or Mark ½) oven for 1 hour.

FLORENCE DE ANDREIS
LA CUISINE PROVENÇALE D'AUJOURD'HUI

Zürich Marzipan Biscuits

Zürcher Marzipanleckerli

If a large number of biscuits are made at one time, they look most attractive if a mixture of colours and flavours are used for the icing: for instance, chocolate, lemon and raspberry. Alternatively, the basic marzipan paste itself may be divided before it is rolled out, and coloured and flavoured with chocolate and pistachio respectively.

To make about 48

550 g	almonds, blanched and ground	1 lb 2 oz
30 g	bitter almonds, blanched and ground	1 oz
550 g	icing sugar, sifted	1 lb 2 oz
2	eggs, yolks separated from whites, both lightly beaten	2
About 2 tbsp	rose-water or orange-flower water	About 2 tbsp
	Icing	
275 g	icing sugar	9 oz
1	egg white	1
2 tbsp	orange-flower water or lemon juice	2 tbsp

Mix the ground almonds and bitter almonds with the icing sugar, add the egg whites and 2 tablespoons of rose-water or orange-flower water, and place the mixing bowl in a saucepan of water over heat. Beat until the mixture begins to come away easily from the bottom of the bowl. Remove the bowl from the heat and add the egg yolks. Dust a board with icing sugar and roll out the paste about 1 cm (⅜ inch) thick. Cut out oblongs about 3 by 5 cm (1¼ by 2 inches) and place them on a board dusted with flour; brush them with more rose-water and leave for two days at average room temperature.

Butter a baking sheet, dust it with flour and place the biscuits on it. Dry rather than bake them for 15 minutes in a cool oven at 150°C (300°F or Mark 2).

Mix the icing ingredients until smooth. After baking, immediately brush the biscuits with the icing.

EVA MARIA BORER
TANTE HEIDI'S SWISS KITCHEN

English Rout Biscuits

The technique of preparing icing sugar glaze is on page 9.

English rout biscuits are modelled from a form of marzipan made entirely with castor sugar and mixed with yolks of egg. This gives the mixture the texture and richness which is characteristic of these little biscuits. The marzipan may be coloured before use and can be shaped in a great variety of ways. A good selection is described here, but the cook's own ingenuity will probably add to the list.

To make about 30

125 g	ground almonds	4 oz
125 g	castor sugar	4 oz
¼ tsp	almond extract	¼ tsp
2 or 3	egg yolks	2 or 3

Combine the almonds with the castor sugar and flavour with the almond extract. Then mix all to a pliable paste of modelling consistency with the egg yolk. Avoid overworking it or it becomes oily. Make up into little biscuits as follows.

Cherry horns: Roll out some of the rout paste fairly thin and cut into circles using a 3 cm (1½ inch) cutter. Brush the centre with egg yolk, lay half a cherry on top and draw the marzipan round horn fashion. Arrange on a greased and floured baking sheet, and put aside for several hours to firm. Brush with egg yolk and bake in a preheated 230°C (450°F or Mark 8) oven just sufficiently long to brown the edges, about 5 minutes.

Rout rings: Colour some of the paste either pink or green and roll out fairly thick. Then cut into small rings using two plain cutters of nearly the same size. Bake as already described and finish with a little white icing and four silver balls placed at the four points of the compass.

Almond rout biscuits: Colour the rout paste and roll out and cut into small fancy biscuits. Brush with egg yolk and stick a split almond on top. Brown in a hot oven as before.

Chocolate sticks: Using coloured rout paste, roll out fairly thick and cut into neat sticks. Without brushing with egg yolk, bake for about 5 minutes in a hot oven, as above; when cold, dip the tips in melted baker's chocolate and then in chocolate vermicelli.

Walnut bon-bons: Roll some coloured rout paste into small balls. Stick a half walnut on either side. After standing, brush the top of each with egg yolk and bake in a preheated oven, as before, for about 5 minutes.

Little loaves: Shape some plain rout paste into little balls, flatten slightly and mark the top with the back of a knife in the form of a cross. After standing, brush with egg yolk and finish off in a hot oven as before.

MARGARET BATES
TALKING ABOUT CAKES WITH AN IRISH AND SCOTTISH ACCENT

French Calisson Biscuits

Calissons d'Aix

Calisson biscuits are traditionally stamped out with a special cutter that gives them an elliptical shape pointed at the ends, but they can also be cut into rounds.

To make about 50

250 g	almonds, blanched	8 oz
4 tbsp	syrup from preserved fruits	4 tbsp
250 g	castor sugar	8 oz
	royal icing (*page 167*)	

In a mortar, pound the almonds fine with the fruit syrup; add the sugar and continue to pound the mixture into a paste. Take the paste out of the mortar, put it into a pan over a low heat and stir it for 5 to 6 minutes, or until the paste is so compact and dry that it will not adhere to your finger. Take it off and spread it on rice paper as evenly as possible, about 1 cm ($\frac{1}{2}$ inch) thick; spread over it a thin layer of icing. Cut into cakes with a calisson cutter or into small rounds. Bake in a preheated 150°C (300°F or Mark 2) oven for 50 minutes or until dried and firm, keeping the oven door ajar.

ÉMILE HÉRISSÉ
THE ART OF PASTRY MAKING

Almond Cakes

Panellets

To make about 70

1 kg	almonds, blanched and ground	2 lb
3	small potatoes, boiled, peeled and mashed	3
775 g	sugar	1 lb 9 oz
30 g	vanilla sugar	1 oz
125 g	coconut, grated	4 oz
4 tbsp	*anis* or any anise-flavoured liqueur	4 tbsp
4 tbsp	brandy	4 tbsp
3	drops orange or lemon extract	3
	whole almonds or pine-nuts	

Mix the ground almonds with the mashed potatoes, adding the sugar and vanilla sugar. Divide the mixture into two parts. To one part, add the grated coconut and the *anis*. In the other half, put the brandy and the orange or lemon extract. Form into little cakes about 4 cm (1$\frac{1}{2}$ inches) across and stick one or two almonds on top of each, or cover with pine-nuts. Place the little cakes on greased baking sheets. Bake in a preheated 200°C (400°F or Mark 6) oven for about 6 minutes or until they are very lightly browned.

IRVING DAVIS
A CATALAN COOKERY BOOK

Almond Cookies

Fregolata

To make about 36

350 g	almonds, blanched	12 oz
350 g	sugar	12 oz
300 g	flour	10 oz
$\frac{1}{8}$ tsp	salt	$\frac{1}{8}$ tsp
1	lemon, rind grated	1
2	eggs, lightly beaten	2
60 g	butter, softened and diced	2 oz
2 tbsp	single or double cream	2 tbsp

Chop the almonds coarsely in a blender, adding sugar as you go along. This is best done by dividing the almonds into eight batches and chopping each batch with 1 tablespoon of sugar— 8 tablespoons in all. In a bowl, combine the almonds, flour, salt and lemon rind, and mix well. Stir in the remaining sugar, the eggs and butter. Mix with a spoon, then knead the dough with your hands, adding 1 tablespoon of cream at a time to make the dough easy to handle.

Break off pieces of dough and roll them with your hands into 2 cm ($\frac{3}{4}$ inch) thick rolls. Cut these rolls into 4 cm (1$\frac{1}{2}$ inch) long pieces. Place the cookies on buttered and floured baking sheets. Bake in a preheated 180°C (350°F or Mark 4) oven for 20 to 25 minutes or until they are barely golden. Do not overbake the cookies or they will be hard.

NIKA HAZELTON
THE REGIONAL ITALIAN KITCHEN

Lady's Kisses

Baci di Dama

You can use Marsala or Lachryma Christi for the liqueur and sandwich the biscuits with jam instead of chocolate.

To make about 36

200 g	almonds, blanched and dried	7 oz
200 g	flour	7 oz
200 g	sugar	7 oz
200 g	butter, melted	7 oz
2 tbsp	semi-dry liqueur	2 tbsp
60 g	dark cooking chocolate, melted over hot water	2 oz

Crush the almonds finely in a mortar. Mix the almonds with the flour and sugar, and make a well in the centre. Pour the butter and the liqueur into the well, and mix together into a smooth dough. Form the dough into balls the size of a walnut, place them on a buttered baking sheet and flatten them with your fingers.

Bake in a preheated 220°C (425°F or Mark 7) oven for 15 minutes. When the biscuits are cooked, leave them to cool, then, to make "kisses", join them together in twos with the melted cooking chocolate.

LAURA GRAS PORTINARI
CUCINA E VINI DEL PIEMONTE E DELLA VALLE D'AOSTA

Small Loaves

Petits Pains

To make about 20

125 g	almonds, blanched	4 oz
250 g	castor sugar	8 oz
100 g	butter	3½ oz
2	eggs	2
250 g	flour	8 oz
½ tsp	vanilla or almond extract, orange-flower water or other flavouring	½ tsp

Pound the almonds in a mortar until finely crushed. Continuing to pound with the pestle, work in the sugar, butter, eggs, flour and flavouring. Mix thoroughly. Form the dough into a ball, sprinkle with flour, and leave to rest for 20 minutes.

Shape the dough into small loaves, oval and pointed at both ends, and slash them down the centre. Place them on a buttered baking sheet and bake in a preheated 180°C (350°F or Mark 4) oven for 20 minutes or until lightly browned. Keep them in a dry place.

MANUEL PRATIQUE DE CUISINE PROVENÇALE

Chocolate Almond Wreaths

Obwarzanki Czekoladowe

To make about 12

90 g	plain chocolate, grated	3 oz
140 g	unblanched almonds, ground	5 oz
2	egg whites	2
140 g	castor sugar	5 oz
40 g	flour	1½ oz
175 g	icing sugar glaze (*page 9*)	6 oz

Make a dough by adding the egg whites to the chocolate, almonds, sugar and flour. Roll into ropes with the palms of your hands on a pastry board and join the ends to form small wreaths 6 cm (2½ inches) in diameter. Bake in a preheated 140°C (275°F or Mark 1) oven for about 30 minutes or until firm. Cover with the icing when cool.

MARJA DISSLOWA
JAK GOTOWAĆ

Bear's Paws or Chocolate Shells

Bärentätzle oder Schokoladenmuscheln

Traditionally, these are shaped by pressing the mixture into wooden moulds similar to madeleine tins. If these are unobtainable, roll out the dough and cut it with cutters.

To make about 12

60 g	plain chocolate, grated	2 oz
60 g	cocoa powder	2 oz
250 g	sugar	8 oz
4	egg whites, stiffly beaten	4
1	lemon, juice strained	1
1 tbsp	vanilla sugar	1 tbsp
250 g	unblanched almonds, ground	8 oz

Fold the sugar into the egg whites and then gradually fold in the other ingredients. Leave the mixture to rest for 1 hour. Work the dough on a sugared and floured board until smooth. Roll into strips about 3 cm (1½ inches) wide and cut each strip into sections making about 12 in all. Sugar the moulds, press the pieces of dough into the moulds, then turn them out on to a greased baking sheet and leave overnight. Bake in a preheated 200°C (400°F or Mark 6) oven for about 10 minutes.

HANS KARL ADAM
DAS KOCHBUCH AUS SCHWABEN

Eulalia Wafers

Bollos Eulalia

Wafers may be purchased at wholesale bakery suppliers and specialist shops. If they are unobtainable, use rice paper cut into convenient sizes.

To make about 36

250 g	ground almonds	8 oz
250 g	sugar	8 oz
250 g	flour	8 oz
250 g	butter	8 oz
6	egg yolks	6
	salt	
½ tsp	ground cinnamon	½ tsp
	wafers	

Mix the almonds with the sugar to make a paste. Sieve the flour on to a pastry board, add the butter, yolks, almond paste and a small pinch of salt. Stir, add the cinnamon and mix well. Spread this preparation fairly thickly on the wafers, put on a baking sheet and bake in a preheated 150°C (300°F or Mark 2) oven for 20 minutes or until firm but not coloured.

VICTORIA SERRA
TIA VICTORIA'S SPANISH KITCHEN

Millennial Cakes

Tausendjahrkuchen

To make 80 to 90

130 g	almonds, blanched	4 oz
4	bitter almonds, blanched	4
1 tsp	egg white	1 tsp
375 g	castor sugar	13 oz
7	eggs	7
130 g	butter, melted	4 oz
1 tsp	ground cinnamon	1 tsp
2	sugar lumps, rubbed over the rind of 1 lemon, then crushed	2
30 g	candied orange peel, finely chopped	1 oz
500 g	flour	1 lb

Pound the almonds finely in a mortar, adding the egg white. Mix with the castor sugar and whole eggs, and whisk until the mixture is thick, white and foamy. Mix in the butter, cinnamon, crushed lemon-flavoured sugar, candied peel and flour. Drop small heaps of the mixture on to a buttered baking sheet. Bake in a preheated 180°C (350°F or Mark 4) oven for 15 minutes or until browned, and remove the cakes from the baking sheet as soon as they come out of the oven.

SOPHIE WILHELMINE SCHEIBLER
ALLGEMEINES DEUTSCHES KOCHBUCH FÜR ALLE STÄNDE

Pistachio Nut Biscuits

Biscottini di Pistacchi

The citron in syrup and grated citron peel may be replaced by 60 g (2 oz) of chopped crystallized citron.

To make about 36

90 g	pistachio nuts, rinsed in hot water and dried	3 oz
45 g	citron in syrup	1½ oz
1½ tsp	grated green citron peel	1½ tsp
7	egg whites, 1 lightly beaten, 6 stiffly beaten	7
150 g	sugar	5 oz
2	egg yolks	2
1 tsp	flour	1 tsp

In a mortar, pound the pistachio nuts, citron in syrup and grated peel together to form a smooth paste. Add the lightly beaten egg white to the paste, little by little. Pour the mixture into a bowl with 100 g (3½ oz) of the sugar and the egg yolks. Stir until combined. Beat the flour into the stiffly beaten egg whites and combine with the nut mixture. Pour into paper moulds or place teaspoonfuls of the mixture on greaseproof paper on a baking sheet. Sprinkle with the remaining sugar and bake in a preheated 140°C (275°F or Mark 1) oven for about 30 minutes or until firm and lightly browned.

IPPOLITO CAVALCANTI, DUCA DI BUONVICINO
CUCINA TEORICO-PRATICA

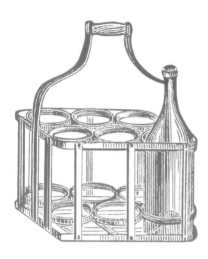

Venetian "Bean" Biscuits

Fave alla Veneziana

These biscuits are traditionally sold in the patisseries of Venice during November. In Trieste, similar biscuits are made using the same paste but shaped like hazelnuts.

To make about 50

300 g	pine-nuts	10 oz
200 g	castor sugar	7 oz
5	egg yolks	5
8 cl	grappa or brandy	3 fl oz
30 g	plain chocolate, finely grated	1 oz
½ tsp	vanilla extract	½ tsp

Pound the nuts to a paste with the sugar. Add the egg yolks, alcohol, chocolate and vanilla. Divide the paste into pieces the shape of a large coin, about 2.5 cm (1 inch) in diameter. Place the "beans" on a greased and floured baking sheet and bake them in a preheated 180°C (350°F or Mark 4) oven for 15 minutes or until just beginning to colour.

RANIERI DA MOSTO
IL VENETO IN CUCINA

Beaten Egg Dough Biscuits

Sponge Fingers

Biscuits à la Cuiller

The technique of making these biscuits is shown on page 68.

To make about 30		
3	eggs, yolks separated from whites, whites stiffly beaten	3
75 g	sugar	2½ oz
	orange-flower water	
75 g	flour	2½ oz
	sifted icing sugar	

Whisk the egg yolks and sugar until pale and fluffy. Add several drops of orange-flower water, then fold in the flour and egg whites. Using a piping bag, pipe 10 cm (4 inch) strips of the mixture on to a buttered baking sheet, leaving plenty of space for them to spread. Sprinkle with icing sugar and bake in a preheated 170°C (325°F or Mark 3) oven for 20 minutes. Take care that the biscuits do not colour.

GINETTE MATHIOT
JE SAIS FAIRE LA PÂTISSERIE

Novara Biscuits

Biscotti di Novara

These are very light biscuits that keep well in an airtight tin. They are best if stored for a few days before eating.

To make about 45		
200 g	castor sugar	7 oz
3	eggs	3
200 g	flour	7 oz
3	sweet, plain, dry biscuits, powdered	3
	salt	

Add 15 g (½ oz) of the sugar to the powdered biscuits and mix well. Thoroughly butter a baking sheet and sprinkle it with flour, shaking off the surplus.

Break two of the eggs into a bowl, then add the yolk and about half the white of the third one, together with the remaining sugar. Beat the mixture until it is thick. Sift the flour and a pinch of salt over the mixture and fold it in lightly. When it is well mixed, pour the mixture into a piping bag fitted with a plain flat nozzle about 2 cm (¾ inch) wide. Squeeze the bag gently and make strips about 8 cm (3 inches) long on the baking sheet, leaving some space between them so that they do not stick together while baking.

Sprinkle the ribbons with the powdered biscuit mixture (take care than none falls on the sheet) and leave them for about 15 minutes. Bake the biscuits in a preheated 180°C (350°F or Mark 4) oven for about 20 minutes or until golden. Then turn them over with a knife and bake them for a few minutes more until quite dry. Leave them to cool on a rack.

FERNANDA GOSETTI
IN CUCINA CON FERNANDA GOSETTI

Light Biscuits

Bizcotelas

To make about 48		
8	eggs, yolks separated from whites, whites stiffly beaten	8
400 g	castor sugar	14 oz
¼ litre	water	8 fl oz
50 g	flour	2 oz

Beat the egg yolks very thoroughly with the sugar and the water until the sugar has dissolved and the yolks are thick. Fold in the flour carefully, and then the egg whites.

Place sheets of greaseproof paper or foil over baking sheets and butter the surface. On the paper place small elongated teaspoonfuls of the mixture and sprinkle with more castor sugar. Bake the biscuits in a preheated 180°C (350°F or Mark 4) oven for 6 to 8 minutes.

MARIA DEL CARMEN CASCANTE
150 RECETAS DE DULCES DE FACIL PREPARACION

Spoon Biscuits

Löffelbiskuits

To make about 48

6	egg yolks	6
100 g	sugar	3½ oz
½	lemon, rind grated	½
5	egg whites, stiffly beaten	5
70 g	cornflour, sifted	2½ oz
100 g	flour, sifted	3½ oz
	sugar or icing sugar	

Beat the egg yolks with 1 teaspoon of the sugar and the grated lemon rind until frothy. Slowly sieve the remaining sugar into the egg whites, beating all the time. Fold the cornflour into the whites and then add the yolk mixture. Finally, add the flour. Place this firm biscuit mixture in a piping bag fitted with a large nozzle. Cover a baking sheet with greaseproof paper and pipe the mixture on to the sheet in 6 to 7 cm (4 to 5 inch) lengths which thicken out at either end. Sprinkle with sugar or sifted icing sugar and bake in a preheated 180°C (350°F or Mark 4) oven for 8 to 10 minutes until golden.

ARNE KRÜGER AND ANNETTE WOLTER
KOCHEN HEUTE

Madeleines

The baking powder will help to raise the batter; it may be omitted for a thinner biscuit.

To make about 36

1	vanilla pod	1
200 g	sugar	7 oz
5	eggs	5
1	lemon, rind grated	1
200 g	flour, sifted	7 oz
1 tsp	baking powder	1 tsp
180 g	butter, melted and cooled	6 oz

Split open the vanilla pod and scrape out the seeds. Whisk together the sugar, vanilla seeds and the eggs until the mixture whitens. Add the lemon rind. Mix the flour and baking powder, sprinkle on to the egg mixture, and fold in gently without making lumps or working the mixture too much. Add the lukewarm butter.

Allow the batter to rest for 15 minutes in a cool place; it can wait for several hours. Butter the madeleine moulds with a pastry brush and flour them. Fill them three-quarters full with the batter. Bake in a preheated 200°C (400°F or Mark 6) oven for 10 to 12 minutes.

LA CUISINE D'ÈVE ET OLYMPE

Citron Sponge Biscuits

Biscottini Ordinari al Cedro

If you cannot obtain a citron, use a large lemon instead.

To make about 120

2	sugar lumps, rubbed over the rind of one citron, then crushed	2
24	eggs, yolks separated from whites, whites stiffly beaten	24
400 g	castor sugar	14 oz
300 g	flour, sifted	10 oz
	jam (optional)	
	icing sugar glaze (*page 9*) or melted chocolate (optional)	

Beat the citron-flavoured sugar, egg yolks and sugar. Continue beating until the mixture is quite firm, then add the flour. Gently fold in the egg whites. Pour the mixture into buttered rectangular tins and bake in a preheated 180°C (350°F or Mark 4) oven for 45 minutes or until the top is golden. Cool and cut into small squares.

If the squares are thick, they may be split in half, spread with jam and covered with icing or melted chocolate.

GIOVANNI VIALARDI
TRATTATO DI CUCINA, PASTICCERIA MODERNA

Pretty Ribbon Biscuits

Beaux Rubans

To make vanilla icing sugar, put two vanilla pods into 500 g (1 lb) icing sugar and leave them for one week. Remove the pods before using the sugar.

To make about 50

8	eggs	8
500 g	vanilla icing sugar	1 lb
250 g	flour	8 oz

Break the eggs into a mixing bowl. Add the sugar, beat well and then gradually beat in the flour. Roll the dough out into a sheet and cut into ribbons, making the strips as narrow as possible. Lay the ribbons on a well-buttered baking sheet and bake in a preheated 200°C (400°F or Mark 6) oven for about 12 minutes or until just beginning to brown. Remove from the oven and immediately wrap the strips of dough round a cylindrical piece of wood to shape them into corkscrews.

MME. ROSALIE BLANQUET
LE PÂTISSIER DES MÉNAGES

Cream Horns

Hohlhippen

For a demonstration of shaping cornucopias with metal moulds see page 52.

To make about 30

30 cl	double cream, whipped	½ pint
5	eggs	5
350 g	sugar	12 oz
1	lemon, rind grated	1
175 g	flour	6 oz
1 tsp	vanilla extract	1 tsp

Beat together the eggs, 300 g (10 oz) of the sugar and the lemon rind until thick and light. Mix in the flour. Roll out the paste quite thin, cut it into strips about the length of a finger and 7.5 cm (3 inches) wide, lay them on a baking sheet which has been rubbed with butter, and bake them in a preheated 180°C (350°F or Mark 4) oven for about 10 minutes or until they are a light yellow colour.

Separate them from the tin and twist them as quickly as possible into the shape of a cornucopia. Leave them in a warm place to get crisp and dry.

Flavour the whipped cream with the vanilla extract and the remaining sugar, and fill the cornucopias with the cream.

LADY HARRIET ST. CLAIR (EDITOR)
DAINTY DISHES

Jasmine Biscuits

Biscotti di Gelsommini

Apricot jam may be used instead of the jasmine conserve, but it will not have the same delicate flavour.

To make about 100

1 tbsp	jasmine conserve	1 tbsp
8	egg yolks	8
550 g	castor sugar	1 lb 2 oz
10	egg whites, stiffly beaten	10
250 g	flour, sifted	8 oz

Put the jasmine conserve in a bowl with the egg yolks and all but 50 g (2 oz) of the sugar. Mix together thoroughly. Fold in the egg whites and, when well combined, add the flour little by little, mixing it in with a spoon.

On baking sheets covered with greased paper, set out teaspoonfuls of the mixture to obtain the maximum number of biscuits. Sprinkle with the remaining sugar and bake in a preheated 150°C (300°F or Mark 2) oven for 30 minutes or until firm and lightly coloured.

IPPOLITO CAVALCANTI, DUCA DI BUONVICINO
CUCINA TEORICO-PRATICA

Jam Biscuits

Biscottini di Confetture

If the citron in syrup is not available, it may be replaced by 125 g (4 oz) of chopped crystallized citron.

To make about 36

2 tbsp	apricot jam, preferably wild apricot	2 tbsp
125 g	citron in syrup	4 oz
5	orange flowers	5
125 g	castor sugar	4 oz
4	eggs, yolks separated from whites, whites stiffly beaten	4

Pound the citron with the orange flowers in a mortar. Add the jam, 90 g (3 oz) of the sugar and the egg yolks. Mix and pass through a mincer, pushing the mixture in with a wooden spoon. Fold in the egg whites.

Place a sheet of greaseproof paper on a baking sheet and drop the mixture on to the paper by teaspoonfuls. Sprinkle with the remaining sugar to form a glaze and bake in a preheated 140°C (275°F or Mark 1) oven for about 30 minutes or until the biscuits are firm.

IPPOLITO CAVALCANTI, DUCA DI BUONVICINO
CUCINA TEORICO-PRATICA

Orange Wafers

To make about 24

½	orange, rind grated	½
1	lemon, juice strained	1
250 g	sugar	8 oz
4	eggs, yolks separated from whites, whites stiffly beaten	4
125 g	flour	4 oz
150 g	marmalade	5 oz

Put the orange rind in a cup and pour the lemon juice over it. After 30 minutes, strain off the juice and reserve it.

Beat the sugar and yolks until light and creamy. Add the juice and fold in the beaten whites. Sift in the flour and fold it in: do not beat any more. Drop spoonfuls of the batter on to a baking sheet lined with greaseproof paper and bake in a preheated 200°C (400°F or Mark 6) oven for 6 to 8 minutes or until light brown. Spread half of the wafers, when cool, with the marmalade and put the others on top of them, pressing them lightly down.

ELIZABETH DOUGLAS
THE CAKE AND BISCUIT BOOK

Orange Biscuits

Krajanki Pomarańczowe

To make about 36

1	orange, rind grated	1
120 g	castor sugar	4 oz
2	eggs	2
2	egg yolks	2
4 tbsp	olive oil	4 tbsp
4 tbsp	rum	4 tbsp
About 250 g flour		About 8 oz

Beat the sugar with the eggs, egg yolks and orange rind until light and thick. Continue mixing, adding the oil, rum and enough flour to make a fairly light dough. Roll out the dough and cut with small, round or fancy-shaped biscuit cutters.

Put the biscuits on to a buttered baking sheet and bake in a preheated 180°C (350°F or Mark 4) oven for 20 minutes or until they begin to brown.

MARJA DISSLOWA
JAK GOTOWAĆ

Anise Caps

Aniskuchen

Instead of mixing the aniseeds into the dough, they can be sprinkled over the biscuits after they are shaped.

Another way of preparing this dough is to mix 600 g (1¼ lb) of sugar with six eggs and four yolks in a bowl set over a pan of simmering water. Whisk the mixture until it is warm and very thick and frothy. Remove from the heat and continue beating until cold. Fold in 600 g (1¼ lb) of flour and the aniseeds, and continue as below.

To make 100 to 120

20 g	aniseeds	¾ oz
500 g	castor sugar	1 lb
7	eggs	7
500 g	flour	1 lb

Beat the sugar and eggs until thick, pale and frothy. Gradually stir in the flour and aniseeds. Butter or grease a baking sheet and, with a spoon, drop pieces of dough about the size of a walnut about 5 cm (2 inches) apart. Leave to stand for several hours in a warm place until the surface of the biscuits is smooth and slightly dried.

Bake in a preheated 180°C (350°F or Mark 4) oven for about 10 minutes or until just beginning to change colour, and remove from the baking sheet while still warm.

SOPHIE WILHELMINE SCHEIBLER
ALLGEMEINES DEUTSCHES KOCHBUCH FÜR ALLE STÄNDE

Drop Biscuits

To make about 100

8	eggs, well beaten	8
500 g	castor sugar	1 lb
350 g	flour	12 oz
1 tbsp	caraway seeds (optional)	1 tbsp

Whisk the eggs and sugar until pale and fluffy, then gradually fold in the flour, beating well after each addition. Drop spoonfuls of the mixture on to floured baking sheets and bake in a preheated 180°C (350°F or Mark 4) oven for 20 minutes. When you see the biscuits rising, watch them carefully and take them out of the oven as soon as they begin to colour; if they are not sufficiently cooked, return them to the oven. The biscuits are done when a white ice forms on them. You may scatter on caraway seeds, if you please. Once the biscuits have been baked, switch off the oven and leave them in the oven until they have become very dry.

E. SMITH
THE COMPLEAT HOUSEWIFE

Springerle

The technique of making and printing springerle *with the traditional carved rolling pin is demonstrated on page 66.*

To make about 50

4	eggs	4
500 g	icing sugar	1 lb
1	lemon, rind grated	1
1 tbsp	arrack or anise-flavoured liqueur	1 tbsp
500 g	flour	1 lb
2 tbsp	aniseeds	2 tbsp

Beat the eggs and sugar until thick; add the lemon rind and arrack. Slowly add the flour and knead the mixture into a dough. Roll the dough out 5 mm (¼ inch) thick. Sprinkle a carved rolling pin with flour and press it firmly on the dough to make patterns. Cut the biscuits along the lines in between the shapes. Grease a baking sheet and sprinkle it with the aniseeds. Place the biscuits on the sheet, cover lightly with a sheet of paper and leave in a cool place overnight to dry.

The next day, cover the biscuits with a sheet of greaseproof paper and bake in a preheated 150°C (300°F or Mark 2) oven for about 20 minutes. They should be white on top and light brown on the bottom. Store in a tin for about three weeks to soften the biscuits slightly.

HEDWIG MARIA STUBER
ICH HELF DIR KOCHEN

White Nuremberg Peppercakes

Weiße Nürnberger Pfefferkuchen

If you use an electric beater, the beating time can be reduced by half. The egg and sugar mixture should be very thick.

To make about 90

500 g	sugar	1 lb
8	eggs	8
500 g	almonds, blanched, dried in the oven and finely chopped	1 lb
500 g	flour	1 lb
1 tbsp	aniseeds, crushed and sieved	1 tbsp
1 tsp each	ground cloves, cardamom and cinnamon	1 tsp each
70 g each	candied lemon and orange peel, finely chopped	2½ oz each

Beat the sugar and eggs together for 1 hour. Mix in the almonds, flour, spices and candied peels. Roll out the dough fairly thin. Cut it into rectangles or rounds, and place the biscuits on baking sheets covered with floured paper. Alternatively, place sheets of the dough on sheets of rice paper and cut out the dough and the rice-paper backing together.

Bake in a preheated 180°C (350°F or Mark 4) oven for 20 minutes or until lightly browned.

SOPHIE WILHELMINE SCHEIBLER
ALLGEMEINES DEUTSCHES KOCHBUCH FÜR ALLE STÄNDE

Orange and Almond Biscuits

Obwarzanki Pomarańczowe

To make about 12

45 g	candied orange peel, finely chopped	1½ oz
100 g	almonds, blanched and chopped	3½ oz
100 g	sugar	3½ oz
2	egg yolks	2

Beat the sugar with the egg yolks and peel until the mixture thickens and lightens in colour. Stir in the almonds. Roll into ropes with the palms of your hands and join the ends to form small, round wreaths 6 cm (2½ inches) in diameter. Place on a baking sheet lined with rice paper. Bake in a preheated 130°C (250°F or Mark ½) oven for about 1½ hours or until dried out.

MARJA DISSLOWA
JAK GOTOWAĆ

Crisp Chartres Biscuits

Croquignoles de Chartres

Add a teaspoonful of egg white to the almonds when pounding them in a mortar to prevent too much oil from being extracted.

To make about 60

75 g	almonds, blanched	2½ oz
2 or 3	bitter almonds, blanched (optional)	2 or 3
250 g	granulated sugar	8 oz
5	eggs, 1 beaten	5
300 g	flour, sifted	10 oz
	salt	
½	lemon, rind grated	½
50 g	butter, melted	2 oz

Pound the almonds and the bitter almonds, if using. Add the sugar and two eggs. Beat the mixture, incorporating two more eggs, a little at a time. Stir in the flour, a pinch of salt, the lemon rind and the butter.

Put the mixture into a piping bag and form little balls, no bigger than a cherry, on a buttered baking sheet. Using a brush, gild the biscuits with the beaten egg. Bake in a preheated 170°C (325°F or Mark 3) oven for 15 minutes or until just beginning to brown.

DOMINIQUE WEBER
LES BONNES RECETTES DES PROVINCES DE FRANCE

Marzipan Figs

Karmous 'l-louz

Marzipan peaches and pears can be made in the same way, using the appropriate food colouring.

To make 15 or 16

500 g	marzipan (*page 167*), tinted with green food colouring	1 lb
	icing sugar	
	Dough	
200 g	sugar	7 oz
60 g	vanilla sugar	2 oz
7	eggs, yolks separated from whites, whites stiffly beaten	7
200 g	flour, sifted	7 oz
	Syrup	
200 g	sugar	7 oz
20 cl	water	7 fl oz
2 tbsp	orange-flower water	2 tbsp

To prepare the dough, beat together 175 g (6 oz) of the sugar, the vanilla sugar and egg yolks until the mixture becomes quite white. Add the remaining sugar to the beaten egg whites and beat again for a moment. Fold the flour and then the egg whites into the dough a little at a time. Using a coffee spoon, make balls of the dough the size of a small peach, and place them on a lightly oiled and floured baking sheet or a sheet of aluminium foil. Bake in a preheated 180°C (350°F or Mark 4) oven for 15 to 20 minutes until very pale gold in colour. Remove from the oven, arrange on a dish and keep covered so that the balls remain soft.

Prepare a fairly light syrup with the sugar, water and orange-flower water. Set aside to cool. Dip the small balls in the syrup and allow them to absorb it.

Place the marzipan on a pastry board sprinkled with icing sugar. Roll it out in a sheet 2 mm ($\frac{1}{16}$ inch) thick. Cut out rounds 8 to 10 cm (3 to 4 inches) in diameter. Wrap each small ball of dough in one of these rounds and shape into a fig. Sprinkle with icing sugar and leave to dry for a few hours.

FATIMA-ZOHRA BOUAYED
LA CUISINE ALGÉRIENNE

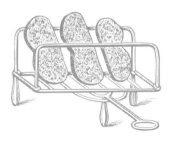

Moroccan Almond Biscuits

Ghoriba aux Amandes

To make 70 to 90

1.5 kg	almonds, blanched	3 lb
5	eggs	5
800 g	icing sugar	1$\frac{3}{4}$ lb
1	lemon, rind grated	1
1$\frac{1}{2}$ tbsp	vanilla sugar	1$\frac{1}{2}$ tbsp
1 tbsp	baking powder	1 tbsp

Pass the blanched almonds twice through a mincer or pulverize them in an electric liquidizer.

Beat the eggs with 750 g (1$\frac{1}{2}$ lb) of the icing sugar until the mixture turns pale. Stir in the lemon rind and vanilla sugar. Add this mixture to the almonds. Mix well and add the baking powder. The resulting dough should be only just malleable.

Grease your hands lightly with butter. Take a small piece of dough and shape it into a ball slightly bigger than a walnut. Flatten the ball and dip one side of it in the remaining icing sugar. Place it on a lightly buttered baking sheet, with the sugared side facing upwards. Repeat, placing the biscuits well apart, until all the dough has been used up. Bake in a preheated 180°C (350°F or Mark 4) oven for 15 to 20 minutes.

AHMED LAASRI
240 RECETTES DE CUISINE MAROCAINE

Pine-Nut Biscuits

Croquets aux Pignons

To make about 24

150 g	pine-nuts	5 oz
125 g	castor sugar	4 oz
2	eggs	2
75 g	flour	2$\frac{1}{2}$ oz
30 g	butter, softened, or 1 tbsp double cream	1 oz

Beat the eggs well, then add the sugar and continue to beat until the mixture is pale and thick. Stir in the flour and pine-nuts, and bind with the butter or cream.

Spread the dough out by hand, to avoid crushing the pine-nuts, and cut it into rounds with a glass. Place on a buttered or oiled baking sheet and bake in a preheated 200°C (400°F or Mark 6) oven for 30 minutes.

ÉLIANE AND JACQUETTE DE RIVOYRE
LA CUISINE LANDAISE

Crisp Nut Biscuits from Périgord

Croquants du Périgord

These biscuits are often made with aniseeds: replace the nuts with 3 tablespoons of aniseeds. The orange-flower water may be replaced by rum, vanilla extract, lemon rind, or another flavouring of your choice.

To make about 18

125 g	walnuts, chopped, or hazelnuts, ground	4 oz
4	eggs	4
250 g	sugar	8 oz
150 g	flour	5 oz
2 tbsp	cream	2 tbsp
1 tsp	orange-flower water	1 tsp

Break the eggs into a bowl and beat with the sugar until well blended. Add the flour and the cream and beat all together until the mixture is a firm homogeneous dough. Add the orange-flower water and the nuts; knead the dough, which will stiffen and leave the sides of the bowl. Place the dough on a pastry board and knead it for 2 to 3 minutes. Then leave it to rest for 10 minutes.

Roll out the dough 2 cm (1 inch) thick. Cut it into small sticks 10 cm (4 inches) by 2 cm (1 inch) and place the sticks on a buttered or oiled baking sheet. Bake in a preheated 150°C (300°F or Mark 2) oven for 30 minutes.

LA CUISINE DU PÉRIGORD

Brazil Nut Crisps

To make 40

200 g	Brazil nuts, coarsely chopped	7 oz
350 g	brown sugar	12 oz
2	eggs	2
250 g	flour	8 oz
$\frac{1}{4}$ tsp	salt	$\frac{1}{4}$ tsp
$\frac{1}{2}$ tsp	baking powder	$\frac{1}{2}$ tsp
1 tsp	vanilla extract	1 tsp

Beat the eggs until very light. Add the sugar gradually, beating all the time. Sift the flour with the salt and baking powder. Add the nuts, flour and vanilla extract to the egg mixture. Chill for several hours. Cut off chunks and roll between your hands into sticks about 5 cm (2 inches) long. If they stick to your hands, keep your hands wet with cold water or dry with icing sugar. The cold water seems to work best for those with moist hands, the icing sugar for those with dry

hands. Place the cookies on a buttered baking sheet (not too close together since they will spread during baking) and bake them for about 15 minutes in a preheated 180°C (350°F or Mark 4) oven. They keep well.

VIRGINIA PASLEY
THE CHRISTMAS COOKIE BOOK

Dutch "Shell Bark" Macaroons

To make about 36

125 g	pecan nuts, chopped	4 oz
75 g	brown sugar	$2\frac{1}{2}$ oz
75 g	granulated sugar	$2\frac{1}{2}$ oz
2	eggs, beaten	2
150 g	flour	5 oz
$\frac{1}{2}$ tsp	baking powder	$\frac{1}{2}$ tsp
1 tsp	milk	1 tsp
$\frac{1}{4}$ tsp	salt	$\frac{1}{4}$ tsp

Add the sugar and other ingredients to the eggs, first the brown then granulated sugar, then the flour, baking powder, milk, salt and finally the nuts, and mix well together. Roll the mixture out to a thickness of 1 cm ($\frac{1}{2}$ inch), cut into 5 cm (2 inch) circles, and bake on a buttered baking sheet for 15 minutes in a preheated 180°C (350°F or Mark 4) oven.

J. GEORGE FREDERICK
PENNSYLVANIA DUTCH COOKERY

Pecan Squares

To make about 24

175 g	pecan nuts, chopped	6 oz
4	eggs	4
500 g	brown sugar	1 lb
175 g	flour	6 oz
$1\frac{1}{2}$ tsp	baking powder	$1\frac{1}{2}$ tsp
1 tsp	vanilla extract	1 tsp

Beat the eggs with the sugar until the mixture is fluffy. Cook in a double boiler for 20 minutes or until thick. Remove from the heat. Sift the flour and baking powder together and add to the mixture with the vanilla extract and the pecan nuts. Spread 1 cm ($\frac{1}{2}$ inch) thick in a greased and floured square tin, and bake in a preheated 200°C (400°F or Mark 6) oven for 12 minutes. Cut into squares.

HARRIET ROSS COLQUITT (EDITOR)
THE SAVANNAH COOK BOOK

Syrup and Honey Biscuits

Florentines

Because chocolate is sensitive to heat and will often be dull rather than glossy if overheated, melt it over hot but not boiling water, never over direct heat.

To make about 30

45 g	butter	1½ oz
12.5 cl	double cream	4 fl oz
125 g	sugar	4 oz
30 g	glacé cherries, soaked in hot water, drained and quartered	1 oz
200 g	almonds, blanched, 150 g (5 oz) finely chopped, the rest slivered	7 oz
100 g	crystallized orange peel, finely chopped	3½ oz
50 g	flour	2 oz
	Topping	
250 g	plain chocolate, chopped	8 oz

Bring the butter, cream and sugar slowly to the boil. Take from the heat and stir in the cherries, chopped and slivered almonds, orange peel and flour. Drop teaspoonfuls of the mixture on to greased and lightly floured baking sheets, leaving plenty of room for spreading, and flatten each portion of the mixture with a wet fork.

Bake for 5 to 6 minutes in a preheated 180°C (350°F or Mark 4) oven. Take from the oven and, with a 7.5 cm (3 inch) plain biscuit cutter, pull in the edges of each biscuit. Return to the oven and bake for 5 to 6 minutes longer or until browned at the edges. Cool a little on the baking sheets; then lift off with a sharp knife and transfer to a rack.

Melt the chocolate in a heatproof bowl over a pan of hot water. Stir with a wooden spoon until smooth and thick. Spread the smooth undersides of the biscuits with chocolate and, if you like, when on the point of setting, mark them with wavy lines, using a cake decorating comb or a serrated knife.

FAYE LEVY
LA VARENNE TOUR BOOK

Gingerbread

To make the gingerbread house shown on page 78, you will need four times the quantities given here. Glacé icing is made in the same way as royal icing (page 8) but using water instead of egg whites; royal icing can be used in this recipe.

If you intend to hang your gingerbread figures from the Christmas tree in the traditional way, take a skewer and make a little hole in the top of each figure before baking. When the cookies are baked and cooled, thread a narrow ribbon through each hole and hang on the tree.

To make about 36

125 g	soft brown sugar	4 oz
125 g	black treacle	4 oz
1 tsp	ground cinnamon	1 tsp
1 tsp	ground ginger	1 tsp
⅛ tsp	ground cloves	⅛ tsp
90 g	butter	3 oz
1½ tsp	baking powder	1½ tsp
500 g	flour, sifted	1 lb
	salt	
1	egg, lightly beaten	1
250 g	glacé icing (optional)	8 oz

Dissolve the sugar with the treacle, spices and butter in a heavy based pan over a low heat, then slowly and carefully bring the mixture to the boil. Cool to room temperature, then mix in the baking powder. Place the flour in a bowl with a pinch of salt and make a well in the centre. Pour in the cooled syrup mixture and the egg, and stir from the centre to incorporate the flour. Turn out on to a floured surface and knead, then wrap in greaseproof paper and leave in the refrigerator for about 30 minutes.

Take out the dough and roll out to about 3 mm (⅛ inch) thick. Using assorted cutters, stamp out people, animals, trees, etc. and place on greased baking sheets. Bake in a preheated 170°C (325°F or Mark 3) oven for 8 to 10 minutes, then remove and cool on a wire rack. Finish the gingerbread men by piping glacé icing round outlines and fill in noses, mouths, eyes, hats and buttons with more glacé icing.

MARGARET WADE
CAKES AND BISCUITS

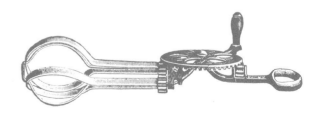

Hunting Nuts

If fresh ginger is unavailable, use 2 teaspoons ground ginger.

To make 50 to 60

250 g	treacle	8 oz
250 g	brown sugar	8 oz
175 g	butter	6 oz
500 g	flour	1 lb
2 tsp	grated fresh ginger root	2 tsp

Melt the treacle, sugar and butter in a saucepan and allow to cool. Add the flour and ginger. Mix all the ingredients well together. Roll small pieces of the dough into balls the size of walnuts. Bake them on a baking sheet in a preheated 170°C (325°F or Mark 3) oven for 15 minutes.

MARY JEWRY (EDITOR)
WARNE'S MODEL COOKERY

Swedish Gingernuts

To make about 72

1 tbsp	ground ginger	1 tbsp
250 g	golden syrup	8 oz
200 g	castor sugar	7 oz
200 g	butter, melted	7 oz
20 cl	double cream	7 fl oz
125 g	candied bitter orange peel, chopped	4 oz
1 tbsp	ground cinnamon	1 tbsp
½ tsp	ground cloves	½ tsp
2 tsp	ground cardamom (optional)	2 tsp
About 500 g	flour	About 1 lb
1 tsp	bicarbonate of soda	1 tsp

Heat the syrup and sugar together until the sugar has dissolved. Add the butter, cream, peel and spices. Sift the flour with the bicarbonate of soda. Work the flour into the other ingredients, adding just enough to make a firm dough. Roll out the dough about 5 mm (¼ inch) thick. Cut into small rounds and bake in a preheated 200°C (400°F or Mark 6) oven for about 15 minutes or until lightly browned.

INGA NORBERG (EDITOR)
GOOD FOOD FROM SWEDEN

Mrs. Gurney's Ginger Snaps

To make about 48

2 tsp	ground ginger	2 tsp
200 g	sugar	7 oz
250 g	golden syrup	8 oz
250 g	butter, or 200 g (7 oz) butter and 50 g (2 oz) lard, melted	8 oz
1 tsp	bicarbonate of soda	1 tsp
2 tbsp	hot water	2 tbsp
About 500 g	flour	About 1 lb

Mix together the sugar, golden syrup, butter or butter and lard, and ginger. Dissolve the bicarbonate of soda in the hot water and add to the ginger mixture. Work in just as much flour as will make a very stiff dough. Roll out on a floured board as thin as possible and cut into small rounds. Bake on a baking sheet in a preheated 180°C (350°F or Mark 4) oven for about 15 minutes, or until beginning to brown.

MAY BYRON
POT-LUCK

Chocolate Cookies, Adventist

The early Dutch settlers baked these chocolate cookies at Thanksgiving time for Christmas use. The result is a soft, chewy cookie with a caramel effect.

To make about 60

140 g	bitter chocolate, grated	4½ oz
¼ litre	molasses or black treacle	8 fl oz
500 g	soft brown sugar	1 lb
250 g	butter, softened	8 oz
1 tsp	bicarbonate of soda	1 tsp
350 g	flour	12 oz

Mix the ingredients to make a stiff batter, using just enough flour to roll out the mixture. Cut with a biscuit cutter about 3 cm (1½ inches) in diameter. Bake the biscuits on greaseproof paper in a preheated 200°C (400°F or Mark 6) oven for 12 minutes or until firm and slightly pliable. When baked and cooled, put in a stone crock or other airtight container in a cool place and *keep for a month or six weeks before eating.*

J. GEORGE FREDERICK
PENNSYLVANIA DUTCH COOKERY

Nut and Honey Biscuits

Honigleckerli

To make about 36

125 g	unblanched almonds, ground	4 oz
125 g	hazelnuts, ground	4 oz
2 tbsp	honey	2 tbsp
275 g	castor sugar	9 oz
60 g	candied peel, chopped	2 oz
2	egg whites	2
	Icing	
4 tbsp	icing sugar	4 tbsp
½	egg white or 1 tbsp lemon juice	½

Mix the almonds, hazelnuts, sugar, honey, candied peel and egg whites and knead into a rollable mixture. Leave in a cool place for 30 minutes or longer. Thickly dust a board with icing sugar, place the paste on it and roll out approximately 5 mm (¼ inch) thick. Cut into diamond-shaped pieces and arrange, not too close together, on a buttered, floured baking sheet. Bake in a preheated 170°C (325°F or Mark 3) oven for 20 to 30 minutes. Mix together the icing ingredients and use to coat the biscuits while they are still warm. Leave in a biscuit tin for some days before eating.

EVA MARIA BORER
TANTE HEIDI'S SWISS KITCHEN

Wild Hazelnut Biscuits

Croquets aux Noisettes Sauvages

To make about 60

200 g	unblanched hazelnuts, ground in a food mill or blender	7 oz
600 g	honey	1¼ lb
½ tsp	ground cinnamon	½ tsp
12	cloves, finely crushed	12
600 g	flour, sifted	1¼ lb
4 tbsp	rum	4 tbsp
1	egg, beaten	1

Heat the honey until liquid, without letting it boil, and pour into a bowl. Add the hazelnuts, cinnamon, cloves, flour and rum, and mix together. Divide the mixture in two.

Roll each piece of dough into the shape of a large sausage. Place on a buttered and floured baking sheet. Flatten the pieces to resemble loaves of bread.

Glaze the dough with the egg and scratch the surface with the tines of a fork for decoration. Place in a preheated 190°C (375°F or Mark 5) oven, reduce the heat to 180°C (350°F or Mark 4) and bake for 20 minutes. When the pieces are a good colour, pierce them with a knife. If they are cooked, the knife blade will come out dry.

Take from the oven, cut into slices while still warm, and cool thoroughly before storing in a biscuit tin.

AMICALE DES CUISINIERS ET PÂTISSIERS AUVERGNATS DE PARIS
CUISINE D'AUVERGNE

Sienese Spiced Biscuits

Cavallucci di Siena

To make about 30

½ tsp each	ground cinnamon and cloves	½ tsp each
2 tsp	ground aniseeds	2 tsp
350 g	sugar	12 oz
15 cl	water	¼ pint
125 g	walnuts, chopped	4 oz
350 g	flour	12 oz
60 g	crystallized orange, chopped	2 oz

Put the sugar into a saucepan and add the water. Cook over a medium heat until the syrup falls in a fine short thread when trickled from a spoon.

Remove from the heat and add the walnuts, flour, crystallized orange and spices. Mix carefully but thoroughly.

Flour a work surface and pour the mixture on to it. Pat down with your hands, then even it with a spatula. It should be 1 cm (½ inch) thick and as even as possible.

Cut the flattened mixture into diamonds, about 3.5 cm (1½ inches) per side. Raise carefully with a narrow metal spatula or wide knife and place each one on a buttered and floured baking sheet, leaving at least 5 cm (2 inches) between them. Bake in a preheated 140°C (275°F or Mark 1) oven for 45 minutes, checking once or twice in order to avoid browning. The resulting biscuits should be white and not too hard.

WILMA PEZZINI
THE TUSCAN COOKBOOK

Original Moravian Christmas Cakes

For many years at Winston-Salem, North Carolina, a little paper-thin spiced cookie has been baked and stored in tins to delight the children at Christmas. The holidays would be incomplete without them. This recipe was given by an experienced Moravian cake-maker who uses the original method. These will keep for weeks if placed in tins and can be made well before Christmas.

To make about 200

175 g	butter	6 oz
175 g	lard	6 oz
350 g	light brown sugar	12 oz
1.7 kg	flour	3¾ lb
1 tbsp	ground mace	1 tbsp
2 tbsp each	ground cloves and cinnamon	2 tbsp each
1 litre	molasses or black treacle, warmed	1¾ pints
30 g	lemon rind, grated	1 oz
17.5 cl	brandy	6 fl oz
30 g	bicarbonate of soda	1 oz
4 tbsp	milk	4 tbsp

Mix together the butter and lard, and cream with the sugar. Add the flour. Mix the mace, cloves and cinnamon with the molasses and add to the flour mixture. Mix all together, using your hands. Add the lemon rind and brandy. Dissolve the bicarbonate of soda in the milk and add to the mixture. This should make a stiff dough. If more flour is needed to stiffen the dough, use it. Roll out very thin and cut cakes in the shape of stars, crescents, animals, etc. Bake in a preheated 180°C (350°F or Mark 4) oven for 10 to 12 minutes.

MARION BROWN
THE SOUTHERN COOK BOOK

Calais Cookies

To make about 72

250 g	lard	8 oz
250 g	sugar	8 oz
1	egg	1
12.5 cl	molasses or black treacle	4 fl oz
12.5 cl	cold water	4 fl oz
500 g	flour	1 lb
1 tsp	ground ginger	1 tsp
1 tsp	salt	1 tsp
1 tsp	bicarbonate of soda	1 tsp

Cream the lard and sugar. Drop in the egg and beat well. Stir in the molasses. Add the water. Sift the flour three times with the ginger, salt and bicarbonate of soda, and add. Mix to a soft dough, kneading as little as possible.

Roll out 1 cm (½ inch) thick for soft cookies, 5 mm (¼ inch) thick for medium crisp, and 3 mm (⅛ inch) for very crisp. Cut out with a 6 cm (2½ inch) cutter and bake in a preheated 190°C (375°F or Mark 5) oven for about 10 minutes. If stored as soon as cool, crisp cookies remain crisp and soft cookies soft.

IMOGENE WOLCOTT (EDITOR)
THE YANKEE COOK BOOK

Honey Kisses

Pierniczki Caluski

To make about 36

3 tbsp	honey	3 tbsp
½ tsp	cloves, crushed in a mortar	½ tsp
½ tsp	ground cinnamon	½ tsp
3 tbsp	water	3 tbsp
300 g	flour	10 oz
20 g	butter or lard	⅔ oz
100 g	icing sugar	3½ oz
1	egg	1
1 tbsp	bicarbonate of soda	1 tbsp

Brown the honey in a saucepan with the cloves and cinnamon. Add 1 tablespoon of the water and allow to cool. Sift the flour on to a pastry board, leaving a little aside to use for rolling out. Add the fat to the flour, chop finely, and mix in the icing sugar. Add the honey and egg. Dissolve the soda in the remaining water, add and mix well. Knead the dough until it is smooth. Divide in half and roll out each half thickly. Cut out biscuits with a small glass. Arrange them on a greased baking sheet, allowing space between them as they spread during baking. Bake the biscuits in a preheated 200°C (400°F or Mark 6) oven for 12 minutes.

ZOFIA CZERNY AND MARIA STRASBURGER
ZYWIENIE RODZINY

Honey Crackers

These are good, but not sweet. If a sweeter biscuit is desired, they should be iced with a mixture of 1 tablespoon of lemon juice and 125 g (4 oz) of icing sugar.

To make about 30

2 tbsp	honey	2 tbsp
250 g	flour	8 oz
$\frac{1}{4}$ tsp	salt	$\frac{1}{4}$ tsp
$\frac{1}{2}$ tsp	allspice	$\frac{1}{2}$ tsp
$\frac{2}{3}$ tsp	bicarbonate of soda	$\frac{2}{3}$ tsp
1 tsp	grated lemon rind	1 tsp
1 tsp	lemon juice	1 tsp
2	eggs	2

Mix the dry ingredients; add the lemon rind, juice, honey and eggs. Beat well. Roll thin and cut into rounds. Bake on a greased baking sheet in a preheated 180°C (350°F or Mark 4) oven for 15 minutes.

LOIS LINTNER SUMPTION AND MARGUERITE LINTNER ASHBROOK
AROUND-THE-WORLD COOKY BOOK

Honey Biscuits

To make about 20

250 g	honey	8 oz
250 g	cornmeal	8 oz
2 tbsp	crystallized orange flowers	2 tbsp
$\frac{1}{2}$ tbsp	pounded coriander seeds	$\frac{1}{2}$ tbsp

Place all the ingredients in a basin and mix well until they form a stiff paste. Divide into portions, shape them into balls about 2.5 cm (1 inch) in diameter, then with a rolling pin roll out to thin oval shapes and trim the edges. Lay the biscuits on a buttered and floured baking sheet a short distance from each other, and bake in a preheated 170°C (325°F or Mark 3) oven for 20 minutes or until lightly browned. When cooked, leave them until cold and if they are to be kept, put them into airtight containers.

OSCAR TSCHIRKY
"OSCAR" OF THE WALDORF'S COOK BOOK

Brandy Snap Curls

To make about 84

3 tbsp	brandy	3 tbsp
12.5 cl	molasses or black treacle	4 fl oz
125 g	butter	4 oz
150 g	flour, sifted	5 oz
1 tsp	salt	1 tsp
165 g	sugar	$5\frac{1}{2}$ oz
1 tbsp	ground ginger	1 tbsp

In a saucepan, heat the molasses to a simmer. Add the butter and stir until the butter is melted. Remove from the heat and stir in the flour, salt, sugar, ginger and brandy.

Oil a baking sheet and drop half teaspoonfuls of the mixture on to the sheet about 7.5 cm (3 inches) apart, making six at a time. Bake in a preheated 150°C (300°F or Mark 2) oven for about 10 minutes. Remove from the oven, cool the wafers for 1 minute, then remove them with a spatula and immediately roll round the handle of a wooden spoon. If removed too soon, the wafers will crush and crinkle; if not soon enough, they will be too brittle to roll. If too brittle, return to the oven for a few minutes to soften.

Repeat until all of the mixture is used, lightly oiling the baking sheet each time with a paper towel and removing any crumbs at the same time.

ANN SERANNE
THE JOY OF GIVING HOMEMADE FOOD

Brandy Snaps

To make about 20

1 tsp	brandy	1 tsp
60 g	butter	2 oz
60 g	sugar	2 oz
2 tbsp	molasses or black treacle	2 tbsp
60 g	flour	2 oz
	salt	
$\frac{1}{2}$ tsp	ground ginger	$\frac{1}{2}$ tsp
$\frac{1}{2}$ tsp	lemon juice	$\frac{1}{2}$ tsp
12.5 cl	double cream, whipped	4 fl oz

Melt the butter, sugar and molasses; allow the mixture to cool. Sift in the flour, a pinch of salt and the ginger. Mix in the lemon juice and brandy. Drop the batter a tablespoonful at a time 10 cm (4 inches) apart on a well-greased baking sheet. Bake in a preheated 170°C (325°F or Mark 3) oven for 7 to 8 minutes or until brown. Remove the sheet from the oven and, after waiting about 1 minute, roll each biscuit carefully round the handle of a wooden spoon, forming a cylinder. Transfer to a plate and allow to cool completely. Fill with the whipped cream just before serving.

J. HOPE NORMAN AND LOUISE A. SIMON (EDITORS)
LOUISIANA ENTERTAINS

—————◆—————

Brandy Snaps or Gauffres

Bake these biscuits in small batches, so that they do not have time to cool and become brittle before they are shaped.

These are delicious filled with ginger-flavoured cream.

To make about 90

1 tbsp	brandy	1 tbsp
125 g	lard or butter, melted	4 oz
500 g	soft brown sugar	1 lb
500 g	flour	1 lb
$\frac{1}{4}$	nutmeg, grated	$\frac{1}{4}$
6	eggs, well beaten	6
1 tbsp	water	1 tbsp

Heat the lard or butter and the sugar together over a low heat until the sugar has dissolved, then mix the ingredients to a soft, dropping batter. Drop two teaspoonfuls for each biscuit on to greased baking sheets, leaving plenty of room for the biscuits to spread (each amount should spread out to saucer size). Bake in an oven preheated to 200°C (400°F or Mark 6) for 10 minutes. Take the baking sheet from the oven, remove the biscuits one by one and wrap them quickly round a stick or the handle of a wooden spoon. They dry and become crisp quickly with a shiny surface; they should be pale toffee-coloured and full of airholes.

DOROTHY HARTLEY
FOOD IN ENGLAND

—————◆—————

Lace Molasses Wafers

To make 50 to 60

12.5 cl	molasses or black treacle	4 fl oz
125 g	sugar	4 oz
125 g	butter	4 oz
125 g	flour	4 oz
$\frac{1}{2}$ tsp	baking powder	$\frac{1}{2}$ tsp
$\frac{1}{4}$ tsp	bicarbonate of soda	$\frac{1}{4}$ tsp

Slowly heat the molasses, sugar and butter to boiling point. Boil for 1 minute and remove from the heat. Sift together the flour, baking powder and bicarbonate of soda and add. Stir

well. Set the pan in a vessel of hot water to keep the batter from hardening. Drop quarter teaspoonfuls of the batter 7.5 cm (3 inches) apart on buttered baking sheets or inverted baking tins. Bake in a preheated 180°C (350°F or Mark 4) oven until brown, about 10 minutes. Cool slightly, then lift carefully with a thin knife. If desired, roll round the handle of a spoon to shape while still warm.

IMOGENE WOLCOTT (EDITOR)
THE YANKEE COOK BOOK

Semolina Pastries

Pâtisserie à la Semoule

Rose-water or orange-flower water can be substituted for the distilled geranium water. Another way to test the consistency of the syrup is to trickle a very little from a spoon; if the syrup makes a thin thread, it is ready.

To make about 60

1.5 kg	fine semolina	3 lb
100 g	sesame seeds	$3\frac{1}{2}$ oz
1 kg	castor sugar	2 to $2\frac{1}{2}$ lb
2 tbsp	lemon juice	3 tbsp
2 tbsp	distilled geranium water	2 tbsp

Brown the semolina in a preheated 180°C (350°F or Mark 4) oven for 15 minutes, turning frequently, or place on a metal tray over a low heat and stir constantly. Toast the sesame seeds in a dry pan over a medium heat, turning them constantly until they brown.

Place the sugar in a pan, cover with water, add the lemon juice and place over the heat. Allow to heat up. From time to time extract a small quantity of syrup between thumb and forefinger. Part your fingers. If the syrup stretches out in a thread, remove the pan from the heat. Otherwise, continue. As soon as the syrup is ready, flavour with the geranium water, pour in the toasted semolina and mix together. Spread the mixture evenly on a baking sheet lined with greaseproof paper. Sprinkle with the sesame seeds and leave to cool, then cut into slices and serve.

MOHAMED KOUKI
LA CUISINE TUNISIENNE D'"OMMOK SANNAFA"

—————◆—————

Graham Crackers

These crackers have a grainy texture and a full wheat-rye flavour. Keep them for at least 24 hours before serving.

To make 24 to 28

140 g	flour	4½ oz
100 g	wholemeal flour	3½ oz
75 g	rye flour	2½ oz
5 tbsp	sugar	5 tbsp
½ tsp	salt	·½ tsp
½ tsp	bicarbonate of soda	½ tsp
1 tsp	baking powder	1 tsp
¼ tsp	ground cinnamon	¼ tsp
40 g	unsalted butter, chilled and cut into small pieces	1½ oz
60 g	solid vegetable fat	2 oz
2 tbsp	honey	2 tbsp
1 tbsp	molasses or black treacle	1 tbsp
4 tbsp	cold water	4 tbsp
1 tsp	vanilla extract	1 tsp

Blend the flour, wholemeal flour, rye flour, sugar, salt, bicarbonate of soda, baking powder and cinnamon in a bowl. With the pastry blender or your fingertips, work in the butter and shortening until small, even particles are formed.

Mix together the honey, molasses, water and vanilla extract in a small bowl. Sprinkle this mixture gradually into the dry ingredients, tossing with a fork until the liquid is evenly incorporated. Press the dough together into a ball. It may be crumbly, but do not add water. Wrap in plastic film and chill for several hours or overnight.

Halve the dough. Let it soften for about 15 minutes.

Sprinkle a sheet of greaseproof paper sparingly with rye flour, place one piece of the dough on top and flatten with a rolling pin. Sprinkle it lightly with rye flour and top with another sheet of greaseproof paper. Roll it out to form a rectangle roughly 18 by 38 cm (7 by 15 inches), rolling slowly and with even pressure so the crumbly dough does not break.

Peel off the top sheet of greaseproof paper and prick the dough all over at 1 to 2.5 cm (½ to 1 inch) intervals, using a skewer or sharp-tined fork. Cut into squares approximately 6 cm (2½ inches) wide. Transfer the squares to a large, ungreased baking sheet with a spatula, placing them very close together—almost touching. Repeat the process with the remaining piece of dough. Re-roll and cut the scraps.

Bake the crackers on the middle shelf of a preheated 180°C (350°F or Mark 4) oven for about 15 minutes, or until they brown lightly on the edges. Transfer to a rack and let cool completely, then store in an airtight container.

HELEN WITTY AND ELIZABETH SCHNEIDER COLCHIE
BETTER THAN STORE-BOUGHT

Oat Crackers

To make about 144

150 g	rolled oats	5 oz
350 g	wholemeal flour	12 oz
⅓ tsp	bicarbonate of soda	⅓ tsp
90 g	honey, warmed	3 oz
1 tsp	salt	1 tsp
125 g	butter	4 oz
17.5 cl	buttermilk, heated	6 fl oz

Mix all the ingredients, except for the buttermilk, and combine them thoroughly. Add the buttermilk to make a biscuit-type dough (a few additional tablespoons of buttermilk may be needed to make a workable dough). Divide the dough in half. Roll it out, one half at a time, between greaseproof paper, to a thickness of 5 mm (¼ inch). Cut the dough into squares or rectangles 2.5 to 4 cm (1 to 1½ inches) across. Prick each one with a fork. Lightly oil a baking sheet and place the crackers on it. Bake them in a preheated 170°C (325°F or Mark 3) oven for about 25 minutes. Store them in an airtight container.

FAYE MARTIN
RODALE'S NATURALLY DELICIOUS DESSERTS AND SNACKS

Country Biscuits

Galletas Campesinas

To make about 60

240 g	fine oatmeal	8 oz
120 g	wholemeal flour	4 oz
50 g	sugar	2 oz
2 tsp	baking powder	2 tsp
	salt	
2	eggs, beaten	2
180 g	honey, melted	6 oz

Put the oatmeal, flour, sugar, baking powder and a pinch of salt in a bowl. Mix well, then form a mound with a well in the centre. Pour in the eggs and honey. Mix and knead thoroughly. Grease and flour a baking sheet; place spoonfuls of the mixture on it, leaving a little space between them. Bake in a preheated 180°C (350°F or Mark 4) oven for 20 minutes.

MARIA DEL CARMEN CASCANTE
MANUAL MODERNO DE PASTELERIA CASERA

Fried Biscuits

Wine Biscuits

Tostones de Monja

To make about 72

17.5 cl	muscatel wine	6 fl oz
500 g	flour	1 lb
17.5 cl	olive oil	6 fl oz
	oil for deep frying	
	icing sugar	
	ground cinnamon	

Mix the flour, olive oil and wine together, and knead to form an elastic dough. Roll the dough out with a rolling pin and cut it into rounds with a pastry cutter. Deep fry the rounds in hot oil. If the dough has been thoroughly worked, the rounds will turn over by themselves when one side has been well fried. Drain the rounds, dust them with icing sugar and ground cinnamon, and serve them hot.

MARIA MESTAYER DE ECHAGÜE (MARQUESA DE PARABERE)
CONFITERIA Y REPOSTERIA

Fried Ribbon Cookies

Crostoli da Friuli

To make 50 to 60

2	eggs	2
60 g	sugar	2 oz
1	lemon, rind grated	1
½ tsp	salt	½ tsp
3 tbsp	grappa or rum	3 tbsp
4 tbsp	milk, warmed	4 tbsp
300 g	flour	10 oz
75 g	butter, melted	2½ oz
	oil for deep frying	
	icing sugar	

Break the eggs into a bowl. Add the sugar, lemon rind, salt and alcohol, and beat thoroughly until light. Stir in 2 tablespoons of the milk. Put the flour into another large bowl and make a well in the middle. Pour in the egg mixture and the butter. Stir to mix well, making a dough that is on the soft side. If necessary, add the remaining milk, a little at a time.

On a lightly floured board, roll out the dough as thin as possible, to a thickness of about 3 mm (⅛ inch). Cut the dough into strips 1 cm (½ inch) wide and 18 cm (7 inches) long. Tie the strips loosely into knots.

Heat the oil to 190°C (375°F) on a cooking thermometer. Fry a few cookies at a time until they are golden and come to the surface. Remove them with a slotted spoon and drain thoroughly on kitchen paper. Sprinkle with icing sugar before serving them on a plate lined with a table napkin.

NIKA HAZELTON
THE REGIONAL ITALIAN KITCHEN

Fried Biscuits

Bignons

If you want even lighter biscuits, add an extra egg and 30 g (1 oz) of fresh yeast, or 1 tablespoon of dried yeast, dissolved in 4 tablespoons of lukewarm milk. Put the ball of dough in a bowl, cover with a cloth and leave to rise in a warm place. Then roll out and cook the dough as below.

To make about 24

250 g	flour	8 oz
3	eggs	3
125 g	sugar	4 oz
50 g	butter, softened	2 oz
2 tbsp	cognac or rum	2 tbsp
	oil for deep frying	

Put the flour on a board and make a well in the centre. Put in the eggs, 50 g (2 oz) of the sugar and the butter. Stir in the cognac or rum. Mix all together, incorporating the flour little by little and kneading to obtain a smooth ball of dough. Leave to rest for about 1 hour.

Roll out the dough about 1 cm (½ inch) thick and cut it into rounds, squares, hearts, etc., according to taste. Drop the biscuits, a few at a time, into hot oil. When they are golden, in about 2 minutes, remove them with a slotted spoon and drain them on kitchen paper. Roll the biscuits in the remaining sugar before serving.

LA CUISINE BOURGUIGNONNE

Fried Biscuits from Lyons

Les Bugnes Comme à Lyon

To make about 40

330 g	flour	11 oz
1 tsp	salt	1 tsp
100 g	castor sugar	3½ oz
60 g	butter	2 oz
3	eggs	3
1 tbsp	baking powder	1 tbsp
	rum	
1	lemon, rind grated	1
	oil for deep frying	

Place the flour on a board, make a well in the centre and put in the salt and half of the sugar. Add the butter, eggs and baking powder, and knead together. Add a few drops of rum and the lemon rind to flavour your dough, which should be fairly firm.

Leave the dough to rest for 1 hour, then roll it out fairly thinly. Cut it into small rectangles and fry them in hot oil for 5 minutes or until golden-brown. Drain and sprinkle with the remaining sugar. The biscuits should be very crisp.

RAYMOND THUILIER AND MICHEL LEMONNIER
LES RECETTES DE BAUMANIÈRE

Fried Pastries

Faramayas

This recipe comes from Galicia, north-west Spain.

To make about 50

250 g	flour	8 oz
	salt	
50 g	castor sugar	2 oz
1	lemon, rind grated	1
50 g	butter	2 oz
2 tbsp	brandy	2 tbsp
1 tbsp	water	1 tbsp
	oil for frying	
	icing sugar	

Sift the flour and a pinch of salt, and blend in the sugar and lemon rind. Lightly rub in the butter, then add the brandy and water, and knead as little as possible to form a dough. Cover with a damp cloth and leave in a cool place for about 2 hours. Roll out very thinly and cut into squares. Leave on a floured baking sheet in a cool place or on a marble top for half an hour. Fry in hot oil about 5 mm (¼ inch) deep until golden-brown, drain well and dust with plenty of icing sugar. The *faramayas* may be eaten hot or cold.

ANNA MACMIADHACHÁIN
SPANISH REGIONAL COOKERY

Rye Drops

To make 30

125 g	rye flour	4 oz
2 tbsp	sugar	2 tbsp
2	eggs, well beaten	2
1 tsp	bicarbonate of soda	1 tsp
35 cl	soured milk	12 fl oz
125 g	flour	4 oz
¼ tsp	salt	¼ tsp
¾ tsp	ground cinnamon	¾ tsp
	oil or fat for deep frying	
	icing sugar mixed with ground cinnamon	

Add the sugar to the beaten eggs and the soda to the soured milk. Combine. Sift together the flours, salt and cinnamon and add. The dough should be stiff enough to drop off the end of a spoon. Drop small spoonfuls into hot oil or fat and fry for 3 to 4 minutes or until puffed and browned. Drain and roll in icing sugar and cinnamon before serving.

ANNETTE LASLETT ROSS AND JEAN ADAMS DISNEY
GOOD COOKIES

Rice Flour Biscuits

Jaggery is coarse brown Indian sugar made from palm-sap.

To make about 40

250 g	rice flour	8 oz
1 tbsp	poppy seeds	1 tbsp
10	cardamom pods, skinned and ground	10
	salt	
300 g	jaggery, grated, or brown sugar	10 oz
½ litre	water	16 fl oz
90 g	*ghee*	3 oz
	double cream	

Mix the flour, poppy seeds, ground cardamom and a pinch of salt in a saucepan. Make a syrup by boiling the sugar and water for a few minutes. Now pour the syrup on to the flour mixture and stir well until a thick doughy mixture is formed. Cover the mixture and keep overnight.

Next day, knead the dough and form it into small balls about 2 cm (¾ inch) in diameter. Flatten each ball to make biscuits. Adding 30 g (1 oz) of *ghee* to the pan at a time, deep fry the biscuits on both sides until golden. Drain the biscuits on kitchen paper and serve with cream.

JACK SANTA MARIA
INDIAN SWEET COOKERY

Date Lozenges

Maqrout'l-farina

To make about 36

	Date paste	
500 g	fresh dates, peeled and stoned	1 lb
	ground cinnamon	
	oil	
	Dough	
750 g	flour	1½ lb
250 g	butter, melted	8 oz
	salt	
About 30 cl	water	About ½ pint
	oil for deep frying	
	Topping	
125 g	honey, melted	4 oz
200 g	sesame seeds or almonds, blanched and ground	7 oz

Put the dates through a meat mincer or the coarse disc of a vegetable mill. Add a pinch of cinnamon and knead well, moistening your hands with oil from time to time. Shape the paste into a ball and set aside.

To prepare the dough, sift the flour on to a pastry board, make a well in the centre and pour in the melted butter and a pinch of salt. Mix well. Knead the mixture, adding water a little at a time, to form a fairly firm, manageable dough. Roll the dough out into a thin sheet. Shape the date paste into a rope the length of the sheet of dough and place on the dough. Roll the paste up in the dough, rolling the dough over on itself two or three times. Flatten the long roll slightly with a *taba'* or *marchame* (a type of small board impressed with a pattern) or, failing that, with a ruler. Cut the roll into lozenges with sides of 5 to 6 cm (2 to 2½ inches). Prick each one with a fork.

Heat the oil in a frying pan. Immerse the lozenges in the oil and fry until golden-brown. Remove from the pan and drain. Pour the melted honey over the lozenges and sprinkle with the sesame seeds or ground almonds.

FATIMA-ZOHRA BOUAYED
LA CUISINE ALGÉRIENNE

Bengali Biscuits

Takti

To make 80 to 90

1 kg	flour	2 lb
1 kg	*ghee*	2 lb
30 cl	water	½ pint
1 kg	sugar	2 lb

Place the flour on a board and, using your fingertips, rub in 250 g (8 oz) of the *ghee* until the mixture is crumbly. Add about 15 cl (¼ pint) of cold water, enough to make a smooth dough. For convenience in working, divide the dough into four batches. Roll out each batch to a thickness of 1 cm (½ inch) and prick it all over with a fork for proper cooking. Cut the dough into pieces about 5 cm (2 inches) square. Gather the trimmings and work them into the remainder of the dough.

Heat the remaining *ghee* and fry the squares in it about five or six at a time. The frying is complete when they are a fawn colour. They must be short and flaky.

Meanwhile, boil the sugar with about 15 cl (¼ pint) of water until the syrup forms threads when dropped from a spoon.

Put the fried biscuits one by one in the syrup; smear each on all sides and lay out on a plate to dry, so that it receives a thin coating of sugar on cooling, like icing sugar on cakes.

MRS. J. HALDAR
BENGAL SWEETS

Twice-Cooked Biscuits

Almond Toast

Mandelbrot

A favourite European café nibble, this crunchy-dry, subtly nutty biscuit is at home with ice cream, dried fruit compotes, espresso, or a glass of light red wine.

To make about 24

175 g	almonds	6 oz
250 g	flour, sifted	8 oz
2½ tsp	baking powder	2½ tsp
½ tsp	salt	½ tsp
¼ tsp	grated nutmeg	¼ tsp
90 g	butter, softened	3 oz
175 g	sugar	6 oz
1 tsp	almond extract	1 tsp
½ tsp	vanilla extract	½ tsp
2	eggs	2

Spread the almonds on a baking sheet and toast them in a preheated 150°C (300°F or Mark 2) oven for 15 minutes, or until barely golden. Remove from the oven and turn the oven heat up to 190°C (375°F or Mark 5).

Sift together the flour, baking powder, salt and nutmeg. Set aside. In a mixing bowl, cream the butter until it is light. Gradually cream in the sugar until the mixture is light and fluffy. Add the almond and vanilla extracts, then beat in the eggs, one at a time. Stir in the flour mixture (on lowest speed, if you are using a mixer). Mix in the almonds thoroughly.

Smooth foil over a baking sheet measuring at least 42 by 28 cm (17 by 11 inches). Spoon two strips of batter on to the sheet, equidistant from each other and the ends of the sheet; they should measure about 22 cm (9 inches) in length and 9 cm (3½ inches) in width. Smooth them and even the sides with a flexible spatula dipped in cold water.

Bake the strips for 15 to 20 minutes, or until they are pale golden. Slide the foil off the sheet and place the strips on a rack to cool for 15 minutes, having first peeled off the foil. Reset the oven heat to 150°C (300°F or Mark 2).

With a very sharp serrated knife, cut the almond toast carefully into slices 2 cm (¾ inch) wide and lay them flat, very close together, on the baking sheet.

Return the biscuits to the oven for 15 minutes, then turn them over and bake for 15 minutes longer, or until they are golden. Cool the almond toast on a rack. Pack in airtight containers; it will keep for a month.

HELEN WITTY AND ELIZABETH SCHNEIDER COLCHIE
BETTER THAN STORE-BOUGHT

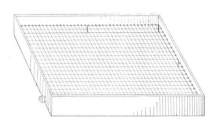

Prato Biscuits

Biscotti di Prato

To make about 150

1 kg	flour	2 lb
1 kg	sugar	2 lb
8	eggs, yolks separated from whites, whites stiffly beaten	8
400 g	almonds, blanched, toasted and chopped	15 oz
100 g	hazelnuts, toasted and chopped	3½ oz
1 tsp	vanilla extract	1 tsp
1	orange, rind grated	1
1 tsp	ammonium bicarbonate	1 tsp

Make a pastry dough by combining the flour and sugar with the egg yolks and whites. Add the nuts and work the dough thoroughly to make it as smooth as possible. Flavour the dough with the vanilla and grated orange rind and add the ammonium bicarbonate to make the mixture light.

Divide the dough into small balls about 5 cm (2 inches) in diameter, shape them into cylinders and flatten them slightly with the palm of your hand. Sprinkle a baking sheet with flour and place the biscuits on it. Bake them in a preheated 200°C (400°F or Mark 6) oven for about 10 minutes. As soon as they change colour, remove from the oven. Reduce the temperature to 180°C (350°F or Mark 4). Let the biscuits cool a little and then cut them like bread into slices 2 cm (¾ inch) thick (make thinner slices if you prefer smaller biscuits).

Return the biscuits to the oven for a further 10 minutes to dry them out and finish baking.

GIOVANNI RIGHI PARENTI
LA GRANDE CUCINA TOSCANA

Russian Biscuits

To make about 80

10	eggs, yolks separated from whites, whites stiffly beaten	10
250 g	castor sugar	8 oz
175 g	flour	6 oz
125 g	ground almonds	4 oz
1 tsp	aniseeds	1 tsp

Whisk the egg yolks and sugar together in a bowl set over simmering water until they present the appearance of a thick batter; lightly stir in the whites, as also the flour, ground almonds and aniseeds. Turn the batter into long, greased tin moulds or, failing these, in stout paper cases 25 cm (10 inches) long by 7.5 cm (3 inches) deep and 6 cm (2½ inches) wide. Bake in a preheated 180°C (350°F or Mark 4) oven for 30 minutes or until lightly browned.

When they are baked, and have been allowed to become thoroughly cold, cut them into rather thin slices, which, being placed on baking sheets, should be again baked for 15 minutes or until of a very light colour on both sides.

FRANCATELLI'S THE MODERN COOK

Jaw-Breakers

Sciappa Denti

To make about 100

1 kg	flour	2 to 2½ lb
30 g	fresh yeast or 1 tbsp dried yeast, dissolved in 3 tbsp warm water	1 oz
250 g	butter, softened	8 oz
6	eggs, yolks separated from whites, yolks slightly beaten, whites stiffly beaten	6
½ litre	milk, warmed	16 fl oz
1 kg	sugar	2 to 2½ lb
2 tbsp	*eau-de-vie* or brandy	2 tbsp
125 g	almonds, blanched, toasted and finely chopped	4 oz
1	orange, rind grated	1
2	egg yolks, beaten with 2 tbsp water	2

Place the flour in a large bowl and make a well in the centre. Add the yeast, butter, the six beaten egg yolks, milk, sugar, *eau-de-vie*, almonds and grated rind. Fold in the egg whites.

Cover the bowl with a cloth and leave for 30 minutes. Cut off chunks of the dough and form them into cylinders about 5 cm (2 inches) thick. Place the cylinders on an oiled baking sheet and bake in a preheated 180°C (350°F or Mark 4) oven for 10 minutes. Brush the cylinders with the egg yolk mixture and bake for an additional 5 minutes or until golden-brown. Cut the cylinders diagonally into 1 cm (½ inch) slices, place the slices flat on the baking sheet and bake for a further 10 minutes or until they are dry and crisp.

MARIA NUNZIA FILIPPINI
LA CUISINE CORSE

Lenten Biscuits from Palermo

Quaresimali

To make about 250

1.6 kg	flour	3½ lb
450 g	sugar	15 oz
50 g	whole pistachio nuts	2 oz
100 g	orange rind, diced	3½ oz
½ tsp	bicarbonate of soda	½ tsp
1 tsp	ammonium bicarbonate	1 tsp
7	eggs	7
1 tsp	cinnamon extract or 2 tsp ground cinnamon	1 tsp

Work all the ingredients together. Divide the dough into two and roll out each piece to fit two 35 cm (18 inch) square greased and floured baking tins. Bake in a preheated 170°C (325°F or Mark 3) oven for 20 minutes. Remove from the oven, cut into slices and return the baking tins to the heat until the slices are golden, about 10 minutes.

PINO CORRENTI
IL LIBRO D'ORO DELLA CUCINA E DEI VINI DI SICILIA

Zwieback

These crisp toasts are marvellous with *café au lait* or at teatime. Store them in airtight containers. They will keep almost indefinitely.

To make 90 to 100

125 g	sugar	4 oz
30 g	fresh yeast or 1 tbsp dried yeast	1 oz
4 tbsp	warm water	4 tbsp
½ litre	milk	16 fl oz
175 g	unsalted butter	6 oz
1 tsp	salt	1 tsp
¼ tsp	ground cinnamon	¼ tsp
⅛ tsp	grated nutmeg	⅛ tsp
¼ tsp	ground mace	¼ tsp
3	eggs, beaten	3
140 g	light or medium rye flour	4½ oz
About 750 to 800 g	unbleached flour	About 1½ to 1¾ lb

Stir together 1 teaspoon of sugar, the yeast and the water in a small bowl. The mixture will rise to several times its original volume while you continue.

In a saucepan, heat together the milk, the remaining sugar, 125 g (4 oz) of the butter and the salt just until the butter has melted. Then cool to 38°C (100°F) or until the mixture feels barely warm.

Combine the milk mixture and the yeast mixture in a large bowl. Stir in the cinnamon, nutmeg and mace, then beat in the eggs, then the rye flour.

A cupful at a time, beat in as much as possible of the unbleached flour. When the dough is too stiff to stir, turn out on to a pastry board dusted with flour and knead in the remaining flour, or as much as necessary to make a smooth, elastic, medium dough, not too stiff. Knead thoroughly for 5 to 10 minutes. Gather the dough into a ball.

Lightly butter a large bowl and turn the ball of dough about in the butter to coat all surfaces. Cover the bowl with plastic film and let the dough rise until doubled in bulk, about 1½ hours. Punch the dough down to expel air, cover again, and let it rise again until doubled, about 45 minutes.

Turn the dough out on to a floured pastry board, knead it a few strokes to expel air, and divide it into five equal parts. Form each part into a smooth cylinder about 25 cm (10 inches) long, rolling the pieces under the palms of your hands.

Lay the cylindrical loaves crosswise on a large, generously buttered baking sheet (about 43 by 28 cm or 17 by 11 inches), leaving 5 cm (2 inches) between them and 2.5 cm (1 inch) of space at the end of the pan. Melt the remaining 50 g (2 oz) of butter. Brush all surfaces of the loaves with the melted butter. Let the loaves rise again in a warm place until they have almost doubled in bulk.

Bake the loaves in the centre of a preheated 180°C (350°F or Mark 4) oven until they are firm and golden and sound hollow when the bottoms are tapped. Remove them from the baking sheet and cool them on wire racks.

When the loaves are almost cool, reheat the oven to 100°C (200°F or under Mark ¼). Slice the cylinders slightly on the bias into 1 cm (½ inch) slices, about 18 to a loaf. Lay the slices flat, close together, on baking sheets or cake racks and dry them in the preheated oven until they are dry throughout; then raise the oven temperature to 150°C (300°F or Mark 2) and allow them to brown delicately, watching closely lest they overbrown. Cool the zwieback on wire racks.

HELEN WITTY AND ELIZABETH SCHNEIDER COLCHIE
BETTER THAN STORE-BOUGHT

Ring Biscuits

Gimblettes d'Albi

To make 50 to 60

500 g	flour	1 lb
50 g	butter, softened and diced	2 oz
	salt	
50 g	sugar	2 oz
30 g	aniseeds	1 oz
20 g	fresh yeast or 1 tsp dried yeast, dissolved in 4 tbsp tepid water	⅔ oz
6	eggs	6

Put the flour in a bowl. Make a well in the centre and add the butter, a pinch of salt, the sugar, aniseeds and yeast. Mix these ingredients together. Add the eggs, one at a time. Knead the dough until smooth and elastic, and leave it to rise in a warm place for 2 hours. Roll out the dough and cut it into rings or triangles with a knife or biscuit cutter. Bring a large pot of water to the boil and drop in the biscuits. As they rise to the surface, take them out and plunge them into cold water. Drain them, place them on a greased baking sheet and bake in a preheated 200°C (400°F or Mark 6) oven for 20 minutes.

NICOLE VIELFAURE AND A. CHRISTINE BEAUVIALA
FÊTES, COUTUMES ET GÂTEAUX

Cracknel Biscuits

Craquelins

This Breton pastry is one of the oldest and most popular in all Brittany; it is also distributed throughout France.

These biscuits may be eaten, as they are, with milk or cider, or they may be garnished with pastry cream and fruits such as cherries in syrup or apple compote. They can also be joined together in twos with a filling.

To make about 60		
30 g	fresh yeast or 1 tbsp dried yeast	1 oz
12.5 cl	warm water	4 fl oz
1 kg	flour	2¼ lb
8	eggs	8
	salt	

Cream the yeast in the water. Make a well in 750 g (1½ lb) of the flour and put the eggs, a pinch of salt and the yeast solution into the well. Knead with your hands, then leave the dough to rest and rise for 1 hour in a warm place.

Rework the dough with a rolling pin; add the remaining flour. Roll out for a second time and cut the dough into 10 cm (4 inch) squares. Bring the four points together on the underside of each square and flatten the top. Smooth with a knife; there should be no roughness.

Bring a large saucepan of water to the simmer. Add the squares; they will rise to the surface one after another. As soon as this happens, take them out. They will be hollow on one side and bulging on the other.

Allow them to cool a little, then dip them into a large bowl of cold water for 30 minutes. Drain, hollow side down. Then bake the biscuits in a preheated 180°C (250°F or Mark 4) oven for 10 minutes to brown them.

LA CUISINE BRETONNE

Poached Biscuits

Echaudés

To make 12		
50 g	granulated sugar	2 oz
	salt	
15 cl	water	¼ pint
5 tbsp	olive oil	5 tbsp
250 g	flour, sifted	8 oz
1	egg yolk	1

Dissolve the sugar and a pinch of salt in the water. Add the olive oil and stir vigorously. Make a well in the centre of the flour and add all the other ingredients. Work the mixture quickly with your fingertips.

Divide the mixture into two and, on a pastry board, push each piece of dough away from you with the heel of the hand. Fold it and repeat the action once more. Then roll all the dough into a ball and leave it to rest in a cool place for 2 hours, wrapped in plastic film or a cloth.

Take small pieces of dough, weighing about 30 g (1 oz) each, and shape them into balls. Flatten them gently and press three fingers into the top to mark a crease.

Fill a large saucepan with water and bring it to the boil. Poach the biscuits in the boiling water, a few at a time, removing them with a slotted spoon when they rise to the surface. Drain them, place on a cloth and leave to dry for 2 hours. Then bake on a greased baking sheet in a preheated 220°C (425°F or Mark 7) oven for about 20 minutes.

DOMINIQUE WEBER
LES BONNES RECETTES DES PROVINCES DE FRANCE

Boiled Biscuits

Obwarzanki Gotowane

To make about 12		
275 g	flour	9 oz
80 g	sugar	3 oz
½ tsp	salt	½ tsp
3	eggs, lightly beaten	3
2	egg yolks, lightly beaten	2
30 g	poppy seeds	1 oz

Mix together the flour, sugar and salt, and add the eggs to make a dough. On a pastry board, roll the dough into ropes with the palms of your hands and join the ends to form small wreaths 6 cm (2½ inches) in diameter. Drop the biscuits into a saucepan of boiling water, a few at a time, for 2 minutes, then transfer them to a baking sheet heated in the oven. Brush the tops with the egg yolks, then sprinkle with the poppy seeds. Bake the biscuits in a preheated 200°C (400°F or Mark 6) oven for 7 minutes or until golden-brown.

MARJA DISSLOWA
JAK GOTOWAĆ

Savoury Biscuits

Norwegian Flatbread

Flattbröd

In the demonstration on page 86, barley flour is substituted for the rye flour used here. The dough is given a resting period after it has been kneaded to make it easier to roll out. If you are in a hurry, this step can be omitted.

Flatbread has been made in Norway for centuries—vast quantities were prepared to be stored for the winter months. It has always been regarded as something of a ritual and in the old days a table was specially kept for making the flatbread—often hung up under the beams of the farm kitchen and lowered for the performance! This particular flatbread makes an excellent cheese biscuit.

Flatbread can be made with almost any mixture of flours and with vegetables too, in the proportion of one-fifth flour to four-fifths sieved, cooked root vegetables, which should be mixed, kneaded well together and made as below.

To make 8

225 g	rye flour	8 oz
225 g	wholemeal flour	8 oz
About ½ tsp	salt	About ½ tsp
About 35 cl	lukewarm water	About 12 fl oz

Sift the flours and salt into a bowl. Stir in sufficient lukewarm water with a wooden spoon to mix to a fairly soft dough. Turn out on to a floured surface and knead well for about 15 minutes or until a little of the dough rolled into a sausage and then bent in half will not crack. Place the dough in a greased bowl, cover the bowl with a folded, damp tea towel and leave the dough to rest for at least 2 hours.

Divide the rested dough into eight equal pieces and roll each piece into a round approximately 25 cm (10 inches) in diameter. Prick each round with a fork. Heat a griddle or large frying pan and when it is very hot place one of the rounds on it. Cook the bread until it is starting to brown in spots on the underside, then turn it over and brown the other side. Now reduce the heat and keep turning the bread until it becomes crisp. Repeat this process with all the rounds. If preferred, the rounds may be placed on baking sheets, pricked well and baked in a preheated 220°C (425°F or Mark 7) oven for about 20 minutes until slightly brown and crisp.

LORNA WALKER AND JOYCE HUGHES
THE COMPLETE BREAD BOOK

Rye Crackers

To make about 30

150 g	stone-ground whole rye flour	5 oz
30 g	fresh yeast or 1 tbsp dried yeast	1 oz
½ tsp	salt	½ tsp
12.5 cl	warm water	4 fl oz
1 tsp	caraway seeds	1 tsp

In a mixing bowl, mix together the yeast, salt and water; add the seeds and flour and mix until you have a cohesive ball.

Put the mixture on a large greased baking sheet and with a rolling pin roll out to about 3 mm (⅛ inch) or less.

Cover with a clean dry towel and set in a warm place for about 1 hour to rise a bit. Do not look for rise; it is too slight to be visible. After the hour, remove the towel, score the mixture with a sharp knife into rectangles and place the baking sheet in a cold oven. Set the heat for very low (under 130°C, 250°F or Mark ½) and bake for 15 minutes. Raise the heat to 180°C (350°F or Mark 4) and bake until crisp and done—perhaps another 15 minutes.

STAN AND FLOSS DWORKIN
THE GOOD GOODIES

Scotch Oatcakes

The scraps which are left over from cutting should be put back into the basin, and made up again.

To make 4 to 6

75 g	fine oatmeal	2½ oz
	salt	
	bicarbonate of soda	
1 tsp	butter or bacon fat, melted	1 tsp
About 8 cl	hot water	About 3 fl oz

Put the oatmeal, with a pinch each of salt and of bicarbonate of soda, into a basin, add the fat and enough water to make a softish paste. Turn this out on a board that has been well sprinkled with oatmeal. Flatten out with your hand or roll with a rolling pin until very thin. Rub over with more oatmeal and cut round with a saucepan lid. Then cut into four or six pieces and slide the cakes carefully on to a hot griddle. Cook them over a medium heat until they begin to curl up, then toast them in front of a fire or under a grill for 1 to 2 minutes, or put them on a baking sheet in a preheated 180°C (350°F or Mark 4) oven for a few minutes until dry and crisp.

FLORENCE B. JACK
COOKERY FOR EVERY HOUSEHOLD

Donegal Oatcake

According to local tradition Donegal oatcake was toasted on an iron stand called a breadiron, also known as a harnen (hardening) stand. The oatcake was put on the stand to toast very slowly for several hours at some distance from the open peat fire. The process is really more of a drying-out operation than toasting proper.

Oatcake keeps well and can be reheated—always at a minimum temperature—as often as you please. The only disadvantages of oatcake are the speed with which it disappears, and the crumbs left scattered all over the table and the floor after an oatcake meal.

Eat the oatcake for breakfast or tea with cold creamy butter. It is wonderfully good also with fresh cream cheese.

To make 1 or 2

500 g	fine oatmeal	1 lb
2 tsp	salt	2 tsp
30 to 60 g	butter or lard	1 to 2 oz
About 45 cl	boiling water	About $\frac{3}{4}$ pint

Put the oatmeal into a mixing bowl, the salt and fat into a measuring jug. Over the latter pour boiling water. Stir until the fat and salt are dissolved. Pour this mixture into the oatmeal. A little more or a little less water may be needed to mix the oatmeal into a pliable cake, which at this stage resembles nothing so much as a mud pie. This is now left overnight, or at least for several hours, until it is dry enough to press out, very thin and flat, into an ungreased baking tin, at least 30 by 20 cm (12 by 8 inches). After a little practice at making oatcake, you find that it can be pressed out almost as thin as card, and then two tins will be needed.

Before baking the oatcake, leave it again to dry out for an hour or two. Press it once more and even out the top with a palette knife or spatula.

Put the tin or tins at the bottom of the slowest possible oven, 130° to 140°C (250° to 275°F or Mark $\frac{1}{2}$ to 1), and leave them for a minimum of 3 hours and longer if it happens to be convenient. Too high a temperature will ruin oatcake; the longer the drying out at a very low temperature, the better it will be. Break the oatcake into wedges to serve it.

ELIZABETH DAVID
ENGLISH BREAD AND YEAST COOKERY

Orford's Water Biscuits

To make about 24

250 g	flour	8 oz
$\frac{1}{2}$ tsp	salt	$\frac{1}{2}$ tsp
1 tsp	baking powder	1 tsp
60 g	lard	2 oz
	water	
	coarse salt	

Sift the flour with the salt and baking powder and rub in the lard finely. Moisten with water to make a firm dough. Roll out very thinly, prick all over with a fork and stamp into large rounds. Sprinkle with coarse salt and bake in a preheated 180°C (350°F or Mark 4) oven for 10 to 15 minutes until the edges are pale golden in colour.

CONSTANCE SPRY AND ROSEMARY HUME
THE CONSTANCE SPRY COOKERY BOOK

Bath Oliver Biscuits

The technique of rolling and folding puff pastry dough is the same as that for rough-puff dough, shown on page 26.

This Biscuit, excellent against indigestion, owed its name to Dr. Oliver, a famous physician of Bath, the friend of Pope, Warburton, and other 18th-century notabilities. When on his deathbed (1749), the doctor called for his coachman and gave him the recipe for such Biscuits, also 10 sacks of flour and 100 sovereigns. The fortunate fellow started a shop, whereat the Biscuits were made, and sold, in Green Street, Bath.

To make about 30

60 g	butter	2 oz
15 cl	milk	$\frac{1}{4}$ pint
	salt	
30 g	fresh yeast or 1 tbsp dried yeast	1 oz
350 g	flour	12 oz

Stir the butter and milk in a saucepan over a gentle heat until the butter is melted; cool to tepid and add a pinch of salt and the yeast. Let the mixture stand for 10 minutes or until the yeast foams. Mix the flour in very smoothly; knead the mixture well, wrap it in a warmed cloth, put it into a bowl, and place it on a warm hearth for 15 minutes.

Roll out the dough eight or nine times, folding it in thirds after each rolling as for puff pastry. Finally roll it out 5mm ($\frac{1}{4}$ inch) thick. Stamp it into biscuits with an ordinary cutter; prick them well with a fork, and bake them on baking sheets in a preheated 180°C (350°F or Mark 4) oven until the biscuits are lightly browned, say, about 30 minutes.

W. T. FERNIE
MEALS MEDICINAL WITH "HERBAL SIMPLES"

Cream Wafers

Serve these cream wafers with the salad course, or as an accompaniment to five o'clock tea.

To make about 24

175 g	flour	6 oz
1 tsp	salt	1 tsp
About 12.5 cl	double cream	About 4 fl oz

Mix and sift the flour and salt. Add, gradually, enough cream to make a dough. Toss on to a lightly floured cloth and knead until smooth. Pat and roll as thin as possible. Prick with a fork and shape with a small round or fancy cutter, first dipped in flour. Arrange the wafers on a buttered baking sheet and bake them in a preheated 180°C (350°F or Mark 4) oven until delicately browned, about 15 minutes.

FANNIE MERRITT FARMER
THE BOSTON COOKING-SCHOOL COOK BOOK

Biscuits with Cracklings and White Wine

Pogaćice Sa Ćvarcima I Belim Vinom

Pork cracklings are made from fresh pork fat, cut into cubes and fried in a large pan with a small amount of milk. When the cubes have turned golden-brown, the liquid fat is poured off and the remaining cracklings are salted while still hot.

To make about 80

175 g	pork cracklings, finely chopped	6 oz
12.5 cl	white wine	4 fl oz
250 g	flour	8 oz
3	egg yolks	3
1 tbsp	dried yeast, dissolved in 12.5 cl (4 fl oz) milk	1 tbsp
	salt and pepper	
60 g	lard, melted	2 oz

Mix the cracklings with the flour. Add the egg yolks, dissolved yeast, salt, pepper and white wine. Knead the dough well. Let stand in a cool place for 30 minutes. Roll the dough out to form a square about 1 cm (½ inch) thick. Brush with lard, fold like a book and roll out again. Repeat this three times, each time allowing the dough to rest for 30 minutes. Finally, roll the dough out until it is less than 2.5 cm (1 inch) thick. Cut into rounds, using a small glass or plain cutter. With a knife, score small squares on top of each biscuit. Bake in a preheated 230°C (450°F or Mark 8) oven for 25 minutes. Serve hot.

INGE KRAMARZ
THE BALKAN COOKBOOK

Poppy Seed Crackers

To make about 96

60 g	poppy seeds	2 oz
6 tbsp	boiling water	6 tbsp
250 g	wholemeal flour	8 oz
½ tsp	bicarbonate of soda	½ tsp
1½ tsp	salt	1½ tsp
⅓ tsp	freshly ground black pepper	⅓ tsp
6 tbsp	oil	6 tbsp
1 tsp	honey	1 tsp
1	egg, lightly beaten	1
60 g	onion, finely chopped	2 oz

In a small bowl, add the poppy seeds to the boiling water; leave to stand until cool. Sift together the flour, bicarbonate of soda, salt and pepper. Add the oil, honey, egg, onion and poppy seed mixture. Stir until a stiff dough forms. Knead this lightly until it is smooth and shape it into two balls.

Roll the dough out 3 mm (⅛ inch) thick on a lightly floured board and cut the dough into rounds with a 4 cm (1½ inch) biscuit cutter. Place the crackers on an ungreased baking sheet and prick each one with a fork. Bake the crackers in a preheated 220°C (425°F or Mark 7) oven for 10 to 12 minutes or until lightly browned. Store them in an airtight container.

FAYE MARTIN
RODALE'S NATURALLY DELICIOUS DESSERTS AND SNACKS

Sesame Seed Wafers

For powdered caraway seeds, pound 1 teaspoon of seeds in a mortar or wrap them in muslin and pound with a rolling pin.

To make about 30

75 g	sesame seeds	2½ oz
250 g	flour, sifted	8 oz
200 g	butter	7 oz
½ tsp	salt	½ tsp
½ tsp	powdered caraway seeds	½ tsp
4 tsp	iced water	4 tsp

Sprinkle the sesame seeds on a baking sheet and toast them in a preheated 180°C (350°F or Mark 4) oven until they are golden-brown, 5 to 10 minutes. Leave them to cool.

Mix together the flour, 175 g (6 oz) of the butter and the salt. Chop with two knives or with a pastry blender until the pieces are about the size of small beans. Add the caraway seeds and mix well. Add the water, a few drops at a time, and toss with a fork. Gather the dough up with your hands and shape it into a ball. Roll it out 1 cm (½ inch) thick on a lightly floured board. Spread the rolled-out dough with the remaining butter, softened. Fold the dough in thirds and press the ends together. Chill for at least 30 minutes.

Roll out again 1 cm ($\frac{1}{2}$ inch) thick. Sprinkle with the sesame seeds and roll them lightly into the dough. Cut with a biscuit cutter about 5 cm (2 inches) in diameter. Place the wafers on an ungreased baking sheet. Bake in a preheated 180°C (350°F or Mark 4) over for 15 to 20 minutes or until golden.

ANTHONY MILLER (EDITOR)
GOOD FOOD FROM SINGAPORE

Indian Fenugreek Crackers

Kasoori Mathari

Dried fenugreek leaves and Indian vegetable ghee can be bought in Asian food stores.

These crackers should rest for two to three days before being served, for the full-bodied aroma of fenugreek to penetrate.

To make about 80

30 g	dried fenugreek leaves (*kasoori methi*)	1 oz
300 g	flour	10 oz
2 tsp	salt	2 tsp
60 g	butter, chilled and cut into tiny cubes	2 oz
60 g	vegetable *ghee*, chilled	2 oz
12.5 cl	water	4 fl oz

In a large bowl, crumble the fenugreek leaves to a rough powder. Add the flour and salt and mix thoroughly. Add the butter and *ghee* and mix in with your fingertips until they are evenly distributed in the flour, with no lumps of butter.

Pour the cold water, about 1 tablespoon at a time, over the flour mixture until it can be gathered into a mass. Place the dough on a floured marble surface or wooden board and knead briefly (about 1 minute) to make a soft, smooth ball. Divide the dough into four equal portions and shape each one into a ball. Place one on the work board and keep the remaining ones covered with plastic film or a moist tea-cloth to prevent a crust forming. Dust each ball in turn lightly with flour and roll it into a 25 cm (10 inch) circle.

Cut the crackers out with a 4 cm (1$\frac{1}{2}$ inch) round or fancy-shaped biscuit cutter. Prick the crackers all over with a fork to prevent them from puffing up during baking. Line two large baking sheets with aluminium foil and place the crackers on them 2 cm ($\frac{3}{4}$ inch) apart. Bake them in the middle of a preheated 190°C (375°F or Mark 5) oven for 10 minutes, until a few light brown spots appear on the underside. Gently turn the crackers with a spatula and bake them for 5 minutes more or until they are lightly browned on the edges.

Transfer the crackers to wire racks and cool them thoroughly before storing them in airtight containers.

JULIE SAHNI
CLASSIC INDIAN COOKING

Caraway, Salt and Cheese Straws

Kümmel, Salz und Käsestangen

To make about 100

	caraway seeds	
	coarse salt	
	grated Cheddar or Gruyère cheese	
	paprika	
250 g	flour	8 oz
	salt	
125 g	butter	4 oz
5 tbsp	soured cream	5 tbsp
1	egg yolk, beaten	1

Place the flour in a bowl with a pinch of salt, cut in the butter until the mixture has the texture of coarse meal, and stir in the soured cream to make a soft, crumbly dough. Chill the dough for about half an hour in the refrigerator. Roll out 5 mm ($\frac{1}{4}$ inch) thick and coat with beaten egg yolk.

For caraway straws, sprinkle the dough with 1 tablespoon caraway seeds and 2 teaspoons coarse salt; for salt straws, sprinkle the dough with 1 tablespoon coarse salt and 2 teaspoons paprika; for cheese straws, sprinkle with 75 g (3 oz) grated cheese and 2 teaspoons paprika. Cut the dough into small straws. Bake in a preheated 200°C (400°F or Mark 6) oven for 12 minutes or until golden.

HEDWIG MARIA STUBER
ICH HELF DIR KOCHEN

Cheese Straws

Brins de Paille

To make about 20

60 g	Gruyère cheese, grated	2 oz
60 g	flour	2 oz
60 g	butter	2 oz
	salt	
2 tbsp	milk	2 tbsp

Place the cheese, flour, butter and a pinch of salt in a bowl, and stir in the milk. Knead the mixture with your hands until it forms a smooth dough; finish by kneading it lightly on a pastry board. Roll the dough into long strips the thickness of a pencil. Cut the strips into sections of equal length and place them on a buttered and floured baking sheet. Bake in a preheated 220°C (425°F or Mark 7) oven for 5 minutes. They will be golden-brown and are delicious eaten hot.

PIERRE HUGUENIN
LES MEILLEURES RECETTES DE MA PAUVRE MÈRE

Ramekins à l'Ude or Sefton Fancies

To make about 30

250 g	rough-puff dough (*page 165*)	8 oz
125 g	Cheddar or Gruyère cheese, grated	4 oz
1	egg yolk, mixed with 2 tbsp milk	1

Roll out the dough rather thinly. Sprinkle the cheese equally over the dough, fold it together, roll it out very lightly twice and continue thus until the cheese and dough are well mixed. Finally, roll out about 5 mm (¼ inch) thick. Cut the ramekins with a small biscuit cutter. Brush them with the egg yolk and milk, and place on a buttered and floured baking sheet. Bake for about 15 minutes in a preheated 200°C (400°F or Mark 6) oven. Serve them very hot.

SHEILA HUTCHINS
ENGLISH RECIPES AND OTHERS FROM SCOTLAND, WALES AND IRELAND

Thick Parmesan Biscuits

This is a little-known recipe from *The Cookery Book of Lady Clark of Tillypronie*, compiled from a treasure-house of note-books left by Lady Clark and published in 1909, nine years after her death. The recipe is an exceptionally good one. Lady Clark makes the point that it is the *thickness* of these biscuits that gives them their character. The Parmesan cheese is also essential. English cheese will not do. The biscuits can be stored in a tin and heated up when wanted.

To make 12

60 g	Parmesan cheese, grated	2 oz
60 g	butter	2 oz
125 g	flour	4 oz
1	egg yolk	1
	salt	
	cayenne pepper	

Rub the butter into the flour. Add the Parmesan cheese, egg and seasoning and work well. Moisten with a little water if necessary. Roll out the dough to the thickness of 1 cm (½ inch). Cut into 2.5 cm (1 inch) diameter rounds. Arrange on a lightly greased baking sheet. Bake in the centre or lower centre of a preheated 170°C (325°F or Mark 3) oven for just on 20 minutes. Serve the biscuits hot.

ELIZABETH DAVID
SPICES, SALT AND AROMATICS IN THE ENGLISH KITCHEN

Stiltonettes

To make about 24

175 g	Stilton cheese, crumbled	6 oz
250 g	flour, sifted	8 oz
2 tbsp	yogurt	2 tbsp
125 g	butter, softened	4 oz
75 g	sweet pepper, finely chopped	2½ oz
4 tsp	finely cut chives	4 tsp

Rub the cheese and butter into the flour and add the yogurt to make a firm dough. Knead it well with floured hands; form the dough into a log, cover the log with plastic film, and chill it for 1 hour in the refrigerator or for 10 minutes in the freezer.

Roll the chilled dough out on a lightly floured board into a rectangular shape about 5 mm (¼ inch) thick. Sprinkle on the sweet pepper and chives and lightly pat them with your hand. Roll up the dough lengthwise, as you would a Swiss roll. Tightly wrap the roll in plastic film and chill it again.

Preheat the oven to 220°C (425°F or Mark 7). When the roll is chilled, remove the film and cut slices approximately 5 mm (¼ inch) thick. Set the slices about 2.5 cm (1 inch) apart on ungreased baking sheets and bake for about 15 minutes.

ANITA MAY PEARL
COMPLETELY CHEESE: THE CHEESELOVER'S COMPANION

Hot Cheese Crackers

Sajtos Izelitö

To make about 30

250 g	Gruyère cheese, grated	8 oz
90 g	flour	3 oz
250 g	butter	8 oz
3 tbsp	soured cream	3 tbsp
½ tsp	paprika	½ tsp
	salt	

Mix the flour and half the butter until the mixture forms crumbs. Add half the cheese, 2 tablespoons of the soured cream, the paprika and a little salt. Knead the dough well, then let it rest in the refrigerator for about 2 hours.

Roll the dough into a sheet 5 mm (¼ inch) thick. Cut the sheet into rounds with a small biscuit cutter. Place on a baking sheet and bake in a preheated 180°C (350°F or Mark 4) oven for 12 to 15 minutes.

Mix together the remaining butter, cheese and soured cream and spread a 5 mm (¼ inch) layer of the mixture on the cooled crackers. Place a second cracker on top, making little sandwiches and serve while still warm.

GEORGE LANG
THE CUISINE OF HUNGARY

Standard Preparations

Shortcrust Dough

The proportion of fat to flour in shortcrust dough can be varied according to the result required. For the standard shortcrust pastry consistency, use the smaller quantity of butter; for a richer and much crisper result, use the larger quantity of butter.

To make 350 to 400 g (12 to 14 oz)

250 g	flour	8 oz
	salt	
125 to 175 g	butter, chilled and cubed	4 to 6 oz
4 to 6 tbsp	cold water	4 to 6 tbsp

Sift the flour with a pinch of salt into a bowl. Add the butter. Rub the butter and flour together with your fingertips until the mixture has a coarse mealy texture, or cut the butter into the flour with two knives. Add half the water and, with a knife or fork, quickly blend it into the flour and butter mixture. Add just enough of the rest of the water to allow you to gather the dough together into a firm ball. Wrap the dough in plastic film and refrigerate it for 15 minutes, or put it into the freezer for half that time, before rolling it out.

Rough-Puff Dough

The liquid used for this dough can be varied according to the result required. Water or milk, cream or egg yolk thinned with water can be used; for a very rich, sweet dough, use a mixture of egg yolk, cream and rum.

To make 500 g (1 lb)

250 g	flour	8 oz
	salt	
1 tbsp	icing sugar (optional, for sweet dough)	1 tbsp
250 g	butter, chilled and cubed	8 oz
15 cl	liquid	$\frac{1}{4}$ pint

Sift the flour, a pinch of salt and the icing sugar, if used, into a bowl. Add the butter and cut it rapidly into the flour with two knives, stopping while the cubes of butter are still quite large.

Quickly stir in just enough liquid for the mixture to cohere, then gather it together with your hands and form it into a ball. Wrap the dough in plastic film and refrigerate it for 45 minutes, or half that time in the freezer.

Place the dough on a cool, floured surface and beat it flat with a rolling pin. Turn the dough over to make sure that both sides are lightly floured. Roll the dough out rapidly into a rectangle about three times as long as it is wide. Fold the two short ends to meet each other in the centre, then fold again to align the folded edges with each other. Following the direction of the fold lines, roll the dough into a rectangle again, fold again in the same way and refrigerate for at least 30 minutes. Repeat this process two or three more times before using the dough. Always let the dough rest in the refrigerator in between the times it is rolled out.

Basic Syrup Dough

The following spices can be used to flavour this dough: ground cinnamon, ground ginger, ground cloves, ground nutmeg, ground coriander, ground black pepper, whole fennel seeds and whole aniseeds. Mix some or all of them, in proportions to suit your taste, to make up the quantity of spice required.

To make about 1 kg (2 to 2½ lb)

250 g	syrup (honey, treacle or molasses)	8 oz
250 g	brown sugar	8 oz
30 g	butter	1 oz
2 tbsp	water	2 tbsp
400 g	flour	14 oz
$\frac{1}{2}$ tsp	bicarbonate of soda	$\frac{1}{2}$ tsp
	salt	
1 to 2 tsp	spices	1 to 2 tsp
125 g	almonds or hazelnuts, chopped (optional)	4 oz
125 g	crystallized peel, chopped (optional)	4 oz

Place the syrup, sugar, butter and water in a saucepan and stir them together over a gentle heat until the sugar has dissolved and the ingredients are blended together, then raise the heat to bring them to the boil. Remove the pan from the heat and allow the mixture to cool to room temperature.

Sift together the flour, bicarbonate of soda, a pinch of salt and the spices. Gradually add these to the cooled syrup, stirring well between each addition. When all the sifted ingredients have been incorporated, add the chopped nuts and peel, if using, and stir them in well.

Turn the dough out of the pan on to a floured board. Flour your hands and knead the dough lightly for a few minutes until it becomes smooth.

Creamed Sugar Dough

This basic dough can be shaped in a variety of different ways. The consistency can be altered by increasing or reducing the amount of egg used in the mixture. For a softer dough, suitable for forcing through a sieve, biscuit press or piping bag, use two eggs; for a dough firm enough to roll out easily, use only one egg.

To make 850 g (1¾ lb)		
175 g	butter, softened	6 oz
300 g	castor sugar or 250 g (8 oz) of sugar and 50 g (2 oz) of vanilla sugar	10 oz
1	egg	1
1	egg yolk	1
1 tsp	grated lemon rind or other flavouring (optional)	1 tsp
350 g	flour	12 oz
	salt	

Cream the butter, add the sugar and vanilla sugar, if using, and beat them together until pale and fluffy. Mix in the egg, egg yolk and flavouring, if using. Sift together the flour and a pinch of salt. Add the flour gradually to the cream mixture, stirring it in. When the dough becomes too stiff to stir, mix in the remaining flour by hand.

Meringue

The technique of making meringues is shown on page 60.

To make about 30		
6	egg whites	6
275 g	castor sugar	9 oz

Beat the egg whites until they form soft peaks. Sprinkle a little sugar over the beaten egg whites and whisk it in. Continue to add the sugar, a very little at a time, whisking continually, until all the sugar is incorporated and the mixture holds stiff peaks. Pipe or spoon small amounts of the mixture on to a baking sheet lined with greaseproof paper and bake the meringues on a low shelf in a preheated 150°C (300°F or Mark 2) oven for at least 3 hours or until completely dry. Allow the meringues to cool completely before removing them from the greaseproof paper.

Hazelnut meringue: Make the meringue mixture as above. Gradually add 500 g (1 lb) of ground hazelnuts, folding them evenly into the mixture. Form the meringues and bake them in the same way as plain meringues.

Nut Filling

Any nuts, or a mixture of several kinds, may be used.

To make 500 g (1 lb)		
250 g	nuts, coarsely chopped	8 oz
250 g	sugar	8 oz
1 tbsp	rose-water or other liquid flavouring	1 tbsp

Place the nuts and sugar in a bowl and mix them together thoroughly. Add the rose-water and stir until the mixture is evenly moistened and resembles coarse breadcrumbs.

Praline Butter Cream

For coffee butter cream, cream 250 g (8 oz) of butter and gradually beat in 350 g (12 oz) of sifted icing sugar. Add 2 tablespoons of strong black coffee. For chocolate butter cream, add 125 g (4 oz) of plain chocolate, melted in a bowl over hot water, to the butter and sugar mixture

To make 750 g (1½ lb)		
250 g	almonds, blanched	8 oz
250 g	sugar	8 oz
250 g	butter	8 oz

In a heavy saucepan, cook the almonds and sugar over a low heat, stirring all the time, until the sugar caramelizes and turns a light golden-brown. Turn the mixture out immediately on to a greased baking sheet to set. When it is cool, place the hard nut mixture in a plastic bag and pound it with a mallet or rolling pin to reduce it to a fine powder. Sieve the contents of the bag so that the powder falls into a bowl; replace any larger remaining pieces in the plastic bag and repeat until all the nut mixture is powdered.

Cream the butter until fluffy. Beat in the praline powder, a little at a time, and continue beating the mixture until the desired consistency is reached.

Citrus Filling

To make about 400 g (14 oz)

2	lemons, rind grated and juice strained	2
300 g	icing sugar	10 oz
1 tbsp	melted butter	1 tbsp

Mix together the icing sugar and lemon rind in a bowl and stir in 4 tablespoons of the lemon juice. Add the melted butter. Place the bowl over a pan of hot water, on a gentle heat, and stir the mixture until all the ingredients are blended smoothly. Turn off the heat and allow the mixture to rest over the water for 10 minutes, stirring from time to time.

Remove the bowl from the pan and beat the mixture for about 5 minutes, until the paste becomes lighter in colour, thick and grainy and easy to spread.

Fig Filling

To make 500 g (1 lb)

250 g	dried figs	8 oz
30 cl	water	½ pint
250 g	sugar	8 oz

Place the figs and water in a saucepan over a moderate heat and simmer for between 10 and 20 minutes, until the figs are soft. Drain the figs, reserving the cooking water, allow them to cool, then remove the stems.

Chop the figs coarsely and return them to the saucepan with the sugar and the reserved cooking water. Bring the mixture to a simmer, stirring all the time, then allow to cook for about 10 minutes over a moderate heat, until the mixture has become a thick paste.

Chocolate Ganache

To make about 1.25 litres (2 pints)

600 g	plain chocolate, broken in pieces	1¼ lb
60 cl	double cream	1 pint

Place the chocolate pieces and cream in a heavy saucepan over a low heat and stir until the chocolate has melted and the mixture is smooth and thick, and an even dark brown in colour. Do not allow the mixture to boil. Pour the chocolate cream into a bowl and allow it to cool completely.

When the cream is cold, whisk it until it has increased in bulk, is a pale colour and light and fluffy in texture.

Marzipan

Other nuts, or a mixture of several kinds, can be used instead of almonds. A finer-textured marzipan can be made by substituting icing sugar for granulated sugar; a lighter result is obtained by binding the marzipan with lightly beaten egg whites instead of whole eggs.

To make about 1 kg (2 to 2½ lb)

500 g	ground almonds	1 lb
500 g	granulated sugar	1 lb
1	lemon, rind grated	1
2	eggs, beaten	2

Mix together the ground almonds, sugar and lemon rind. Pour in the beaten eggs, a little at a time, stirring the mixture with a fork or knife. When the mixture becomes moist, start to mix it by hand until all the egg has been added. Gather the mixture into a ball and knead it quickly by hand to produce a paste with a smooth consistency.

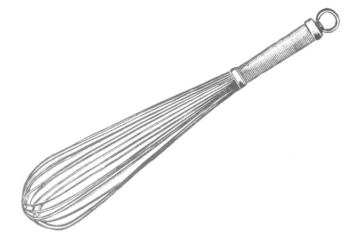

Royal Icing

To make 60 cl (1 pint)

1 kg	icing sugar, sifted	2 lb
4	egg whites	4
½	lemon, juice strained (optional)	½

Using a wooden spoon, stir about half the icing sugar into the egg whites. Add the lemon juice, if used. Beat the mixture with the wooden spoon until it is smooth, then add the remaining icing sugar, a little at a time, beating well after each addition. When all the sugar has been incorporated, beat the mixture until it is stiff—about 15 minutes. The icing can be used immediately, or it can be kept for up to 30 minutes, covered with a damp cloth to prevent it from drying out. If kept for longer, the icing will begin to set.

Recipe Index

English recipe titles are listed by categories such as "Almonds", "Brandy Snaps", "Cheese", "Drop Biscuits", "Filling", "Marzipan" and "Simple, Dough or Paste Biscuits", and within those categories alphabetically. Foreign recipe titles are listed alphabetically without regard to category.

General Index/Glossary

Included in this index are definitions of many of the culinary terms used in this book: definitions are in italics. The recipes in the Anthology are listed in the Recipe Index on page 168.

Recipe Credits

The sources for the recipes in this volume are shown below. Page references in brackets indicate where the recipes appear in the Anthology.

Adam, Hans Karl, *Das Kochbuch aus Schwaben.* © copyright 1976 by Verlagsteam Wolfgang Hölker. Published by Wolfgang Hölker, Münster. Translated by permission of Verlag Wolfgang Hölker (*pages 114, 137*).
Amicale des Cuisiniers et Pâtissiers Auvergnats de Paris, *Cuisine d'Auvergne (Cuisines du Terroir).* © 1979 Denoël, Paris. Published by Éditions Denoël. Translated by permission of Éditions Denoël (*pages 96, 148*).
Andreis, Florence de, *La Cuisine Provençale d'Aujourd'hui.* © Rivages 1980. Published by Éditions Rivages, Marseille. Translated by permission of Éditions Rivages (*pages 98, 134*).
Aoun, Fayez, *280 Recettes de Cuisine Familiale Libanaise.* © 1980, Jacques Grancher, Éditeur. Published by Jacques Grancher, Éditeur, Paris. Translated by permission of Jacques Grancher, Éditeur (*pages 107, 111*).
Artocchini, Carmen, *400 Ricette della Cucina Piacentina.* Published by Stabilimento Tipografica Piacentino, Piacenza, 1977. Translated by permission of the author, Piacenza (*page 106*).
Autumn, Violeta, *A Russian Jew Cooks in Perú.* Copyright © 1973 Violeta Autumn. Published by 101 Productions, San Francisco. By permission of 101 Productions (*pages 115, 134*).
Barker, William, *The Modern Pâtissier.* © William Barker and Northwood Publications Ltd., 1974 and 1978. Published by Northwood Publications Ltd., London. By permission of Northwood Publications Ltd. (*page 112*).
Bates, Margaret, *Talking about Cakes with an Irish and Scottish Accent.* Copyright © 1964 Pergamon Press Ltd. Published by Pergamon Press Ltd., Oxford. By permission of Pergamon Press Ltd. (*pages 95, 130 and 135*).

Besson, Joséphine, *La Mère Besson "Ma Cuisine Provençale".* © Éditions Albin Michel, 1977. Published by Éditions Albin Michel, Paris. Translated by permission of Éditions Albin Michel (*page 129*).
Blanquet, Mme Rosalie, *Le Pâtissier des Ménages.* Published by Librairie de Théodore Lefèvre et Cie/Émile Guérin, Éditeur, Paris, 1878 (*pages 107, 113, 127 and 140*).
Borer, Eva Maria, *Tante Heidi's Swiss Kitchen.* English text copyright © 1965 by Nicholas Kaye Ltd. Copyright © 1981 Kaye & Ward Ltd. Published by Kaye & Ward Ltd., London. First published as "Die Echte Schweizer Küche" by Mary Hahns Kochbuchverlag, Berlin W., 1963. By permission of Kaye & Ward Ltd. (*pages 99, 118, 135 and 148*).
Bouayed, Fatima-Zohra, *La Cuisine Algérienne.* Published by S.N.E.D. (*Société Nationale d'Édition et de Diffusion*), Algiers, 1978. Translated by permission of the author, Algiers (*pages 107, 144 and 155*).
Boyd, Lizzie (Editor), *British Cookery.* © 1976 by British Tourist Authority and British Farm Produce Council. Published by Croom Helm Ltd., London. By permission of the British Tourist Authority, London (*page 126*).
Břízová, Joza and Klimentová, Maryna, *Tschechische Küche.* © by Verlag PRÁCE, Praha/CSSR, and Verlag für die Frau, Leipzig/DDR. Published by PRÁCE, Prague and Verlag für die Frau, Leipzig, 1977. Translated by permission of DILIA, Theatrical and Literary Agency, Prague, for the authors (*pages 99, 119*).
Brown, Catherine, *Scottish Regional Recipes.* Published by The Molendinar Press, Glasgow 1981. By permission of Richard Drew Publishing Limited, Glasgow (*pages 94, 95*).
Brown, Marion, *The Southern Cook Book.* © 1968 The University of North Carolina Press. Published by The University of North Carolina Press, Chapel Hill. By permission of The University of North Carolina Press (*page 148*).
Brownstone, Cecily, *Cecily Brownstone's Associated Press Cook Book.* © Copyright 1972 by The Associated Press. Published by David McKay Company, Inc., New York. By permission of David McKay Company, Inc. (*page 126*).
Byron, May, *Pot-Luck.* Copyright by Hodder and Stoughton Limited. 7th Edition published by Hodder and Stoughton

Limited, London 1926. By permission of Hodder and Stoughton Limited, Kent (*page 147*).
Carême, Antonin, *Le Pâtissier Royal Parisien.* First published in Paris, 1841. Published by Laffitte Reprints, Marseille 1980. Translated by permission of Laffitte Reprints (*pages 128, 129 and 133*).
Cascante, Maria del Carmen, *150 Recetas de Dulces de Fácil Preparación.* © Editorial De Vecchi, S.A., 1975. Published by Editorial De Vecchi, S.A., Barcelona. Translated by permission of Editorial De Vecchi, S.A. (*pages 115, 139*).
Cascante, Maria del Carmen, *Manual Moderno de Pastelería Casera.* © Editorial De Vecchi, S.A., Barcelona, 1978. Published by Editorial De Vecchi, S.A. Translated by permission of Editorial De Vecchi, S.A. (*pages 132, 152*).
Cavalcanti, Ippolito, Duca di Buonvicino, *Cucina Teorico-Pratica.* Tipografia di G. Palma, Naples. Second edition, 1839 (*pages 138, 141*).
Ceccaldi, Marie, *Cuisine de Corse (Cuisines du Terroir).* © 1980, by Éditions Denoël, Paris. Published by Éditions Denoël. Translated by permission of Éditions Denoël (*page 102*).
Chanot-Bullier, C., *Vieilles Recettes de Cuisine Provençale.* Published by Tacussel, Éditeur, Marseille. Translated by permission of Tacussel, Éditeur (*page 98*).
Cobbett, Anne, *The English Housekeeper.* Originally published by A. Cobbett, Strand, sixth edition, 1851. Reprinted in facsimile by EP Publishing Limited. Copyright © 1973 by EP Publishing Limited, Wakefield, Yorkshire (*page 120*).
Colquitt, Harriet Ross (Editor), *The Savannah Cook Book.* © 1933 by Harriet Ross Colquitt. © 1960 by Harriet Ross Colquitt. Eighth edition 1974 published by Colonial Publishers, Charleston, South Carolina. By permission of Colonial Publishers (*page 145*).
Comelade, Éliane Thibaut, *La Cuisine Catalane.* © Éditions J. Lanore CLT. Published by Éditions Jacques Lanore, CLT, Paris 1978. Translated by permission of Éditions Jacques Lanore, CLT, Malakoff (*page 113*).
Correnti, Pino, *Il Libro d'Oro della Cucina e dei Vini di Sicilia.* Copyright © 1976 U. Mursia Editore, Milano. Published by Ugo Mursia Editore S.p.A., Milan. Translated by permission of Ugo Mursia Editore S.p.A. (*page 157*).

Craig, Elizabeth, *Scandinavian Cooking.* © Elizabeth Craig 1958. Published by André Deutsch Limited, London. By permission of André Deutsch Limited (*pages 95, 105*).
Cuisine Auvergnate, La, *(L'Encyclopédie de la Cuisine Régionale).* © Presses Pocket, 1979. Published by Presses Pocket, Paris. Translated by permission of Les Presses de la Cité, Paris (*page 97*).
Cuisine Bourguignonne, La, *(L'Encyclopédie de la Cuisine Régionale).* © Presses Pocket, 1979. Published by Presses Pocket, Paris. Translated by permission of Les Presses de la Cité, Paris (*page 153*).
Cuisine Bretonne, La, *(L'Encyclopédie de la Cuisine Régionale).* © Presses Pocket, 1979. Published by Presses Pocket, Paris. Translated by permission of Les Presses de la Cité, Paris (*page 159*).
Cuisine du Périgord, La, *(L'Encyclopédie de la Cuisine Régionale).* © Presses Pocket, 1979. Published by Presses Pocket, Paris. Translated by permission of Les Presses de la Cité, Paris (*page 145*).
Cuisine d'Ève et Olympe, La, © Éditions Mengès. Published by Éditions Mengès, Paris 1980. Translated by permission of Éditions Mengès (*page 140*).
Czerny, Zofia and Strasburger, Maria, *Żywienie Rodziny.* Copyright by Zofia Czerny and Maria Strasburger. Published by Czytelnik Spoldzielnia Wydawnicza 1948. Translated by permission of Agencja Autorska, Warsaw, for the heiress to the authors (*pages 104, 149*).
David, Elizabeth, *English Bread and Yeast Cookery.* Copyright © Elizabeth David, 1977. First published by Allen Lane. Published by Penguin Books Ltd., London 1979. By permission of Penguin Books Ltd. (*page 161*).
David, Elizabeth, *Spices, Salt and Aromatics in the English Kitchen.* Copyright © Elizabeth David, 1970. Published by Penguin Books Ltd., London. By permission of Penguin Books Ltd. (*page 164*).
Davidis, Henriette, *Praktisches Kochbuch.* Newly revised by Luise Holle. Published in Bielefeld and Leipzig, 1898 (*page 132*).
Davis, Irving, *A Catalan Cookery Book.* Lucien Scheler, Paris, 1969. By permission of Lucien Scheler, Libraire (*page 136*).
Deschamps, B. and Deschaintre, J.-Cl., *Le Livre de l'Apprenti Pâtissier.* © Éditions J. Lanore CLT 1979. Published by Éditions Jacques Lanore CLT, Paris. Translated by permission of Éditions Jacques Lanore CLT, Malakoff (*page 132*).
Deschamps, B. and Deschaintre, J.-Cl., *Pâtisserie, Confiserie, Glacerie: Travaux Pratiques.* © Éditions J. Lanore CLT – 1979. Published by Éditions Jacques Lanore CLT, Paris. Translated by permission of Éditions Jacques Lanore CLT, Malakoff (*page 96*).
Disslowa, Marja, *Jak Gotować.* Published by Wydawnictwo Polskie R. Wegnera, Poznań, 1938. Translated by permission of Agencja Autorska, Warsaw, for the author (*pages 137, 142, 143 and 159*).
Donati, Stella (Editor), *Le Famose Economiche Ricette di Petronilla.* © Casa Editrice Sonzogno 1974. Published by Casa Editrice Sonzogno S.P.A., Milan. Translated by permission of Gruppo Editoriale Fabbri Bompiani Sonzogno Etas S.P.A. (*pages 97, 103*).
Dorset Federation of Women's Institutes, *What's Cooking in Dorset.* Published by the Dorset Federation of Women's Institutes, 1972. By permission of the Dorset Federation of Women's Institutes (*page 94*).
Douglas, Elizabeth, *The Cake and Biscuit Book.* Published by Alexander Moring Ltd./The de la More Press, London, c. 1910 (*pages 116, 141*).
Douglas, Joyce, *Old Derbyshire Recipes and Customs.* © Joyce Douglas, 1976. Published by Hendon Publishing Co. Ltd., Hendon Mill, Nelson, Lancashire. By permission of Hendon Publishing Co. Ltd. (*page 102*).
Dowson, Mrs. Aubrey (Editor), *The Women's Suffrage Cookery Book.* Published by Women's Printing Society Limited, London (*pages 101, 102*).
Duckitt, Hildagonda J., *Hilda's "Where is it?" of Recipes.* Published by Chapman and Hall Ltd., London, 1903. By permission of Associated Book Publishers Ltd., London (*page 101*).
Dworkin, Stan and Floss, *The Good Goodies.* Copyright © 1974 by Stan and Floss Dworkin. Published by Rodale Press, Inc., Book Division, Emmaus, Pa. By permission of Rodale Press, Inc. (*page 160*).
Elkon, Juliette, *The Chocolate Cookbook.* Copyright © 1973 by Juliette Elkon. Published by The Bobbs-Merrill Co., Inc., Indianapolis/New York. By permission of The Bobbs-Merrill Co., Inc., Indianapolis (*pages 124, 125 and 129*).
Fance, Wilfred J. (Editor), *The New International Confectioner.* © Copyright English language Editions Virtue and Company Limited, London and Coulsdon. © Copyright International Editions Rene Kramer publisher, Lugano-Castagnola, Switzerland. 4th Edition with revisions published in 1979 by Virtue and Company Limited. By permission of Virtue and Company Limited (*page 109*).
Farmer, Fannie Merritt, *The Boston Cooking-School Cook Book.* Copyright, 1896, 1900, 1901, 1902, 1903, 1904, 1905, 1906, 1912, 1914 by Fannie Merritt Farmer. Copyright, 1915, 1918, 1923, 1924, by Cora D. Perkins. Published by Little, Brown and Company, Boston 1924. By permission of The Fannie Farmer Cookbook Corporation, Bedford, MA (*page 162*).
Fernie, W. T., *Meals Medicinal with "Herbal Simples".* Published by John Wright & Co., Bristol 1905. By permission of John Wright and Sons Limited, Bristol (*page 161*).
Filippini, Maria Nunzia, *La Cuisine Corse.* Published by Société d'Éditions-Serena, Ajaccio, 1978. Translated by permission of Société d'Éditions—Serena (*page 157*).
Flexner, Marion, *Out of Kentucky Kitchens.* Copyright, 1949 by Marion Flexner. Published by Franklin Watts, Inc., New York. By permission of Franklin Watts, Inc. (*pages 120, 122*).
Francatelli's The Modern Cook (1846). Copyright © 1973 by Dover Publications, Inc. Published by Dover Publications, Inc., New York (*page 157*).
Frank, Dorothy C., *Cooking with Nuts.* © 1979 by Dorothy C. Frank. Published by Clarkson N. Potter, Inc./Publishers, New York. By permission of Clarkson N. Potter, Inc. (*page 122*).
Frederick, J., George, *Pennsylvania Dutch Cookery.* Copyright, 1935, by The Business Bourse. Published by The Business Bourse Publishers. A Reprint of the Original © Favorite Recipes Press, Inc., 1966. By permission of Favorite Recipes Press/Nashville Educational Marketing Services, Inc., Nashville, Tennessee (*pages 145, 147*).
Garcia, Maria Luisa, *El Arte de Cocinar.* © M. Luisa Garcia. 8th edition Published by Edival Ediciones, Valladolid 1977. Translated by permission of the author, Mieres, Asturias (*page 112*).
Gaspero, Josh (Editor), *Hershey's 1934 Cookbook.* © Copyright 1971 by Hershey Foods Corporation. Published by Hershey Foods Corporation, Hershey, Pennsylvania. By permission of Hershey Foods Corporation (*page 124*).
Gavotti, Erina (Editor), *Millericette.* © Copyright 1965 by Garzanti Editore. Published by Garzanti Editore, Milan. Translated by permission of Garzanti Editore s.p.a., (*page 118*).
Gérard, Jacqueline, *Bonnes Recettes d'Autrefois.* © Librairie Larousse, 1980. Published by Librairie Larousse, Paris. Translated by permission of Société Encyclopédique Universelle, Paris (*pages 117, 130*).
Girl Guides' Association, Fiji, The (Editors), *South Sea Islands Recipes.* Published by The Girl Guides' Association, Fiji 1958. By permission of Fiji Girl Guides' Association (*page 95*).
Giusti, Giorgio (Editor), *Centonovantadue Ricette dell'800 Padano.* Published in Modena 1970. Translated by permission of the author, Modena (*page 130*).
Good Housekeeping Institute, The (Editor), *Good Housekeeping Cookery Book.* © The Hearst Corporation 1944, 1966, 1972, 1976. First published in Great Britain 1948. Reprinted by Ebury Press, London 1977. By permission of National Magazine Co., Ltd., London (*page 105*).
Gosetti, Fernanda, *In Cucina con Fernanda Gosetti.* © 1978 Fabbri Editori, Milano. Published by Fabbri Editori. Translated by permission of Gruppo Editoriale Fabbri Bompiani Sonzogno Etas, Milano (*pages 116, 117 and 139*).
Haitsma Mulier-van Beusekom, C. A. H. (Editor), *Culinaire Encyclopédie.* Copyright © 1957/1971 by Elsevier Nederland, Amsterdam. Published by Elsevier 1957. Revised edition 1971 by Elsevier Nederland B.V. and E.H.A. Nakken-Rovekamp. Translated by permission of Elsevier Nederland B.V. (*page 127*).
Haldar, Mrs. J., *Bengal Sweets.* Fifth edition. Published by Industry Publishers Ltd., Calcutta, 1948 (*page 155*).
Hartley, Dorothy, *Food in England.* © Copyright 1954 by Dorothy Hartley. Published by Macdonald and Jane's, London, 1954. Adapted by permission of Macdonald Futura Publishers Ltd., London (*page 151*).
Hazelton, Nika, *The Regional Italian Kitchen.* Copyright © 1978 by Nika Hazelton. Published by M. Evans and Company, Inc., New York. By permission of Curtis Brown Ltd., New York (*pages 136, 153*).
Henderson, H. H. F., Toors, H. and Callenbach, H. M., *Het Nieuwe Kookboek.* © 1948/1972 Zomer & Keuning-Wageningen. Published by Zomer & Keuning-Wageningen. Translated by permission of Zomer & Keuning Boeken B.V., Ede, the Netherlands (*page 100*).
Hérissé, Émile, *The Art of Pastry Making.* Published by Ward, Lock, Bowden, and Co., London, 1893 (*page 136*).
Hewitt, Jean, *The New York Times New England Heritage Cookbook.* Copyright © 1972 and 1977 by The New York Times Company. Published by G. P. Putnam's Sons, New York. By permission of Curtis Brown Ltd., New York (*page 108*).
Huguenin, Pierre, *Les Meilleures Recettes de ma Pauvre Mère.* Published by Comité de la Foire Gastronomique de Dijon, Dijon, 1936. Translated by permission of Maître Patrice Huguenin, heir to the author, Beaune (*page 163*).
Hutchins, Sheila, *English Recipes and Others from Scotland, Wales and Ireland.* © 1967 by Sheila Hutchins. First published by Methuen & Co. Ltd. Published by The Cookery Book Club, 1970. By permission of the author (*page 164*).
Jack, Florence B., *Cookery for Every Household.* Published by Thomas Nelson and Sons, Ltd., London and Edinburgh 1934. By permission of Thomas Nelson and Sons Ltd., Walton-on-Thames, Surrey (*pages 94, 160*).
Jekyll, Lady, *Kitchen Essays.* © Lady Freyberg. Published by Collins Publishers, London and Glasgow 1969. By permission of Collins Publishers, London (*page 116*).
Jewry, Mary (Editor), *Warne's Model Cookery.* © Copyright F. Warne (Publishers) Limited. Published by Frederick Warne and Co. London and New York 1872. By permission of Frederick Warne (Publishers) Limited (*page 147*).
Junior Charity League of Monroe, Louisiana, The (Editors), *The Cotton Country Collection.* Copyright 1972 Junior Charity League, Monroe, Louisiana. Published by The Junior Charity League of Monroe. By permission of The Cotton Country Collection, Junior Charity League, Inc. (*pages 124, 125 and 126*).
Junior League of Memphis, Inc. (Editors), *The Memphis Cook Book.* Copyright 1952 The Junior League of Memphis, Inc. Published by Memphis Junior League Publications of the Junior League of Memphis, Inc., Memphis, Tennessee. By permission of Memphis Junior League Publications of the Junior League of Memphis, Inc. (*page 122*).
Junior League of Spartanburg, Inc. (Editors), *Spartanburg Secrets II.* Published by the Junior League of Spartanburg, Inc., Spartanburg, South Carolina 1964. By permission of the Junior League of Spartanburg, Inc. (*page 124*).
Khawam, René R., *La Cuisine Arabe.* © Éditions Albin Michel, 1970. Published by Éditions Albin Michel, Paris. Translated by permission of Éditions Albin Michel (*page 110*).
Kouki, Mohamed, *La Cuisine Tunisienne d'"Ommok Sannafa".* © by Mohamed Kouki. Published in collaboration with L'Office National des Pêches, Tunis, 1974. Translated by permission of the author, Tunis (*page 151*).
Kramarz, Inge, *The Balkan Cookbook.* © 1972 by Crown Publishers, Inc. Published by Crown Publishers, Inc., New York. By permission of Crown Publishers, Inc. (*pages 98, 117 and 162*).
Krüger, Arne and Wolter, Annette, *Kochen Heute.* © by Gräfe und Unzer Verlag München. Published by Gräfe und Unzer GmbH. Translated by permission of Gräfe und Unzer GmbH (*page 140*).
Kürtz, Jutta, *Das Kochbuch aus Schleswig-Holstein.* © Copyright 1976 by Verlagsteam Wolfgang Hölker. Published by Verlag Wolfgang Hölker, Münster. Translated by permission of Verlag Wolfgang Hölker (*page 114*).
Laasri, Ahmed, *240 Recettes de Cuisine Marocaine.* © 1978, Jacques Grancher, éditeur. Published by Jacques Grancher, éditeur, Paris. Translated by permission of Jacques Grancher, éditeur (*pages 104, 144*).
Ladies Auxiliary of The Lunenburg Hospital Society, The, *Dutch Oven.* Published by The Ladies Auxiliary of The Lunenburg Hospital Society, Nova Scotia, 1953. By permission of

The Ladies Auxiliary of The Lunenburg Hospital Society (*page 115*).

Lang, George, *The Cuisine of Hungary.* Copyright © 1971 by George Lang. Published by Atheneum Publishers, Inc., New York. By permission of Atheneum Publishers, Inc. (*page 164*).

Levy, Faye, *La Varenne Tour Book.* © 1979 La Varenne U.S.A., Inc. Published by Peanut Butter Publishing, Seattle, Washington. By permission of Latoque International Ltd., Gladwyne, Pennsylvania (*pages 131, 146*).

MacMiadhacháin, Anna, *Spanish Regional Cookery.* Copyright © Anna MacMiadhacháin, 1976. Published by Penguin Books Ltd., London. By permission of Penguin Books Ltd. (*page 154*).

Madame Elisabeth, *500 Nouvelles Recettes de Cuisine.* Copyright by Éditions Baudinière, Paris, 1938. Published by Éditions Baudinière. Translated by permission of Nouvelles Éditions Baudinière (*page 98*).

Maffioli, Giuseppe, *Cucina e Vini delle Tre Venezie.* © Copyright 1972 U. Mursia & C. Published by U. Mursia & C., Milan. Translated by permission of Ugo Mursia Editore (*page 106*).

Magyar, Elek, *Kochbuch für Feinschmecker.* © Dr. Magyar Bálint. © Dr. Magyar Pál. Originally published in 1967 under the title "Az Ínyesmester Szakácskönyve" by Corvina Verlag, Budapest. Translated by permission of Artisjus, Agence Litteraire Theatrale et de Musique, Budapest, on behalf of the legal successors of Elek Magyar (*pages 108, 110*).

Manuel de la Friandise, Le, *(ou les Talents de ma Cuisinière Isabeau Mis en Lumière).* Attributed to author of "Le Petit Cuisinier Économe". Published by Janet, Libraire, rue Saint-Jacques, Paris, in 1796 and 1797 (*pages 103, 108 and 133*).

Manuel Pratique de Cuisine Provençale. © Pierre Belfond, 1980. Published by Pierre Belfond, Paris (*pages 131, 132 and 137*).

Martin, Faye, *Rodale's Naturally Delicious Desserts and Snacks.* Copyright © 1978 Rodale Press, Inc. Published by Rodale Press Inc., Emmaus, Pennsylvania. By permission of Rodale Press Inc. (*pages 152, 162*).

Mathiot, Ginette, *Je Sais Faire la Pâtisserie.* © 1938 Albin Michel, Éditeur, Paris. Published by Éditions Albin Michel. Translated by permission of Éditions Albin Michel (*page 139*).

McCormick Spices of the World Cookbook, The, Copyright © 1979 by McCormick & Co., Inc. Published by McGraw-Hill Book Company, New York. By permission of McGraw-Hill Book Company (*page 119*).

Mestayer de Echagüe, Maria (Marquesa de Parabere), *Confiteria y Reposteria (Enciclopedia Culinaria).* 7th Edition published by Espasa-Calpe, S.A., Madrid 1950. Translated by permission of Editorial Espasa-Calpe S.A. (*page 153*).

Miller, Anthony (Editor), *Good Food from Singapore.* Second edition 1960. Published by J. Ay-Buch & Co., Ltd. (*page 162*).

Mosto, Ranieri da, *Il Veneto in Cucina.* © Di Aldo Martello Editore-Milano. Published by Aldo Martello Editore, 1974. Translated by permission of Giunti Publishing Group, Florence (*page 138*).

New Jersey Recipes, Olde & New. Published by Jersey Central Power & Light Company. By permission of Jersey Central Power & Light Company, Morristown, New Jersey (*pages 116, 123*).

Norberg, Inga (Editor), *Good Food from Sweden.* Published by Chatto & Windus, London 1935. By permission of Curtis Brown Ltd., London, Agents for the editor (*page 147*).

Norman, Hope J. and Simon, Louise A. (Editors), *Louisiana Entertains.* Menus and Recipes from The Rapides Symphony Guild, Alexandria, Louisiana. Copyright © 1978 by Rapides Symphony Guild, Alexandria, Louisiana. Published by Rapides Symphony Guild. By permission of Rapides Symphony Guild (*page 150*).

Ortiz, Elisabeth Lambert, *The Complete Book of Mexican Cooking.* Copyright © 1967 by Elisabeth Lambert Ortiz. Published by M. Evans and Company, Inc., New York. By permission of the author (*page 101*).

Parenti, Giovanni Righi, *La Grande Cucina Toscana.* Copyright © SugarCo Edizioni Srl., Milano. Published by SugarCo Edizioni. Translated by permission of SugarCo Edizioni (*page 156*).

Pasley, Virginia, *The Christmas Cookie Book.* Copyright 1949 by Virginia Pasley. Published by Atlantic Little, Brown and Co. By permission of the author, Westwood, California (*page 145*).

Pearl, Anita May, *Completely Cheese: The Cheeselover's Companion.* Co-authors: Constance Cuttle and Barbara B. Deskins. Edited by David Kolatch. Copyright © 1978 by Jonathan David Publishers, Inc. Published by Warner Books by arrangement with Jonathan David Publishers, Inc., New York. By permission of Jonathan David Publishers, Inc. (*page 164*).

Pezzini, Wilma, *The Tuscan Cookbook.* Copyright © 1978 by Wilma Pezzini. Published by J.M. Dent & Sons Ltd., London. By permission of Hughes Massie Limited, London (*pages 130, 148*).

Portinari, Laura Gras, *Cucina e Vini del Piemonte e della Valle D'Aosta.* © Copyright 1971 U. Mursia & C. Published by U. Mursia & C., Milan. Translated by permission of Ugo Mursia Editore (*pages 100, 134, and 136*).

Ramazani, Nesta, *Persian Cooking.* Copyright © 1974 by Nesta Ramazani. Published by Quadrangle/The New York Times Book Company, New York. By permission of the author, Virginia (*page 105*).

Rao, Nguyen Ngoc, *La Cuisine Chinoise à l'Usage des Français.* © 1980, by Éditions Denoël, Paris. Published by Éditions Denoël. Translated by permission of Éditions Denoël (*pages 100, 104*).

Rey-Billeton, Lucette, *Les Bonnes Recettes du Soleil.* © by Éditions Aubanel 1980. Published by Éditions Aubanel, Avignon. Translated by permission of Éditions Aubanel (*pages 102, 134*).

Richardson, Mrs. Don (Editor), *Carolina Low Country Cook Book of Georgetown, South Carolina.* © 1947 Mrs. Don Richardson, Georgetown. S.C. Printed by Walker, Evans & Cogswell Co., Charleston, S.C., 1963, 1975 for Women's Auxiliary, Prince George, Winyah, Protestant Episcopal Church, Georgetown, S.C. By permission of Mrs. Don Richardson (*pages 105, 123 and 128*).

Ripoll, Luis, *Nuestra Cocina. 600 Recetas de Mallorca, Menorca, Ibiza y Formentera.* © by Luis Ripoll. Published by Editorial H.M.B., S.A., Barcelona, 1978. Translated by permission of the author, Palma de Mallorca (*page 99*).

Rivoyre, Éliane and Jacquette de, *La Cuisine Landaise.* (*Cuisines du Terroir*). © 1980, by Éditions Denoël, Paris. Published by Éditions Denoël. Translated by permission of Éditions Denoël (*pages 133, 144*).

Ross, Annette Laslett and Disney, Jean Adams, *Good Cookies.* Copyright © 1963 by Annette Laslett Ross and Jean Adams Disney. Published in England by Faber and Faber Limited, London 1963. Published in America as "The Art of Making Good Cookies Plain and Simple" by Doubleday & Co. Inc., New York. By permission of Doubleday & Co. Inc. (*pages 119, 121, 124 and 154*).

Sahni, Julie, *Classic Indian Cooking.* Copyright © 1980 by Julie Sahni. Published by William Morrow and Company, Inc., New York. By permission of Jill Norman & Hobhouse Ltd., London (*page 163*).

Santa Maria, Jack, *Indian Sweet Cookery.* © Jack Santa Maria 1979. Published by Rider and Company, London. By permission of Rider and Company (*page 154*).

Scheibler, Sophie Wilhelmine, *Allgemeines Deutsches Kochbuch für Alle Stände.* Published by C.F. Amelangs Verlag, Leipzig 1896 (*pages 109, 138, 142 and 143*).

Schuler, Elizabeth, *Mein Kochbuch.* © Copyright 1948 by Schuler-Verlag, Stuttgart-N, Lenzhalde 28. Published by Schuler Verlagsgesellschaft mbH, Herrsching. Translated by permission of Schuler Verlagsgesellschaft mbH (*page 123*).

Seranne, Ann, *The Joy of Giving Homemade Food.* Copyright © 1978 by Ann Seranne. Published by David McKay Company, Inc., New York. By permission of David McKay Company, Inc. (*page 150*).

Serra, Victoria, *Tia Victoria's Spanish Kitchen.* English text copyright © by Elizabeth Gili, 1963. Published by Kaye & Ward Ltd., London, 1963. Translated by Elizabeth Gili from the original Spanish entitled "Sabores: Cocina del Hogar" by Victoria Serra Suñol. By permission of Kaye & Ward Ltd. (*page 137*).

Smith, E., *The Compleat Housewife: or, Accomplish'd Gentlewoman's Companion.* Fifteenth edition, London 1753. Facsimile edition first published 1968 by Literary Services and Production Limited, London (*page 142*).

Spry, Constance and Hume, Rosemary, *The Constance Spry Cookery Book.* First published 1956 by J.M. Dent & Sons Ltd., London. Published by Pan Books Ltd., London 1972. By permission of J.M. Dent & Sons Ltd. (*page 161*).

St. Clair, Lady Harriet (Editor), *Dainty Dishes.* Eleventh edition published c. 1880 by John Hogg, London (*page 141*).

Stechishin, Savella, *Traditional Ukrainian Cookery.* Copyright, 1957, 1959 by Savella Stechishin. Published by Trident Press Ltd., Winnipeg, Canada 1979. By permission of Trident Press Ltd. (*page 108*).

Stoll, F. M. and Groot, W. H. de, *Het Haagse Kookboek.* © 1973 Van Goor Zonen. © 1979 Elsevier Nederland B.V., Amsterdam/Brussels. Published by Gebroeders van Cleef, den Haag. Translated by permission of Elsevier Nederland B.V. (*page 112*).

Stuber, Hedwig Maria, *Ich Helf Dir Kochen.* © BLV Verlagsgesellschaft mbH, München, 1955. Published by BLV Verlagsgesellschaft mbH, Munich. Translated by permission of BLV Verlagsgesellschaft mbH (*pages 114, 115, 142 and 163*).

Sumption, Lois Lintner and Ashbrook, Marguerite Lintner, *Around-the-World Cooky Book.* Published by Dover Publications, Inc., New York 1979. Originally published under the title "Cookies and More Cookies" by Chas. A. Bennett Co., Peoria, Illinois 1948 (*pages 113, 150*).

Thuilier, Raymond and Lemonnier, Michel, *Les Recettes de Baumanière.* © 1980, Éditions Stock. Published by Éditions Stock, Paris. Translated by permission of Éditions Stock (*page 154*).

Toklas, Alice B., *The Alice B. Toklas Cook Book.* Copyright, 1954, by Alice B. Toklas. By permission of Harper and Row Publishers, Inc. (*page 96*).

Tschirky, Oscar, *"Oscar" of the Waldorf's Cook Book.* Published by Dover Publications, Inc., New York 1973. Originally published under the title "The Cook Book of 'Oscar' of the Waldorf" by The Werner Company in 1896 (*page 150*).

Vence, Céline, *Encyclopédie Hachette de la Cuisine Régionale.* © Hachette 1979. Published by Librairie Hachette, Paris. Translated by permission of Librairie Hachette (*page 97*).

Vialardi, Giovanni, *Trattato di Cucina, Pasticceria Moderna* (*page 140*).

Vielfaure, Nicole and Beauviala, A. Christine, *Fêtes, Coutumes et Gâteaux.* © Christine Bonneton Éditeur. Published by Christine Bonneton Éditeur, Le Puy. Translated by permission of Christine Bonneton Éditeur, Paris (*page 158*).

Vitalis, M., *Les Bases de la Pâtisserie, Confiserie, Glacerie.* © Éditions CLT J. Lanore. Published by Éditions Jacques Lanore CLT, Paris 1980. Translated by permission of Éditions Jacques Lanore CLT, Malakoff (*pages 111, 112, 113 and 127*).

Wade, Margaret, *Cakes and Biscuits.* © 1977 Phoebus Publishing Company/BPC Publishing Limited, London. Published by The Hamlyn Publishing Group Limited, London. Adapted by permission of Macdonald Educational Limited, London (*page 146*).

Walker, Lorna and Hughes, Joyce, *The Complete Bread Book.* © Copyright The Hamlyn Publishing Group Limited 1977. Published by The Hamlyn Publishing Group Limited, London. By permission of The Hamlyn Publishing Group Limited (*page 160*).

Weaver, Louise Bennett and LeCron, Helen Cowles, *A Thousand Ways to Please a Husband.* Copyright, 1917 by Britton Publishing Company, Inc. Copyright, 1932 by A.L. Burt Company. Published by Blue Ribbon Books, Inc., New York (*page 118*).

Weber, Dominique, *Les Bonnes Recettes des Provinces de France.* © Bordas, Paris, 1979. Published by Éditions Bordas, Paris. Translated by permission of Éditions Bordas (*pages 110, 133, 143 and 159*).

White, Florence, *Good English Food.* First published by Jonathan Cape Ltd., London 1952. By permission of Jonathan Cape Ltd. (*page 103*).

Wifstrand Selma (Editor), *Favorite Swedish Recipes.* Published by Dover Publications, Inc., New York 1975. Originally published under the title "Swedish Food" by Esseltes Goteborgsindustrier AB. By permission of Dover Publications, Inc. (*page 118*).

Witty, Helen and Colchie, Elizabeth Schneider, *Better Than Store-Bought.* Copyright © 1979 by Helen Witty and Elizabeth Schneider Colchie. Published by Harper and Row Publishers, Inc., New York. By permission of Harper and Row Publishers, Inc. (*pages 121, 152, 156 and 158*).

Wolcott, Imogene (Editor), *The Yankee Cook Book.* Copyright 1939, © 1963, by Imogene Wolcott. Published by Ives Washburn, Inc., New York (*pages 126, 149 and 151*).

Acknowledgements and Picture Credits

The Editors of this book are particularly indebted to Gail Duff, Maidstone, Kent; Ann O'Sullivan, Deya, Mallorca; Dr. R. H. Smith, Aberdeen.

They also wish to thank the following: Danielle Adkinson, London; Bagpuss Antiques, Grays Antique Market, London; Baker Smith (Cake Decorators) Ltd., Farnham, Surrey; Maggie Black, London; Nora Carey, Paris; Marisa Centis, London; Carol Charlton, London; Josephine Christian, Stoke St. Michael, Bath, Somerset; Lesley Coates, Seven Kings, Essex; Emma Codrington, Richmond, Surrey; June Dowding, Seven Kings, Essex; Mimi Errington, Screveton, Nottinghamshire; Jay Ferguson, London; Nayla Freeman, London; Julian Hale, London; Annie Hall, London; Maggi Heinz, London; Maria Johnson, Sevenoaks, Kent; Sarah

Kelly, London; Wanda Kemp-Welch, Nottingham; Philippa Millard, London; Sonya Mills, Oxford; Wendy Morris, London; Dilys Naylor, Kingston-upon-Thames, Surrey; Winona O'Connor, North Fambridge, Essex; Sylvia Robertson, Surbiton, Surrey; Stephanie Thompson, London; Fiona Tillett, London; Tina Walker, London; Rita Walters, Seven Kings, Essex.

Photographs by Bob Komar: cover, 4, 6—bottom, 16—top right, 24—bottom left, 25—top and bottom right, 36—bottom, 52—bottom, 54, 56 to 64, 70 to 72, 76—top, 77. Photographs by John Elliott: 6—top, 7, 8, 9—bottom, 10 to 13, 38—top, 39—top, 40 to 42, 44, 45, 46—top and bottom left and middle, 47 to 49, 74, 75, 76—bottom, 80 to 82, 84 to 87, 90 to 92.

Photographs by Tom Belshaw: 9—top, 14, 16—top left and bottom, 17, 18—top right, 20 to 23, 24—top and bottom middle and right, 25—bottom left, 26 to 34, 38—bottom, 39—bottom, 43, 46—bottom right, 78, 79, 88, 89.

Other photographers (alphabetically):
John Cook: 50—top, 51—top, 52—top, 66, 67, 68—top and bottom left and middle, 69—top. Alan Duns: 18—top left and bottom right, 19, 36—top, 37, 50—bottom, 51—bottom, 53, 68—bottom right, 69—bottom. Louis Klein: 2.

All line cuts from Mary Evans Picture Library and private sources.

Colour separations by Gilchrist Ltd., Leeds, England
Typesetting by Camden Typesetters—London, England
Printed and bound by Brepols S.A.—Turnhout, Belgium.